Playing with Anger

**Recent titles in
Race and Ethnicity in Psychology**

Sources of Stress and Relief for African American Women
Catherine Fisher Collins

Playing with Anger

*Teaching Coping Skills to
African American Boys through
Athletics and Culture*

EDITED BY
HOWARD C. STEVENSON JR.

Race and Ethnicity in Psychology
Jean Lau Chin, John D. Robinson, and Victor De La Cancela,
Series Editors

**Westport, Connecticut
London**

Library of Congress Cataloging-in-Publication Data

Playing with anger : teaching coping skills to African American boys through athletics and culture / edited by Howard C. Stevenson Jr.
    p. cm.—(Race and ethnicity in psychology, ISSN 1543–2203)
    Includes bibliographical references (p.) and index.
    ISBN 0–275–97517–7 (alk. paper)
    1. African American boys—Social conditions. 2. African American boys—Psychology. 3. Anger in adolescence—United States. 4. Life skills—United States. 5. Physical education for youth with social disabilities—United States. 6. Youth with social disabilities—Rehabilitation—United States. 7. African Americans—Race identity. I. Stevenson, Howard C., 1958– II. Series.
E185.86.P57   2003
305.235—dc21   2002044996

British Library Cataloguing in Publication Data is available.

Library of Congress Catalog Card Number: 2002044996
ISBN: 0–275–97517–7
ISSN: 1543–2203

First published in 2003

Praeger Publishers, 88 Post Road West, Westport, CT 06881
An imprint of Greenwood Publishing Group, Inc.
www.praeger.com

Printed in the United States of America

The paper used in this book complies with the Permanent Paper Standard issued by the National Information Standards Organization (Z39.48–1984).

10 9 8 7 6 5 4 3 2 1

To Simone,
an angel God thought too beautiful to let go

Contents

Preface

I will never forget the bonding that was developed so richly between my brother and me as we played sports with each other in our country backyard—our own makeshift Madison Square Garden where tree limbs became screaming fans as we replayed last-second buzzer beaters in slow motion. The combination of playful competitiveness and challenge, along with caring and support frame the key liberating memories of my childhood. The game, any game, where the chance to show off our skills or just yell and release the tensions of the day, would hold so many possibilities for healing that doing anything else to pass the time would have been unthinkable. When I became a psychologist in training I realized that getting children and youth to talk about their problems was often much easier when we walked together, or played together, or were engaged in some seemingly competitive movement activity. I would often sneak in questions and comments to my clients while they were preoccupied with the athletic demand at the time, and their resistance would seem to be lessened and often less necessary.

Eventually, the combination of play and "work" in a clinical sense was a great fit for me although I was aware that play increased the avenues for instantaneous resistance and influence; for frustration and the tolerance of frustration; for failure and success. Besides the fact that I am addicted to sports activities, I felt there was much more therapeutic promise in the integration of athletic movement with clinical intervention. This integration was not a hypothesis as much as an appreciation of my own experiences as an athlete and as a coach of children and adolescents. Since my son was four, I have been coaching him and other youth in soccer and basketball and it has never ceased to amaze me that these little bundles of legs and arms can take in so much information and learn so many skills simply because they are so eager to learn. I came to understand that any lack of learning was primarily the result of my holding back in coaching skills I expected to be used only by much older youths. No! In coaching youth and athletes, there are so many pregnant emotional moments in which a person is begging for information, for a chance to learn. But not just information on how to play the game. These minds, bodies, and spirits are eager to receive information on how to be.

I had the wonderful experience of playing semiprofessional soccer in California for three and a half years in the Greater Los Angeles Soccer League. It was wonderful for two reasons. One, it was competitive enough to satisfy both my romantic notions of a professional career around the world and my physical need to work out my athletic gifts. Second, it helped to clarify for me how multiple gifts can be integrated so that I didn't need soccer to pay for food and clothing. Now, soccer is a sport that can bring the most skilled player to his or her emotional boiling point in just seconds. This is understandable given some of the aggression that people can get away with beyond the gaze of officials and coaches. For every team that I have ever played on from high school to college, besides a scorer, my role has been that of a peacemaker or intermediary. I have never had a problem coming between or stopping two other players fighting—except on one day.

While playing in a game against a team in this soccer league, a player who was guarding me kept kicking at my shins and the back of my legs when the ball was on the other side of the field. I used my usual set of coping strategies which included, (1) telling him to stop, (2) warning him calmly (with a sick smile) that if he did not stop there would be retaliation in a way he would not be able to prepare for (that is, retaliation while his back was turned or while he was in a vulnerable position and would be unable to see me coming); and (3) retaliating in a short but direct physical way (while no one was looking). Rarely did I ever have to go to Step 3 because the fear of a half-crazed smiley "way-too-calm" Black man (sometimes with a fake, high-pitched, but convincing West African accent) was usually enough to keep my opponents from pushing it too far, and the assaults would stop. But this one time, after going through to Step 3, I still could not get this man to stop and I was defenseless—my particular set of strategies just did not work. I was unprepared for someone who did not heed my warnings, and my emotions got the better of me. Before I knew it, my right hand was around his neck.

Now, you must know, I am not a fighter or a boxer. So if I get into a fight, it's meant to be temporary. It'll be a fight long enough for me to find daylight to run. But this time I had snapped and my aggressive teammates, the ones I usually had to keep from fighting in every game, were grabbing my wrist trying to pry it free from the guy's throat. When they finally pulled me free after considerable force, I came back to consciousness, more or less, in time to hear my teammates, say, "What's up with you? You're so violent, man!" I had to laugh because they couldn't see that their own game rituals, inciting aggression from others and fist-fighting during every game, were violent and my momentary and rare "losing it" experience couldn't compare, in my opinion. But maybe they were right. I was more aggressive than I had given myself credit. Or maybe we all are and rather than see the different ways we express our anger, I needed to understand it for each person.

The lesson I took from this story is that so many emotional moments occur in athletic events that athletics can't be understood just from the standpoint of sports. The emotional elements of the individual players must be taken into consideration. It so happened that I was angry about a lot of things that day. I had an argument with a friend earlier that morning. I was late for the practice before the game and was nagged for that and other things in my life had just gone badly—experiences my opponent could not have known. But what if someone had known that I had had a bad day or a few bad weeks? Would that information have been useful? Would my expression of this anger in a rare unexpected way have told others anything about my personality (besides the fact that at that moment I was a half-crazed "way-too-calm" smiley Black man with my own accent) or better yet, my openness to intervention and feedback?

Such is the thrust of this book and the Preventing Long-term Anger and Aggession in Youth (PLAAY) project. We seek to identify in boys who are having good or bad days what key issues "make them tick." How can we get to know them so that their aggressive behavior is explainable without categorizing it according to race and gender stereotypes? Athletics is one avenue to find out who boys are—not just how well they play. Culture is an avenue to bring understanding to their unique struggles and their unique potential. Finding out the identities of Black boys is as an important culturally relevant psychological intervention as any other. It is the most human—especially when the world these boys live in is quick to see and judge only their limitations. Too often, these judgments are inhumane and their consequences are life-threatening. Who are they? They are—boys—brothers, just like my brother and me who need and needed what all boys and brothers and sisters, all humans need—appreciation for their right to exist in the midst of chaos or calm. But in a world that would rather see image before presence and needs no proof before it has "truth," perhaps a better question to address in working with African American boys is "Who are they not?"

Acknowledgments

There are so many people who have contributed to this project and to the writing of this book. First, I wish to give honor to God who sees farther than we can imagine and makes all things possible. I would like to especially acknowledge the work of the staff members of the PLAAY project. These are wonderful women and men who decided to take a leap of faith on many occasions about this work. Many coauthored the chapters of the book. To believe that it was possible to engage Black males through unconventional methods like basketball and martial arts and interactive group therapy was no simple feat. They all provided their unique styles, talents, and personalities to make the program very successful and very enlightening. I appreciate how they took risks to come out of their safety zones and explore different ways of engaging.

Gwendolyn Davis, was a steadfast carrier of the knowledge and vision of the Project when the rest of us would lose sight of that. I love you and your commitment to the ethical care of the boys and the development of the CPR curriculum, which is the most important of the PLAAY components. Special acknowledgment goes to Margaret Beale Spencer, a colleague and friend, who was emotionally and intellectually supportive of the PLAAY project endeavors and always made room for us at the table.

I would also like to thank all of the staff and teachers of Behavior Academy who supported the PLAAY project. We cannot include all of their names here but mention some which include Robert Yancey, Dan Rizen, Barry Elko, Jeanette Dupriest, Hadiya Rashied, Robert Williams, Ethel McGhee, Antoine Terrell, Beatrice Watson, Olivia Twyman, Mr. Gathers,

Marcia Roye, Ernie Green, Ms. Love, and Herbert Chandler. We wish them nothing but the best in their endeavors. Thanks go to the graduate research assistants Avi Winick, Wanda Sabir-Lassiter, Nikki Edgecombe, and Dana Fry who aided in the data collection and development of the procedures.

Special thanks go to Rudy Mendoza-Denton and Valerie Purdie for their early work on observing aggression and interactions on the basketball courts of New York City, for their contributions to the conceptualization of the PLAAY project, and for their frequent visits to Penn to practice the basketball strategies. I hope y'all still got game, 'cause we still do.

To the wonderful undergraduate research assistants who were not afraid to get in the mix of the PLAAY project and connect with the boys, I give special acknowledgment. Some showed remarkable natural intuitive clinical talents. Besides Erick Espin and Juana Gatson for their stellar work, these undergraduates include Jamarah Leverette, John Fraser, Abram Williams, Chris Padilla, Danielle Bourget, and Jerri Ann Heath. Thanks goes to the wonderful folks at the Graduate School of Education at the University of Pennsylvania including Dean Susan Fuhrman for her support of the project and especially to the helpful folks in the Business Office. Many thanks go to Edith Arrington, my post-doctoral Fellow who helped sharpen my ideas on socialization through our weekly forum on race and racism.

I would like to thank Emilene Otey, grants officer at the National Institute of Mental Health, which provided the funding for the PLAAY Project (PO1 #57136). I am grateful for her constant support for the creative ideas embedded in the project. Thanks also go to the staff and directors of the Faculty Scholars Award program of the William T. Grant Foundation that supported the early seeds of the project ideas.

Bryan, my brother, I thank you for all the times we've grown closer as we played together. To Bryan, my son, I love you dearly and thank you for inspiring me and keeping me focused on what is really important in life.

Finally, to all the boys in the PLAAY Project, we pray God's blessings on your future and your life. We believe in you with our highest hopes and ask that you might remember our moments together and remember us— because we will not forget you.

Howard C. Stevenson Jr.

PART I

"An Hour of Play": Theoretical Frames for the PLAAY Project

INTRODUCTION

Boys, Not Men: Hypervulnerability in African American Youth

Howard C. Stevenson Jr., Gwendolyn Y. Davis, Teresa Herrero-Taylor, and Russell Morris

Fortunately, somewhere between chance and mystery lies imagination, the only thing that protects our freedom, despite the fact that people keep trying to reduce it or kill it off altogether.

—Luis Buñuel, *My Last Sigh*

Being Black and male is surreal. You are desired and you are despised. You are mostly hunted for sport and for the development of others. Your rarity in certain contexts makes you a marketable commodity worthy of desire and loathing. You are assumed to be hostile and you are assumed to be careless. You are followed as often as you are left alone. You want what everybody else wants but it feels as if the world looks upon you as if you want it with malice. Like W. E. B. DuBois once said, "in amused contempt and pity," you feel ashamed of wanting what everyone wants. Peace from the hunting comes too often as you give up, stop running, and face every attacker with such ferocity, that you agree to die in a blaze of glory. Or you make a secret pact with every onlooker and attacker to die in a blaze of glory just to save face. If the attacker is a shoe commercial, a shoe, or an evil eye glance from a policeman, or another brother on your neighborhood block, your biggest struggle will be to ponder whether your fight for life and death will match or surpass the meaning of your surreal existence.

Our musings here reflect how identity struggles for Black young men can often reveal a life-and-death debate. To be fortunate enough to have identity musings without a polarized life-and-death struggle is rare for many African American boys. Racial profiling of young Black males while they drive, walk, shop, talk, stand, and gather in groups has reached such epidemic proportions that even paranoid Black Panthers might underestimate its magnitude (ACLU Pedestrian and Car Stop Audit, 2000; Schmitt, Langan, & Durose, 2002). It's become another of America's interesting pastimes. Even America's overindulgence of aggressive masculinity and male gender patriarchy yields no protection for Black men. A person can't simply be male if he is Black. We have yet to observe a male code of silence and camaraderie like the "blue wall" evident in many police forces which requires the threat of imprisonment before it will crumble.

The struggle of African American identity or identities in the bodies, souls, and minds of male adolescents is a complex one. For one, scholars and identity researchers from anthropology to psychology, using a variety of empirical methods ranging from ethnography to survey research, are debating whether such an identity even exists. Social theorists who apply no particular empirical research strategies still use keen insight, observation, and analysis of the social and historical expressions of contemporary culture as evidence (Asante, Crouch, Early, Hooks, West, etc.). The arguments often center on whether to consider identity a unified entity since context influences our self-expressions and self-interpretations. Frankly, gender and race are inseparable as far as identity is concerned, or so we will argue, if youth accept the larger definitions of what Black manhood means. That is, we believe, if the larger societal definitions, questions, and ponderings of Black maleness are accepted, life and death struggles are the only identity options.

THE ESSENTIALISTIC "BECOMING" OF BLACK MALE IDENTITY

Some argue that because Black youth can behave very differently depending on the context, to conceptualize group identity is to be an *essentialist,* which to some scholars is a fate worse than death. Essentialist views are those that suggest the cultural expressions and strivings of a group of people can be identified from a particular set of values and behaviors with enduring historical and relational connections. The other extreme of the perspective is that there is no need to structure any one sense or definition or construction of identity or culture and to do so only simplifies a very complex reality. Those who propose the multiple identity perspectives are rarely eager to entertain any essentialist notions. Those who propose a strictly essentialist viewpoint are not willing to concede that a lack of cultural cohesion exists among African Americans apart from their contextual interactions.

With respect to African American boys, the intellectual debate on identity is often lost in the natural and unpredictable realities of racism in America (Meeks, 2000). Some researchers and clinicians barely acknowledge the gendered impact of racism and others ignore the topic altogether. Many see it as an excuse that supports a learned helplessness ideology. We do not. Black boys must manage in a world that fears and falsely idolizes their identity projections. Their stylistic machinations, verbiage, protests, and movements are feared and desired, desired and feared. What we are proposing is that both essentialistic and multiple identity perspectives and the derivatives of them are relevant. This "both-and" perspective has some African American psychology underpinnings, has been written by the authors elsewhere, and will be discussed in more detail in chapter 1 (Nobles, 1991; Stevenson, 1998b; Stevenson & Davis, 2003).

To settle solely on the essentialist viewpoint would be to narrow the possibilities and multiple expressions of Black youth as they move from one challenging social context to another. To settle solely on the multiple identity perspective is to adopt a Foucaultian view that identity is "becoming" without acknowledging that Black youth live in a static world that expects them to be somebody specific and somebody static. That is, while Black youth are becoming, the world is imaging them in some very rigid ways, and they unfortunately are also imaging themselves in some of the same rigid ways. Why? Because they are engaged mostly in reacting and doing, as opposed to simply reflecting. Power, thus, or empowerment becomes possible primarily if they step outside and reflect upon the straight-jacketed images or boxes, the rigidity, the stasis and be somebody who is dynamic and undefinable.

In fact, in the mind of the adolescent, doing rather than being may best represent the identity striving. This becoming occurs in abstract and across time, but most youth are being or doing, not solely becoming. In fact, all of us are being and doing. The difference for adults is a keener ability to reflect upon experience so choices are choices and not rush judgments (or at least we like to lie to ourselves that our judgments are superior). The luxury of acknowledging the becoming process is one that requires reflection, looking back, on one's life. Black adolescent development in urban contexts in which family support is limited rarely allows for such reflection when the fight for identity expression and the social demands to be or do are so great and so weighty. It is a burden to carry the mantle of growing when ducking is your priority.

THE "DOING" OF BLACK MALE IDENTITY

Multiple identity theorists miss the boat, in our opinion, because although they are right to think theoretically about the phenomenon of multiple identities, they are often wrong about how youth appropriate or access or express these identities in a racist, sexist, misogynistic world. It is less comforting to consider a world in which some of us are freer to express multiple identities in contexts that encourage this expression.

Conversely, others of us must enjoy the "playground" that is available to us—the front step in neighborhoods where playing down the street is a dangerous thing. Social interactions, in our opinion, push all of us, and Black youth in this instance, to be, not become, to do, not just plan what to do. Black youth are often pressured to present a clarified identity with specific actions, not an ambiguous or multidimensional one, because the social interactions and context often demand it. Cunningham (1999) and Spencer, Cunningham, and Swanson's (1995) work on reactive coping helps to illuminate this idea of doing as an integral part of one's identity striving. In Spencer's *Phenomenological Variant of Ecological Systems Theory* (PVEST), identity striving *is* coping. This model appreciates the static and dynamic nature of identity for Black youth (Spencer, 1999; Youngblood & Spencer, 2002). In PVEST, there is an opportunity to appreciate identity within a "both-and" reality.

Sometimes for poor Black boys, there are serious emotional, social and psychological costs to shifting their presented identity. It could mean that they face, ever so momentarily, the perceptions of animalism and criminality of a Black-male-phobic public as well as the abyss of nothingness or nihility in themselves. To shift may represent some reflection of their current lesser position in society as well as their future. It could also mean a diminution of social status among peers and a change in presentation could give them reason for distrust (Stevenson, 1997). Cunningham (1999) has found that when Black adolescent males are using exaggerated macho identity stances, they are in fact—coping. This coping is essential in social and ecological environments in which danger to their personal and familial safety is high. Maintaining a stable identity presentation allows predictability among peers, provides a set of strategies (albeit limited) to manage societal hostility (e.g., cool pose and reactive coping), and builds a fragile and temporary but demonstrably confident self in socially stressful contexts. To summarize, identity shifting has some very powerful and scary consequences for young Black boys. The very angst of having to monitor these public and private identities leaves many boys "missed, dissed, and pissed" (Kunjufu, 1983; Stevenson, 1997; Wilson, 1990).

"Pissed" is defined as an underlying expressed and unexpressed seething anger related to conscious but mostly unconscious feelings of devaluation experienced since early childhood from societal, familial, and interpersonal rejection. "Missed" is defined as the societal systematic conundrum of *misrepresentation* and *misinterpretations* of Black male behavior. "Dissed" represents the *disrespect* and distortion of Black male imaging across the American image landscape. This distortion is like identity quicksand for males who are unaware of or unprepared to manage this reality. The feeling that one has to constantly fight life's battles by oneself, must always be "on guard," and must retaliate against multiple attackers reflects a heightened sense of fear that represents being dissed. Doing Blackness and maleness with intensity is one way Black boys cope with being missed, dissed, and pissed.

"LOOKING THROUGH A GLASS DIMLY": HOW RACIAL PROJECTIONS OF SOCIAL SYSTEMS HURT BLACK BOYS

In mental health and other social institutions, there are several reasons to account for the missed, dissed, and pissed reality of African American male adolescents and the way social systems respond to them, but one stands out above the rest. A phenomenon that has caused more confusion for effective psychological assessment and treatment of African American males is the strict reliance on either-or principles. Those values influence how we conduct assessment and treatment strategies, the most popular of which involves the separation of internalizing and externalizing behaviors. This separation is very much situated in Western dichotomies of spirit and flesh, thoughts and feelings, good and bad, strong and weak, and normal and abnormal. Often, clinical psychologists and other mental and social health clinicians and researchers are trained to understand that there are two kinds of troubled youth in our world—internalizers and externalizers. Internalizers are often known to be anxious, depressed, withdrawn, shy, sullen, bored, unconscious, quietly irritable, catatonic, and compulsive.

Externalizers are often believed to be aggressive, outwardly angry, hostile, conduct disordered, oppositional defiant, loud, active, remorseless, and volitional. Mental health and juvenile justice systems reflect these dualistic diagnostic categories when judgments are made as to the appropriate "treatment" for acting-out versus non-acting-out youth. Kunjufu was absolutely correct to consider this mental health reality as a conspiracy to murder African American boys. Black emotions are aggressive and violent while White youth aggression is "a pain in the ass." The fear of the potential violence of disenfranchised, gun-toting angry White males in high schools has not reached the level of heightened extreme fear and stereotype that has accompanied the public images of Black male youth, in our opinion. Who could forget Kip Kinkel, the 15-year-old White male from Thurston High School in Springfield, Oregon, who on May 21, 1998, fired 51 rounds of ammunition at a hundred or so students in the cafeteria, wounding 22 and killing 2. What is most relevant about this case here is not the shooting violence at the school, but the fact that Mr. Kinkel was not thoroughly searched by detectives at the scene of the crime. This "mistake" led to Kinkel almost killing a police officer at the police station when he took a knife he had taped to his leg, and lunged to stab him. Thanks to pepper spray and nifty police work, Kinkel was subdued and then thoroughly searched. It appeared that despite Mr. Kinkel's shooting spree of gun violence, murder, and assault, he was not deemed dangerous enough to warrant a thorough body search. We wonder if a Black male caught in the same circumstances would have been so easily dismissed. We think not.

Thus, we have considered that Black youth are struggling within a narrow and surreal existence. While many, not all, but significantly more White youth have greater latitude for psychological development, experimentation and meaning-making through mistakes, most Black youth do not have such luxury, especially if they are poor (Baer & Chambliss, 1997). While White male youth have the equivalent of two football fields worth of freedom with which to make serious life-changing mistakes (e.g., property crimes, misdemeanor, interpersonal aggression, substance abuse, and school disruption) without the risk of losing their future, Black males have a long yard. In fact, to carry this football analogy further, every day could be labeled "Fourth and long." But to bring it back to the "hood" analogy, the only safe space to play is on the front steps or stoop of their houses.

Black males are twice as likely to be arrested and seven times more likely to be held in detention facilities as White youth (Children's Defense Fund, 2000). Black males consistently receive more severe and lengthier punishments than White males who commit the same offenses (Children's Defense Fund, 2000). Black males are overrepresented at every level of the juvenile justice system, constituting 70 percent of all juveniles in American correctional facilities (Children's Defense Fund, 2000). In Pennsylvania, a recent civil rights report found that a Black youth is six times more likely to be locked up than a White peer, even when charged with a similar crime and when neither has a prior record (Steffensmeier, Ulmer, & Kramer, 1998). Moreover, Black males report experiencing racial discrimination at higher levels than any other group (Krieger, Sidney, & Coakley, 1998). The *Wall Street Journal* reported on a study that found that a white ex-con was called back for a second job interview as a dishwasher or driver 17% of the time, while a crime-free Black applicant was called back 14% of the time (Wessell, 2003).

Our systems are flawed as to identifying adequately the social and mental health needs of African American youth for several reasons. One reason can be found in the insidious nature of racism. Research shows that African Americans, especially Black boys are often feared as criminalizing men or animals (Baer & Chambliss, 1997; Finkelman, 1992; Greenberg & West, 2001; Kennedy, 2001; Meeks, 2000; Sampson & Laub, 1993). Sampson and Laub (1993) found through investigation of juvenile court proceedings and records that black males are perceived as threatening members of society who need to be controlled. Romer, Jamieson, and de Coteau (1998) found that the percentage of crime committed by African Americans in a northeast city is significantly lower than the percentage of news coverage on three major local news networks compared to Whites. A viewer could form the impression simply by watching the local news that African Americans commit crime at higher levels. Furthermore, African American males are often targeted as threats and menaces to society by many social authority figures ranging from police to school teachers and that this social construction of Black males as "menace" has both public health and economic marketing implications (Gibbs, 1988; McIntyre & Pernell, 1985; Potts, 1997; Rowan, Pernell, & Akers, 1996; Sampson & Laub, 1993).

Anne Ferguson's (2000) telling account of how 11- and 12-year-old Black boys are criminalized and expected to land in jail as a group is even more chilling when you consider her book *Bad Boys* is focused on how schools can be the culprits of the projections. The rash of police shootings and killings of innocent, unarmed Black males, the subsequent media whitewash of the social implications of the loss of Black life compared with Whites (West, 1993), and the refusal of major institutions (police) to admit wrongdoing or change their practices in the face of overwhelming statistical or video evidence are just a few of the evidentiary issues to support the racism argument (ACLU Pedestrian and Car Stop Audit, 2000).

A recent ACLU Audit and Monitoring Report on Police Pedestrian and Car Stops in Philadelphia County revealed that African Americans and Latinos are being stopped at 2 to 3 times (in some districts, up to 10 times) their rates of population compared with Whites and that this is most pronounced in Philadelphia districts in which African Americans and Latinos make up less than 10 percent of the population (ACLU Pedestrian and Car Stop Audit, 2000). Despite the percentage of African Americans in a particular district, the arrest rates for Blacks exceeds the expected population percentage in each of the 23 districts in Philadelphia County and in only 2 districts does the arrest rate of Whites exceed the White population percentage.

Serious researchers and clinicians interested in the identity development and psychological intervention with Black boys cannot wait for "White" power structures or people in powerful positions to actually understand and challenge a systemic view of racism. To wait for this phenomenon is akin to watching polar ice melt and reveals only an ignorance and inability to interpret the American racial milieu across the past three centuries. It may happen, but why wait for it? Why wait for more Black male youth to fall prey to stereotypes that have daily negative physical and mental health consequences? Questions like these and answers to these questions represent key reasons why this book was written.

Intervening with racism may require a psychological arming of the victims more than it involves the upending of the social status quo (White & Jones, 1999). Too often, Black interventionists, civil rights leaders, and protesters leave the children unprotected while going to fight on the race-relations battlefield. The understandable explanation is that children will pick up meaning by watching, by implication, or by indirect socialization. Mostly this is true, but when we win some of the battles and lose the war, our children suffer the most, because all children witness is their loved ones withering slowly to nothing. The message to helpers, Black or otherwise, should be, "Don't leave the children unprotected." Besides, you can't upend the status quo if the status of the children is suspect, because no child will be left behind to follow in your footsteps. As in the "in the event of an emergency the oxygen mask will fall from the ceiling" pre-takeoff speech on most airlines, we should breathe first, then give the masks to the children, rather than first leave our seat to try to fly an oxygen-depleted plane. Socialization of culture, in our opinion, should be explicit, not assumed if we realistically expect to reduce the psychologically asphyxiating effects of racism.

A second observation of the way the "either-or" projections of American social systems hurt Black boys is that professionals and researchers remain clueless about the social and cultural context demands of Black males, about the functionality of violent behavior, and about how this information is translated into action. Moreover, who cares about the intellectual debate between various identity perspectives when our societal media landscape perpetually essentializes violence and attaches it as endemic to Black manhood? While social scientists and activists say and do nothing? The intellectual conundrum of the public fight for understanding Black male identity ought not to be discussion of whether Black identity is essentialistic or multidimensional. This is an important but insufficient discussion. The key intellectual debate or challenge ought to be about the fact that Black male identity is conspicuously invisible and too often structurally attached to the most violent behaviors we abhor (see chapter 2; Franklin, 1999; Franklin & Franklin, 2000). "Hostile attribution bias" as a term has been very helpful in distinguishing aggressive and nonaggressive youths, but it may not be as applicable to the behaviors of male youths who live in dangerous contexts. The training of professionals is helpful but can't fully encompass the larger subtlety of modern societal racism. True intervention in this conundrum of missed, dissed, and pissed requires that Black families start the training at home first. To expect the mental health establishment to appreciate these larger societal machinations is overly optimistic.

A third way projections hurt Black youth is the consistent and predictable insistence of professionals (from education to mental health to juvenile justice) that internalizing and externalizing behaviors are different diagnostic categories and do not tend to coexist in an individual. This insistence is coupled with the ignorance of how ecological contexts influence behavior. Most of the aggression we see in Black youth is accompanied by depression symptoms, fear of annihilation, loss of family support and psychological distress. It is not sociopathic, which is the common misconception of professionals who have no training in the complexity of urban youth culture, who avoid discussion of race and racism, or who fear getting their intellectual and physical hands dirty in the nexus of intervention and education. So, approaches that attempt to understand and address the depression rather than control the aggression are more likely to be successful. Unfortunately, our culture has moved toward control and patrol, not understanding the synthesis of opposite emotional struggles. Therefore, there is a narrowing of the ways in which Black youth are treated based on the narrow diagnostic expectations in traditional mental health and educational contexts.

"DOING" HYPERVULNERABILITY: WHERE THE FEAR OF NOTHINGNESS MEETS INSECURE MASCULINITY

Cornell West discusses the problem of nihilism in poor, minority communities as a danger too often overlooked. Nihility is defined here as the state of or fear of nothingness or nonexistence (West, 1993). We believe that we have observed this in African American boys who have a history of anger- and aggressive-laden social conflicts. We believe that the fear of nonexistence often underlies their actions and presented identities. It is these being or presented identities that we are most interested in as we understand the hypermasculinity, hypervulnerability, and fears of nonexistence for African American males in high-risk urban contexts. Majors and Billson (1992) have applied Goffman's (1959) notions of "impression management" to Black male identity strivings. They discuss the phenomenon of dramaturgy and the pressure to present and perform one's identity and the stress raised by this presentation to the world. Unfortunately, false images of manhood perpetuate hypervulnerability. But what is hypervulnerability?

Our experiences with the boys have taught us that their emotional lives are under siege daily. The constant verbal assaults from peers, friends, and sometimes family about their physical features, fashion, walk, talk, or ideas bring about a hypersensitivity to humiliation. Hypervulnerability is a combination of feelings and experiences that surround potential humiliation. Specifically, hypervulnerability includes but is not exclusive to the following situations or experiences:

- Lack of racial socialization skills
  - alertness to discrimination, coping with antagonism, cultural pride reinforcement, cultural legacy appreciation, endorsement of mainstream culture
- Heightened sensitivity and reactivity to rejection
- Sole responsibility to protect one's image
- Disproportionately identified as a societal problem
- Exaggeration or devaluation of one's self
- Undervalued fear of calamity
- Over-reliance on insecure masculinity
- Barriers to trusting closest friends or family
- Internalization of negative images of racial and/or gender inferiority and dehumanization
- Masked mild to moderate depression related to loss and overwhelming manhood development demands

- View and treatment of women as subservient to male demands
- Homophobia and hostility towards phenomenon outside of narrow masculinity

When we use the term "hypervulnerability" this is what we mean. Hypervulnerability is the intense psychological and physical exposure of one's cognitions, feelings, and actions to annihilation and dehumanization from one's family, friends, neighborhood, society, and the various images that these social institutions blatantly and unwittingly promulgate and manufacture.

IT IS BETTER TO LOOK GOOD THAN TO FEEL GOOD

We believe that the more males experience the pressure to show themselves and demonstrate masculine competency, the greater the hypervulnerability. The problem with these dynamics and the "drama" that accompanies them is that African American boys and men are borrowing from the American society's ideas of insecure masculinity that reside in popular icons like the Marlboro Man, James Bond, Wallstreet Man, and the President. These images and the drive to emulate them are not without reward, mind you, because to accomplish these images can yield much in material and social advancements. The tragic reality is that *all* men (financially successful or not) in America fall short of being what these men represent. The goal of insecure masculinity is to "look good" despite any internal reality to the contrary—much to the delight of Fernando (played by Billy Crystal) of *Saturday Night Live,* whose life motto is "If you don't feel good, at least look good." Another oft-quoted phrase "All men are great in their imagination" is especially apropos for these dynamics. The failure fear of men of all ethnic and racial backgrounds who quietly idolize these images across the socioeconomic spectrum as evidenced by the concomitant power struggles of domestic violence, alcoholism, substance abuse, and child abandonment only solidify the futility of placing one's trust in insecure masculinity development (McCreary & Wright, 1997; Oliver, 1984; 1989).

Boys cannot be expected to develop into men if the rituals, strategies, communications, and relationships are based on a historically moribund, culturally enslaving, intergenerational dynamic of insecure masculinity (Kindlon & Thompson, 2000; Pollack, 1998). The goal of this theme is to "look good" and approximate *being* "The Man." While Black youths add some "cool pose" flavor to the mix of insecure masculinity, it is our belief that they do not change the basic nature of it. And yes, given the way in which suburban White youth buy rap music and borrow urban fashion strategies, other young boys and men of every ethnic, racial, and socioeconomic group seek to emulate the cool pose. But this amounts to no more than the phenomenon of the cool pose blind leading the blind, who are all being led by the simple, but life-polarizing mission of insecure mas-culinity. Here the ongoing identity struggle between life and death raises its ugly head. Childhood should be full of surprises not solely choices between good and bad. We ask Black boys to become men without a child-hood or a tear and wonder why they die so young. Well? It's hard to be what you don't see, but it's even harder for boys to be men before they fin-ish living or doing boyhood.

The fear of the future is not addressed and is often denied because it raises too many questions and too much pessimism that "now" preoccu-pies the minds and actions of many Black youth. Now is the most impor-tant moment not just because I'm an adolescent, but because tomorrow is bleak. So how can I be now? What must I do now, in order to be now? Vul-nerability is now-oriented. So many boys ask, "How do I protect my vul-nerability now?" So it is our assertion that it is not that poor Black youth don't think about their future, it's that for many poor Black youth who have not engaged or been engaged by the educational institutions of our society, the future is bleak, and to ponder it is too emotionally disturbing. So protecting one's vulnerability *is* being the man.

The best that many of the Black male youths we work with can hope for is to fool most of the people, most of the time. They have surmised this over time, often without adult feedback and supervision—but again they are pondering how to cope in the world with blinders on, with only limited knowledge. The problem for African American boys pretending to be young men is that their access to the tools and resources to "look good" are limited and so the cost of pretending is greater and requires greater risk, imagination and ego-boosting psychological resources. To wear cool fashion and to make money in the quickest means possible is not original, individualistic, or entrepreneurial, if the only jobs and occupations for Black youth are narrowly scripted. This presents what Stevenson & Davis (2003) have defined as a "Catch-33." They are not "leading a charge" or "making their mark" so much as they are follow-ing a script that is not as developed and broad as the scripts that the rest of the adolescent and male world has to follow; thus, the relevance of the concepts of cool pose or reactive coping or "bad boys" for African Amer-ican boys and men (Ferguson, 2000; Majors & Billson, 1992; Spencer et al., 1995).

Unfortunately, the script is designed within White society's projected fears of Black manhood, not the self-determined efforts, experiences, and potential of Black manhood. As such this script is corrupt and any Black male who follows it or lives his life to reject it may be corrupted along with it. To do this script or to play this role or its antirole evil twin brother is to self-destruct in the most consistent historical fashion. Lurking behind this identity striving is DuBois's brilliant rhetorical question of "How does it feel to be a problem?" (DuBois, 1903).

TURNING SOCIETY'S PROJECTIONS INTO SELF-DESTRUCTION: HYPERVULNERABILITY AS PROTECTION

The vulnerability that African American young males experience is overwhelming (Meeks, 2000). We believe that it is this vulnerability that precipitates violence and negative social interactions. That is, vulnerability at multiple levels and the need to protect oneself from the reality, tragedy, or possibility of one's limitations takes precedence over social etiquette or civility. The now calls one to fight the fight. The fear of despair and nonexistence underlies the need for immediate protection. The work of Hawkins, Hawkins, Sabatino & Ley (1998) and Simons et al. (2002) shows that lower perceived future opportunity and discrimination predicts depression in Black males and females. This blocked opportunity despair may be at the heart of the nothingness fear.

"Imagination is the last great weapon in the war against reality" (White, 2000). From a clinical perspective, however, we observe that the abundant expenditure of psychological resources to self-defend one's insecure masculinity through cool pose strategies is simultaneously self-destructive. To use a less than adequate *Star Trek* analogy, most of the resources that Black male youth expend, are in self-defense, not self-development. The ability to reflect, ponder, and face their situation is there, but it is not refined enough to manage the larger complexities of a White supremacist society. They cannot fight back with adequate weapons because all of their psychological and physical energies are focused on the shields of preservation.

This raises the issue of the "both-and" theoretical constructions of reality presented earlier. What must it be like to live as a Black male in a world in which the very "necessary" strategies known to be effective in promoting dominance and competence as a "real man" are the very same nihilistic strategies that ignite self-destruction, or at least ignite the fear of self-destruction?

And for what—to fool most of the people, most of the time? What's up with that? What if only some of the people are fooled some of the time? What if nobody is fooled? All this to avoid feeling the despair, the nihility, the nothingness? What then? What level, quality, and type of psychological reconceptualization or imagination or behavior must be created to remasculinize? These are a few of the relevant questions we find to be central to understanding how to reconceptualize hope for young Black males.

The lack of access to the goals and means for men on the periphery of societal existence and on the outskirts of the mainstream experience has been written by sociologists for decades (Merton, 1959), but often without a contemporary focus on the cultural-ecological implications for Black boys and men (Majors & Billson, 1992). The struggle of African American identity in the bodies, souls, and minds of adolescent boys is unique beyond comparison. Erickson has been quoted as saying that "A bad identity is better than no identity at all." Kierkegaard, the nineteenth century religious philosopher states it differently when he says, "At the bottom of enmity between strangers lies indifference." This statement is true for loved ones as well as strangers. It is this indifference to self and fear of obsolescence that many of our youth struggle to avoid at all costs.

The fear of despair or the thought that they are without identity or existence rests at the heart of most of the conflicts we see among the young boys in our work. Many are just a step below clinical depression. And without intervention, support, or what is better thought of as love, it is the "dancing with the devil" or "flirting with death" that brings about the most meaning. Kierkegaard remarks again regarding death when he states, "Because of its tremendous solemnity death is the light in which great passions, both good and bad, become transparent, no longer limited by outward appearances." It is our contention that the outward appearances of Black male youth are limited and truncated compared to others and while they can reshape these appearances, true freedom can come only if they re-create their image and redefine the questions for themselves. They must expend most if not all of this energy on their own perceptions, not the perceptions of others. History teaches us that it is a humongous waste of time and talent to try to reshape the larger societal racist perception. "Hate the game, not the player" is a familiar retort among young folks today. We think the creation of another game is in order because as the African proverb goes, "By the time the fool has learned the rules of the game, the players have dispersed."

In social and developmental contexts where the demands for dominance and male superiority rank higher than loving one's family, the "bad identity or no" phrase is no small statement (Oliver, 1984; 1989). For Black male youth who could kill each other for disputes involving sneakers and who live in a society in which American men and women kill each other under the influence of road rage and domestic insecurities, the fear of nothingness is no small social problem. Yet, we Americans are more afraid of Black angst than American angst and we are illiterate and blind to any similarity it has to our own angst (Baer & Chambliss, 1997). We just rarely apply these existential ideas to the arena of Black male psychological functioning.

WHEN DOING RUGGED INDIVIDUALISM IDENTITY TURNS TO VIOLENCE

One issue we have consistently found to precipitate Black-on-Black violence is that for many boys, the homies many boys trust the most are ultimately not trustworthy. Again, another example of hypervulnerability is the fear that the friends you "hang with" or your family could betray you. This reality fits with the finding that friend-acquaintance homicide is six times higher for Black youth than for Whites (Children's Defense Fund, 1999). We expect that this is true for those youth who haven't developed bonding relationships with homies beyond the superficial hanging together types of relationships. The recent alleged murder of Baylor basketball star, Brian Dennehey at the hands of a best friend, during the summer of 2003, is but one of many accounts of friends turning on each other. Of course, there are friendships that develop that are closer than family and that have long-lasting and life-supportive characteristics. But where the fear of betrayal or the withholding of trust predominates one's best friend relationships, we propose that hypervulnerability is mediating this experience. Hypervulnerability is the flimsy crazy glue that holds this relationship together and fighting against the ultimate death is the cause celebre.

So in the oldest of American male traditions—the rugged individualism of Marlboro Man, Lone Ranger, and James Bond, many Black male youth with serious hypervulnerability challenges, are left to protect themselves at all costs, and at all times—alone. It is not uncommon in our CPR (Cultural Pride Reinforcement) group therapy component to have the boys get "touchy" and snap at the group leaders or each other over minute misunderstandings. It is clear that they are defending themselves when no defense is necessary, at least in the eyes of outside observers. Lurie (1999) raises this when he discusses conversations among psychiatrists regarding the lack of emotional connections with others that conduct disordered youth experience. One of the psychiatrists reports:

In effect, they have learned that their emotional distress is dangerous to them, and this is why they have difficulty forming close relationships with other people. Furthermore, even minimally stressful situations (especially those that involve humiliation) can provoke a fight-or-flight response, in which a child reacts violently toward other people, behaving as though they were dangerous objects in the environment.

These dynamics reflect what researchers have identified as "hostile attributional bias," but the overwhelming sense of vulnerability is more cultural and environmental than that term suggests (Garber, Quiggle, Panak, & Dodge, 1991). It presupposes that the threat experienced by these boys is not present in-the-moment or in their immediate existential experience (going to school, waking up, going to the corner store). We take a slightly different view of these phenomena. In a both-and psychological reality, boys (or anyone for that matter) who are under stressful situations do not experience fight or flight reactions, but experience both fight and flight reactions—in the moment. If a person is fearful of engaging the aggression then we assume the potential for prevention is high. The minute misunderstandings are able to be corrected and understood. Unfortunately, out of fear or ignorance, our mental health profession refuses to go deeper with these youth and is culturally misattuned to their dilemmas (Zamel & Stevenson, 2003). Moreover, hostile attribution bias is not a bias if a person is living within a dangerous context, which is why even depressed individuals might evoke it but not act on it (Garber et al., 1991). The bias is present because of real threat in the environment. Even the toughest Black males are afraid of being victimized (May & Dunaway, 2000). That is why we prefer hypervulnerability as it may more accurately reflect what is psychologically going on within the Black male youth before, during, and after angry and aggressive conflicts and within their surroundings.

STRATEGIES FOR NURTURING BOYS, NOT MEN: "AN HOUR OF PLAY"

Plato (427 b.c.–347 b.c.) said that "You can discover more about a person in an hour of play than in a year of conversation." Traditional culturally incompetent strategies of psychoeducation, psychotherapy and intervention are not effective for Black male youth who live in a different world than the one that created these strategies (Lurie, 1999; The President's New Freedom Commission on Mental Health, 2003). This is not to say that Black male youth cannot be insightful, cannot appreciate discussing their emotional pain, or cannot learn how to increase self-control through the therapeutic challenge of cognitive distortions. On the contrary, African American boys are still boys who desire and respond to affection, protection, *and* correction (Stevenson, Davis, & Abdul-Kabir, 2001). It simply means that our strategies have missed the mark of what is psychologically and dynamically going on for them. In the article, "Missed, Dissed, & Pissed," Stevenson (1997) points out how Black youth are misunderstood, disrespected, and angry at their misrepresentation and unique struggles in American society—due often to the fact that they undergo different experiences than other groups. So different and culturally relevant intervention strategies are not only necessary, but without them, other traditional approaches are likely to perpetuate the perception that Black male youth require control and prison, not caring and prevention.

Given our view on the detrimental effects of societal and institutional racism, culturally relevant interventions must become meta-analytic, culturally socialization-based, and relationship-centered (Stevenson, 1998a; Stevenson & Davis, 2003). Black males must relearn that they are not members of a lost generation; that they deserve to be touched emotionally, physically, and intellectually; and that they are capable of learning about and critically outmaneuvering the subtleties of American racism. That is, playing a different game. They need to be reminded that they are still boys who need what all boys need not by accident or as an afterthought, but in perpetuity—care and compassion. Affection, correction, and protection. Imagine that—that one major contribution to the health of African American male identity is to challenge all relationships that seek to dehumanize them and image them as something else besides who they really are— boys. One project, PLAAY (preventing long-term anger and aggression in youth), which attempts to address these issues through the use of athletic movement and cultural socialization, is the subject of this book.

As Desmond Tutu once said, "We tend to see children as statistics, but they really are not. They are somebody's child. And if we do not do all that we can to salvage them, it is as if we are spitting in the face of God."

REFERENCES

ACLU Pedestrian and Car Stop Audit. (2000). *ACLU Report/Study on Racial Profiling in Pennsylvania*. Available: http://www.aclupa.org/report.htm.

Baer, J. & Chambliss, W. J. (1997). Generating fear: The politics of crime reporting. *Crime Law and Social Change, 27*, 87–107.

Buñuel, L. (1984). *My last sigh*. New York: Random House.

Children's Defense Fund. (2000). *Disproportionate minority confinement (DMC)*. Available: http://www.childrensdefense.org/ss_violence_jj_dmc.htm.

Cunningham, M. (1999). African American adolescent males' perceptions of their community resources and constraints: A longitudinal analysis. *Journal of Community Psychology, 27(5)*, 569–588.

DuBois, W. E. B. (1903). *The souls of Black folk*. Kraus International Publications.

Ferguson, A. A. (2000). *Bad boys: Public schools in the making of black masculinity*. Ann Arbor: University of Michigan Press.

Finkelman, P. (1992). *Lynching, racial violence, and law*. New York: Garland Publishing.

Franklin, A. J. (1999). Invisibility syndrome and racial identity development in psychotherapy and counseling African American men. *Counseling Psychologist, 27(6)*, 761–793. Sage Publications.

Franklin, A. J. & Franklin, N. B. (2000). Invisibility syndrome: A clinical model of the effects of racism on African American males. *American Journal of Orthopsychiatry, 70*, 1, 33–41.

Garber, J., Quiggle, N. L., Panak, W., & Dodge, K. A. (1991). Aggression and depression in children: Comorbidity, specificity, and social cognitive processing. In D. Cicchetti & S. L. Toth (Eds.), *Internalizing and externalizing expressions of dysfunction. Rochester Symposium on Developmental Psychopathology, 2* (225–264). Hillsdale, NJ: Erlbaum.

Gibbs, J. R. (1988). *Young, Black and male in America: An endangered species*. Dover, MA: Auburn House.

Goffman, E. (1959). *The presentation of self in everyday life*. Garden City, NY: Doubleday.

Greenberg, D. F. & West V. (2001). State prison populations and their growth, 1971–1991. *Criminology—An Interdisciplinary Journal, 39(3)*, 615–654

Hawkins, W. E., Hawkins, M. J., Sabatino, C., & Ley, S. (1998). Relationship of perceived future opportunity to depressive symptomatology of inner-city African American adolescents. *Children and Youth Services Review, 20*, 757–764.

Kennedy, R. (2001). Racial trends in the administration of criminal justice. In N. J. Smelser, W. J. Wilson, & F. Mitchell (Eds.), *America Becoming: Racial trends and their consequences, 2, 1–21.* Washington, D.C.: National Academy Press.

Kindlon, D. & Thompson, M. (2000). *Raising Cain: Protecting the emotional life of boys.* New York: Ballantine Books.

Krieger, N., Sidney, S., & Coakley, E. (1998). Racial discrimination and skin color in the CARDIA study: Implications for public health research. *American Journal of Public Health, 88(9),* Sep. 1998, 1308–1313.

Kunjufu, J. (1983). *Countering the conspiracy to destroy Black boys.* Chicago: African American Images.

Lurie, S. (1999). Child psychiatrists address problem of youth violence. *The Journal of the American Medical Association, 282,* 1906.

McCreary, M. L. & Wright, R. C. (1997). The effects of negative stereotypes on African American male and female relationships. *Journal of African American men, 2,* 25–46.

McIntyre, L. D. & Pernell, E. (1985). The impact of race on teacher recommendations for special education placement. *Journal of Multicultural Counseling & Development, 13(3),* 112–120.

Majors, R. & Billson, J. M. (1992). *Cool pose: The dilemmas of Black manhood in America.* New York: Lexington Books.

May, D. C. & Dunaway, G. R. (2000). Predictors of fear of victimization at school among adolescents. *Sociological Spectrum, 20,* 149–168.

Meeks, K. (2000). *Driving while black; What to do if you are a victim of racial profiling.* New York: Broadway Books.

Merton, R. K. (1959). *Social theory and social structure, Part Three: The Sociology of Knowledge,* 2nd ed. Glencoe, Ill: The Free Press.

Nobles, W. (1991). African philosophy: Foundations for Black psychology. In R. L. Jones (Ed.), *Black Psychology.* Hampton, VA: Cobb & Henry Publishers.

Oliver, W. (1984). Black males and the tough guy image: A dysfunctional compensatory adaptation. *Western Journal of Black Studies, 8,* 199–203.

Oliver, W. (1989). Black males and social problems: Prevention through Afrocentric socialization. *Journal of Black Studies, 20,* 1, 15–39.

Pollack, W. S. (1998). Mourning melancholia, and masculinity: Recognizing and treating depression in men. In W. S. Pollack and R. F. Levant (Eds.), *New psychotherapy for men.* New York: John Wiley & Sons.

Potts, R. G. (1997). The social construction and social marketing of the "Dangerous Black Man." *Journal of African American Men, 2,* 11–24.

The President's New Freedom Commission on Mental Health (2003). *Achieving the Promise: Transforming mental health care in America.* New Freedom Commission on Mental Health, U.S.

Romer, D., Jamieson, K. H., & de Coteau, N. J. (1998). The treatment of persons of color in local television news: Ethnic blame discourse or realistic group conflict? *Communication Research, 25(3),* 286–305.

Rowan, G. T., Pernell, E., & Akers, T. A. (1996). Gender role socialization in African American Men: A conceptual framework. *Journal of African American Men, 1,* 3–22.

Sampson, R. J. & Laub, J. H. (1993). Structural variations in juvenile court processing: Inequality, the underclass, and social control. *Law & Society Review, 27,* 285–311.

Schmitt, E. L., Langan, P. A., & Durose, M. R. (2002). Characteristics of drivers stopped by police, 1999. Washington, DC: U.S. Bureau of Justice Statistics.

Simons, R. L., Murry, V., McLoyd, V., Lin, K., Cutrona, C., & Conger, R. D. (2002). Discrimination, crime, ethnic identity, and parenting as correlates of depressive symptoms among African American children: A multilevel analysis. *Development and Psychopathology, 14,* 371–393.

Spencer, M. B. (1999). Social and cultural influences on school adjustment: The application of an identity-focused cultural ecological perspective. *Educational Psychologist, 34(1),* 43–57.

Spencer, M. B., Cunningham, M., & Swanson, D. P. (1995). Identity as coping: Adolescent African American males' adaptive responses to high-risk environment. In H. W. Harris, H. Blue, E. E. H. Griffith (Eds.), *Racial and ethnic identity: Psychological development and creative expression.* New York, NY: Routledge.

Steffensmeier, D., Ulmer, J., & Kramer, J. (1998). The interaction of race, gender, and age in criminal sentencing: The punishment cost of being young, black, and male. *Criminology, 36,* 763–797.

Stevenson, H. C. (1997). "Missed, Dissed, & Pissed": Making meaning of neighborhood risk, fear and anger management in Black youth. *Cultural Diversity and Mental Health, 3,* 37–52.

Stevenson, H. C. (1998a). Raising Safe Villages: Cultural-ecological factors that influence the emotional adjustment of adolescents. *Journal of Black Psychology, 24,* 44–59.

Stevenson, H. C. (1998b). The confluence of the "both-and" in racial identity theory. In R. Jones (Ed.), *African American Identity Development: Theory, Research, and Intervention.* Hampton, VA: Cobb & Henry.

Stevenson, H. C. & Davis, G. Y. (2003). Racial socialization. In R. Jones (Ed.), *Black Psychology,* 5th Edition. Cobb & Henry: Hampton, VA.

Stevenson, H. C., Davis, G. Y., & Abdul-Kabir, S. (2001). *Stickin' To, Watchin' Over, and Gettin' With: African American Parent's Guide to Discipline.* San Francisco: Jossey-Bass.

Wessell, D. (2003). Racial discrimination is still at work in United States. Wall Street Journal Online, Sept. 4.

West, C. (1993). Race matters. Boston, MA: Beacon Press.

White, G. (translator). (2000). *An Unspeakable Betrayal: Selected Writings of Luis Bunuel.* Berkeley, CA: University of California Press.

White, J. L., & Jones III, J. H. (1999). *Black man emerging: Facing the past and seizing a future in America.* New York: Routledge.

Wilson, A. N. (1990). *Black-on-black violence.* Bronx, NY: African World InfoSystems.

Youngblood, J. & Spencer, M. B. (2002). Integrating normative identity processes and academic support requirements for special needs adolescents: The application of an identity-focused cultural ecological (ICE) perspective. *Applied Developmental Science, 6(2),* 95–108.

Zamel, P. & Stevenson, H. C. (2003). *Cultural attunement and the reduction of rejection sensitivity in Black youth: Effects of the PLAAY project.* Pre-Doctoral Research manuscript: University of Pennsylvania.

CHAPTER 1

Remembering Culture: The Roots of Culturally Relevant Anger

Howard C. Stevenson Jr., Garland Best,
Elaine F. Cassidy, and Delores McCabe

There is a wonderful West African story called "The Cow-Tail Switch" (Coulander & Herzog, 1947) that tells of African village life. It is the story of a hunter named Ogaloussa, who went hunting one day but did not return. He had many sons, one of whom, Puli, was born after Ogaloussa was lost. When Puli could speak, he asked "Where is my father?" This set off a torrent of questions and eventually a search for the father by all of the children. Upon finding Ogaloussa's remains from a tiger attack, the sons used their magic powers to help put their fathers' bones together. The children whose talents varied from the ability to put sinews and flesh back on bones to breathing life into a body continued this magic until eventually Ogaloussa was brought to life again.

On Ogaloussa's return to the village, there was much celebration. Ogaloussa carried a very much sought after cow-tail switch, because of its significance and beauty. During one celebration, he announced that the child who had done the most to bring him back alive would receive the switch as a symbol of thanks. While much arguing went on among the children and villagers about who should receive the honor, since they all had various life-giving powers, Ogaloussa concluded that it was Puli who had done the most because he asked, "Where is my father?" The summarizing proverb of the story is "People are never really dead unless they are forgotten."

Too often, the culturally unique strategies, language, and worldviews of Black male youth are forgotten as we develop "helpful" intervention technologies. Several theoretical frameworks are essential in developing a culturally relevant set of principles (Potts & Watts, 2003), but it is our view that some African-centered principles have a greater potential to shift the very nature of how we apply, evaluate, and maintain our influence on the lives of young Black males. We will review a few of the frameworks that provide fertile ground for culturally relevant interventions and give support to the PLAAY project, and then we will review African-centered psychology implications for psychological interventions.

THEORETICAL FRAMEWORKS THAT CAN GUIDE CULTURALLY RELEVANT INTERVENTIONS

Several culturally relevant theories proposed are sensitive to appreciating psycho-historical racism, cultural-ecological politics, within-race diversity, racial identity development, anger and stress management, and neighborhood social capital (e.g., village support). Those theoretical frameworks include African and cultural psychology, Spencer's phenomenological variant of ecological systems theory (PVEST), and community social disorganization theory.

African psychology places culture, socialization, and empowerment in the center of the explication and amelioration of Black youth behavior (Akbar, 1985; Asante, 1987; Murrell, 2002; Myers, 1988; Nobles, 1991). African psychology posits many principles that are akin to the symbolic interactionism principles of George Herbert Mead (1956) in that the self is viewed as reflexive and active. Yet, the self does not act apart from the values of the significant others from family, neighborhood, society, or world (Burke, 1980; Lal, 1995; Nobles, 1991). Within the African psychology concept of diunitality (both-and), opposites are synthesized not contrasted as in either-or conceptualizations (Potts & Watts, 2003). The key culturally relevant aspects of African psychology are: the importance of cultural capital (Franklin, 1992), extended self, family cultural socialization, physical movement, spirituality, and quality relationships with young and older adults (Asante, 1987; Boykin & Toms, 1985; Dixon, 1976; Dixon & Foster, 1971; Nobles, 1991).

A key flaw in traditional violence prevention research is that very few studies address culture as a factor in youth emotional functioning or understanding youth violence and delinquency (U.S. Department of Health and Human Services, 2001a, 2001b). Furthermore, quality of neighborhood and family practices and relationships as well as the varying influences of ethnicity may better predict how youth become associated with violence (Gorman-Smith et al., 1996; Kuperminc & Reppucci, 1996). Better quality neighborhood and family relationships can prevent or delay youth involvement with violence even in violent neighborhoods (Overstreet, Dempsey, Graham, & Moely, 1999; Stevenson, 1998).

In addition to the lack of consideration of ethnicity in the conceptualization, intervention, and interpretation of violence and violence prevention processes for youth of color, we believe that researchers still err in making surface meaning implementations and interpretations of culture in violence assessment and interpretation. There is still a need to see cultural processes as more central to the functioning of Black youth engagement and rejection of violence as a means of emotional adjustment. Moreover, the development of interventions must consider at deeper levels how to integrate the culturally unique ways in which Black youth make meaning of their adolescent worlds.

Cultural style and identity often mediate the peer interaction aggression of Black youth. Terrell and Taylor (1980) found that young Black men with a strong racial identity were less likely to commit crimes against persons. It is our belief that an explicit focus on culture can address the emotional dynamics linked with anger and aggression. We also believe racism is a stressor and contributor to poor anger management and health (Outlaw, 1993). The role of cultural socialization in improving adolescent emotional adjustment is promising (Stevenson, Reed, Bodison, & Bishop, 1997; Stevenson, Cameron, Herrero-Taylor, & Davis, 2002; Stevenson & Davis, 2003).

Empowerment theory proposes that individuals who "gain mastery and control over their lives and a critical understanding of their environment" are likely to be more psychologically and behaviorally adjusted than those who do not (Zimmerman, Israel, Schulz, & Checkoway, 1992). In particular, empowerment is essential for coping with stress as defined by young African American males and emphasizes interventions that work through existing hip-hop cultural images as well as target contemporary social oppressions to change behavior.

Spencer's PVEST model presupposes five components: risk contrib-utors, stress engagement, coping methods, emergent identities, and life stage outcomes (Spencer & Markstrom-Adams, 1990). This model advances the understanding of and intervention with the meaning-making experiences of minority youth. Risk contributors include variables of race, sex, socioeconomic status (e.g., poverty), and physical status (e.g., early maturation). Stress engagement variables include neighborhood stress, social supports, and daily hassles. Coping methods include maladaptive problem-solving strategies such as exaggerated sex role orientation (e.g., machoism), reactive ethnocentrism, and personal orientation (e.g., social superiority) and adaptive solutions such as achieved social status, interpersonal competence, and self-acceptance. The fourth component stresses the ways in which youth will integrate cultural goals and perceived available means such that emergent identities become extensions of the coping methods used.

PVEST encompases person-environment fit theories view stress as related to how the individual perceives, responds to and is influenced by social, physical, and emotional environments (Kaminoff & Proshansky, 1982; Pearlin, 1982). The stress felt in life in America depends on an individual's overall person-environment fit with American institutions (Kaminoff & Proshansky, 1982). What African American youth perceive to be dangerous, oppressive or empowering in their immediate and not-so-immediate environments is often dangerous or empowering in its impact on identity development, psychological integrity, physical health, anger expression, and community survival (Outlaw, 1993; Russell, 1983; Stevenson et al., 1997). In PLAAY, young adult coaches conduct "on-the-spot" empowerment talks, encourage accurate interpretation of social cues and interaction, and refocus adolescent behavior and emotions to complete athletic game tasks.

When youth are perceived to be "extremely dangerous," their stress levels are increased and their senses become hypervigilant. The PVEST model gives justification for the multisystemic nature of PLAAY. Each component of the intervention (e.g., peer-, parent-, and community-mediated) includes strategies to assess and influence risk contributors, stress engagement, coping methods, identity formation, and life outcomes.

Social disorganization theory emphasizes the need for socially meaningful adult relationships in the lives of youth, and posits that the more socially disorganized a community is in supervision, closeness, and participation, the greater is the risk of negative youth health outcomes (Blackwell, 1991; Bursik and Grasmick, 1993; Jensen, 1972; Massey, 1990; Matseuda & Heimer, 1987; Sampson, 1992). Massey found that high crime rates, inadequate schools, and high rates of mortality are associated with poverty and racism. Several researchers found that males who perceive more trouble occurring in their neighborhood were more likely to be involved in delinquent acts (Jenson, 1972; Matseuda & Heimer, 1987). Black males are known to be victims of racism in disproportionate ways and these authors feel there is a strong link between neighborhood conditions, racism, and delinquency (Blackwell, 1991). Neighborhood context is also related to childhood aggression over and above family characteristics (Coie & Jacobs, 1993); Kupersmidt et al., 1995.

Social capital is the sum total of positive relationships including relationships with kin and neighbors who are buffers against the danger in the immediate environment. Crime rates have been found to be lower in neighborhoods in which significant social capital exists (Sampson, 1992). Stevenson (1998) found depression to be lower among African American adolescents who reported a high degree of neighborhood social capital compared with teenagers who scored low on that measure. This work justifies the use of diverse role models in disciplining, supervising, and nurturing youth, thus reducing emotional disturbance and promoting health.

In summary, the theoretical underpinnings of PLAAY stress the importance of a multiple systems (peers-, young and elder-, family, and community leaders) intervention to reduce long-term anger expression. Particular foci involve empowering youth and parents, strengthening their racial identity and social supports, challenging cognitions about when aggression is appropriate, and tooling them with anger management skills through in vivo intervention. Our theoretical framework would not be complete, however, without further examination of how African-centered principles are key to explicating the behaviors and thinking of Black male teens.

AFRICAN-CENTERED: UNIQUENESS, INTERRELATEDNESS, AND MULTIPLE WAYS OF KNOWING PSYCHOLOGY

There has been resurgence in the social sciences for the support of African-centered psychology as a major theoretical framework to explain the thoughts and behaviors of African Americans (Akbar, 1985; Asante, 1987; Asante & Asante, 1992; Boykin & Toms, 1985; Hilliard, 1983; Murrell, 2002; Nobles, 1991). Resurgence applies here in that focused attention on African American cultural differences and their implications for education and psychology did not arise recently. There is much in African American literature, thought and critique that facilitates the merging of psychological and educational practices through the works of Paul Lawrence Dunbar, W. E. B. DuBois, Ralph Ellison, Alice Walker, Carter G. Woodson, and Maya Angelou, to name a few.

Paradigmatic claims of an Africentric orientation have set the foundation for an agenda with the potential for developing novel psychological strategies. In reviewing this literature, we will focus on three broad themes of Africentric thought: (1) the uniqueness of African or African American cultural expression; (2) the interrelatedness of various dimensions of experiential reality with a major both-and theme; and (3) the multiple ways of knowledge acquisition.

The literature on the uniqueness of African American cultural values and behaviors has contrasted these values from a Euro-American framework with respect to various domains including worldviews, paradigms, and values (Akbar, 1985; Myers, 1988; Nobles, 1974), the rhythm and style of oratorical discourse (Asante, 1987), psychological states and conditions (Akbar, 1981; Nobles, 1974); experiential dimensions (Jones, 1991); learning styles (Hale-Benson, 1985); information processing (Shade, 1991); parenting styles (Spencer, 1983; 1990); language (Hilliard, 1983); and inter- and intragenerational family compositions (Boyd-Franklin, 1989; Nobles, 1974; Wilson, 1986). Despite substantive discussion, these differences have not been adequately tied to clear program development, education reform or psychological interventions.

There are expressions of an African American human nature that are unique and different from Eurocentric cultural expressions (Toldson & Pasteur, 1982; White & Cones, 2000; White & Parham, 1990). These unique expressions present a challenge to the varied but rigid traditional definitions of abnormality simply because they are different. Traditional psychology and the education influenced by it still view the "atypical" as deficient (Potts & Watts, 2003). Moreover, an Africentric orientation redefines the notion of "atypical" as behavior that is budding with potentialities. As Asante (1987) has said, "A truly African-centered rhetoric must oppose the negation in Western culture" (p. 170). Uniqueness or expressive individualism, as Boykin and Toms (1985) point out encompasses freedom of individual creative expression without asserting rugged individualism, which embodies taking on the world alone.

Secondly, an Africentric psychological agenda does not rigidly stipulate a hierarchical arrangement in and between behavioral, cognitive, affective, material, and spiritual domains. These domains are interrelated in diverse and sometimes complex ways that aren't easily measurable. The notion of interrelatedness presents a challenge to the pervasive reductionistic view of the behavioral sciences. Behaviors, thoughts, and emotions, interpersonal and intrapersonal aspects of personality, and the role of nature and the role of humanity are continua that are not separated in a psychology that is informed by African-centered tenets. Consider the African view of time compared with the Western views. Time is believed to be a slave to humanity rather than the other way around (Jones, 1991). In much of African and African American life, time is a part of a person's life, not an entity in and of itself to control or be controlled.

Another implication of the theme of interrelatedness for psychology is that alternate paradigms (yes, even Eurocentric paradigms) are expected to exist alongside an African-centered worldview. Wade Noble's use of the concept of consubstantiation is important here (Nobles, 1974). One example comes in the understanding of self as not a concept of the individual but a concept of a community of ancestors who simultaneously exist from the past, in the present, and toward the future. Furthermore, it is quite possible and important to view Eurocentric paradigms as useful and as working alongside African-centered paradigms in an African-centered approach without the threat of attaching deficiency labels to the co-abiding paradigms. Asante (1987) emphasizes this concept of wholeness in African-centered rhetorical or oratorical discourse when he refers to the oppressive history of African Americans.

Its foundation is necessarily the slave narrative. Its rhythms are harmonious, discordant only to those who have refused to accept either the truth of themselves or

the possibility of other frames of reference. Afrocentric rhetoric, while it is in opposition to the negative in Western culture, allows other cultures to co-exist, and in
that particular aspect is substantially different from Western rhetoric. It is neither
imperialistic nor oppressive. Therein lies its invigorating power (p. 170).

The interrelatedness of an African-centered worldview also posits a
reality that appreciates how opposites are blended to make a whole. Traditionally, in psychology, we often have modeled our definition of healthy
after the image of the white, middle class male who created a fair and
democratic American society (Akbar, 1985; DuBois, 1903, 1928, 1944). Our
traditional view of intelligence has followed a similar path, yet we have
added the dimension of hierarchy and determinism. That is, we tend to
overapply the concept of either-or in our Westernized conceptions of reality, health, and intelligence, to name a few dimensions. We often understand these dimensions in an either-or framework—that people are either
normal or abnormal, smart or "not too bright." And despite our desires to
view individuals along a continuum of say, "plus or minus 6 or 7 IQ
points," teachers and psychologists still judge intelligence based on the
category that an IQ of 90 falls in—the "not too bright" range.

An African-centered psychological model of human functioning challenges an either-or typology and assumes an interrelated both-and reality.
That is, people are not simply good or bad, they are both. In fact, folks are
not just normal or abnormal. They can be both, particularly given how life
can be stressful at different points in time. In a both-and reality, while
some of us are brilliant in some matters, we are absolutely clueless in others. Finally, a both-and reality orientation presupposes circular in contrast
to linear conceptualizations.

The application of both-and theoretical principles to traditional psychology creates a paradigm shift anomie and anxiety that is absolutely
necessary in our mind (Akbar, 1985; Stevenson & Davis, 2003). Consider
the possibility that psychology as a profession constructs itself around its
own either-or biases. What implications would a both-and orientation
have for the way we provide diagnoses, how we raise Black males, or how
we intervene in their challenging lives?

Finally, these domains constitute varied and alternate methods, styles,
and views of knowing (Semaj, 1985). The constant forgetting about the
contributions of ancient African civilization to the modern world only
perpetuates a distortion in the dissemination of information in our education system and through our psychological practices with ethnic minority and majority individuals and families. What might be the impact on a
fourth grader's attitude toward education if during her history class, she
were to discover that ancient Egyptian and Ethiopian civilizations of black
people were existing long before Europe became civilized? Or for her to
find out that the culture of ancient Egypt set the foundation for many of

the ways we attack the physical and metaphysical sciences around the world today? Many of today's African American children find school irrelevant because there is nothing in education that is "black like me," although we know that there is plenty of world history and epistemology that is exclusively for and about them as persons of color (Murrell, 2002). A worldview in the school system that presents a multicultural origin to world civilization is the most ethical and least distorted alternative.

Education is usually thought of as a place to gather specific knowledge, instead of a way to think about how to gain and create knowledge. Myers (1988) says that an African-centered paradigm supports the notion that self-knowledge is the basis of all other knowledge. Thus, any knowledge that teaches a person only what to think instead of how to think is ultimately corruptible. It will eventually become miseducational. An interesting way to look at conflicts between minority children and the schools they attend is to perhaps see that instead of being unaware of what is happening in their school environment, they are hypersensitive in their awareness that their education is out of step or alienating. This "strength" perspective takes into account the effect parents have had in raising their children to challenge existing modes of information dissemination and content.

Racial socialization is a process whereby parents, peers, communities, and society are active (in direct and indirect ways) in teaching children values and ways to critique the hostility of the outside world (e.g., school, establishments, etc.) and to promote positive racial self-esteem in the child. By definition, racial socialization presents an alternative way of knowing the world that may contrast with a traditional school curriculum. Consider the topic of Columbus and the discovery of the new world, for instance. Parents who actively engage in racial socialization are attempting to psychologically prepare their children by increasing their templates of meaning from which to evaluate the mass of epistemological strategies they will receive from others who may be insensitive to their unique cultural histories and beliefs.

The catastrophes that result from a monocular view of "truth" or "knowledge" are numerous. Negative or absent images of Africa and African America can create among African American youth self-esteem devaluation, cultural alienation/misperception, and a sense of community antipathy. The most tragic, however, is the derailing of a person's legitimate search for knowledge. Miseducation, as Carter Woodson has said, is the largest tragedy. In essence, this distorted view of human acquisition of knowledge redefines the journey toward knowledge as a one-way dirt road instead of what it is——a system of freeways, airways, and subways with limitless exits, stops, and altitudes to the same destination.

Of the three themes mentioned, the most challenging to a Euro-American culture is the third, multiple ways of knowing. If, as Asante asserts, Eurocentricity posits itself as the sole avenue of knowledge, one question that flows from our previous discussion is "What are the implications of African-centered thinking for legitimating alternative knowledge and intervention paths?"

AFRICAN-CENTERED PSYCHOLOGY CLARIFIED

Asante (1987) has discussed the definition of African-centered within a larger framework of Afrology—the "Afrocentric study of African concepts, issues and behaviors." He extends this definition by explaining how Afrology would integrate the three existential postures of humanity—feeling, knowing, and acting—instead of separate them, which may be more notably practiced by a reductionistic European ideology. Moreover, to study any social event, the African-centered student must be prepared to integrate those three aspects.

Furthermore, the Afrocentric set of methods is concerned with addressing the struggles of an oppressed people who have through their persecuted status continued and developed traditional (that is, African) but multiple ways of knowing (Asante, 1987). In particular, researchers are cautioned not to parcel out the impact that oppression, the perception of oppression, or living in a racially stratified social structure has on many persons of color because these are key influences in child-rearing, self-esteem, and survival (Nobles, 1974; Ogbu, 1985). As such, some traditionally aberrant behaviors and cognitions, including a healthy cultural paranoia, may be understood when the impact of racism is included in psychological and educational research as an authentic covariate (Grier & Cobbs, 1992; Ridley, 1984).

But where does one find the epistemology to see oppression in a context of health and wellness instead of detriment and despair? Asante (1987) warns that "the hallowed concepts of Western thought—rationality, objectivity, progress—are inadequate to explain all of the ways of knowing (p. 163)." In an African-centered paradigm alternate methods of research such as naturalistic observations and ethnographic studies do not negate but more adequately satisfy the conditions of pragmatic validity, ecological fit, or phenomenological focus expected of qualitative knowledge (Akbar, 1985; Hoshmand, 1987). It is not surprising that an overwhelming theme for many African American thinkers and practitioners is the uncovering of the impact of oppression and struggle in all of African American behavior.

As yet, there has been little attempt to isolate the various components of African American life and see their relative impact on behavior. Eurocentric methodology may offer some ways to address this dilemma. There are many questions raised, however. Would engaging in any experimental psychological exercise to determine the relative effectiveness of treatment strategies in an African-centered framework be possible? Wouldn't accepting a Eurocentric methodology lead only to the misinterpretation of African American behavior? Converse arguments include "Isn't it possible to emphasize African-centered strengths in the context of a research design such that the effectiveness of a particular educational or therapeutic strategy can be maximized for Black participants? Given that mainstream psychology is unlikely to forgo its dependence on experimental ideology, does it not behoove some African American researchers to keep the baby and throw out the bath water (Boykin, 1991)?

An African-centered thinker must acknowledge that some knowledge is hidden or tacit (Myers, 1988). It only follows, however, that an African-centered methodology must be consistent with its worldview. A challenge before the African-centered researcher is to develop a methodology that can identify, for example, the tacit and observed socialization messages unique to African American families (Boykin & Toms, 1985).

More damaging still has been the inability of European thinkers, particularly of the neo-positivist or empiricist traditions, to see that human actions cannot be understood apart from the emotions, attitudes, and cultural definitions of a given context. The Afrocentric thinker understands that the interrelationship of knowledge with cosmology, society, religion, medicine, and traditions stands alongside the interactive metaphors of discourse as principal means of achieving a measure of knowledge about experience (p. 164).

While there are some parallels between an African-centered agenda and the agenda of early phenomenologists and existentialists in their emphasis on experiential definitions and the appreciation of knowing the world from the client's perspective, there are significant differences. The avid reader of Sartre, Nietszche, Carl Rogers, and Rollo May will still find these authors quite European in their emphasis on the individual, and their focus on cognitive interventions and strengths that are intrapersonal, verbal, nonaffective, and nonspiritual. Even Rogers with his background as the child of an intensely religious church-going family, fails to give credence to a supreme Creator in his understanding of unconditional positive regard, a phenomenon many Black folk believe can be possible only from a Divine entity who comes from a spiritual Reality.

There are several paradigms that have attempted to apply African-centered thinking to the social issues affecting African Americans. A few of them will be reviewed here briefly.

REVIEW OF AFRICAN-CENTERED CULTURAL PSYCHOLOGY PARADIGMS

There is no limit to the wealth of paradigms to explain unique African American values (Akbar, 1985; Boykin & Toms, 1985; Jones, 1991; Nobles,

1974). The call for revolution in the sciences is being heard by some and ignored by others (Akbar, 1985) and even African American researchers are no less prone to forget the diversity of African American culture, and more importantly how this diversity affects upon human behavior (Akbar, 1985; Asante, 1987). This hearing comes as a function of the relative impotence of traditional psychological interventions in minority communities. Poverty, crime, substance abuse, poor health, and school dropouts run rampant in many minority communities and the obvious absence and mismatch of treatment strategies forces these communities to cry out for relief.

In challenging the data on the academic achievement of Black children, Boykin (1986) identifies nine characteristics of African American life that if integrated into educational systems may be more helpful in the successful academic achievement of Black children than the existing Eurocentric system. He suggests that these nine aspects of African American culture are related to traditional African culture and are distinct. They include the following:

1. *Spirituality*—Realization that there are forces in the universe that are powerful and are not mechanistic. Optimal functioning of behavior and belief is achieved when a person is well-connected to a very real spiritual life force.

2. *Harmony*—Notion that a person is not separate from his or her environment. Assumes that a person functions optimally if he or she seeks to contribute to harmonious interactions with others; exercising versatile behaviors may be involved.

3. *Movement*—Reflects the rhythmic-music-movement orientation toward life and self-expression. Music and other demonstrations such as dance and movement are not events to be produced or turned on and off, but are integrated in a lifestyle.

4. *Verve*—Related to the movement dimension but emphasis is on novelty and liveliness and away from routine and sequence. A simultaneous focus on multiple concerns rather than on only one is assumed.

5. *Affect*—Represents the interrelationship of feelings, thoughts, and actions and suggests that expression of emotions is a healthful exercise, not an example of poor impulse control; a keen discernment for the emotional expressions of others is also implied.

6. *Communalism*—Assumes that people are interdependent, social beings who hold allegiance to each other and to a group that outweighs personal liberties. Optimal functioning occurs as a person recognizes this but participates in sharing with and supporting the group.

7. *Expressive individualism*—Relates to the individual's stamp of uniqueness in style and behavior; assumes that although people are interdependent, they can demonstrate a style that others may not be able to or are not as efficient with. This aspect also emphasizes spontaneity, personal signature, and creative artistry as opposed to systematic planning and mechanistic operations.

8. *Orality*—Refers to the esteemed value of verbal and oral genius. Suggests that meanings can be communicated best through the speaking and hearing dimensions primarily if the interaction of speaking and hearing is a mutually agreed on interpersonal event. This aspect represents the awesome responsibility of how traditions and culture are communicated through the process of orality and the fact that words by themselves are not enough to command attention.

9. *Social time perspective*—Assumes that humankind and the completion of its social events should take precedence over time rather than become slaves to time categories. It is in fact a more meaningful experience if more homage can be paid and more time given to the essence of traditional and cultural human and environmental interactions and time can be allowed to bend around this essence.

Of the many schemes for identifying African American behavior, Boykin (1986) is the most comprehensive and applicable to experimental methodology. Table 1.1 represents selected examples of authors who have studied Black cultural style and expression. These tables might help readers to gain a beginner's perspective on the growing literature on the psychological importance of cultural expression and style in the coping of African American youth. The categories of Black cultural expression are divided into five knowledge arenas: divine, worldview, affect, self-other relationships, and personal style. These areas are discussed in detail in Stevenson & Davis, 2003, and in chapter 2 but are presented here to help bring some uniformity to the vast body of knowledge on Black cultural expression. The reader should pay more attention to the diversity of ways cultural expression is identified in the life of African Americans and how often these ways are missing in our research and intervention endeavors. Akbar (1985) critiques Eurocentric ideology and calls for a paradigm shift for African American behavior. He suggests that traditional psychology avoids affective experience, spiritual realities, subjective knowledge, and integrated past and present time orientations. Jones (1991) rearticulates his TRIOS model which provides a breath of fresh air in the discussion of worldview differences. TRIOS stands for the following dimensions: time, rhythm, improvisation, oral expression, and spirituality. Jones (1991) has provided these dimensions to set the stage for a multidimensional view of cultural experience and to give psychology a way to move beyond its truncated view of human behavior. White and Parham (1990) have found that interrelatedness of nature and humanity are key aspects of healthy functioning. Myers's (1988) model of optimal functioning elucidates the futility of suboptimal functioning and posits self-knowledge as key to effective functioning regardless of a person's racial or ethnic background.

Nobles (1974) isolates two major themes from African philosophy that many argue are persistent in the Black community today; they are survival of the tribe and oneness of being. These tenets of an African ethos have several accompanying notions. One notion suggests that the family system is horizontal and vertical in its orientation to the world and to its members. A person's relationship to his or her family or tribe is based on interpersonal relationships with other family members. This virtue takes on a vertical notion and mirrors the spirituality dimension of Boykin when one considers that these interpersonal relationships include those with family members who are dead or not yet born. The vertical aspect gives credence to religious and spiritual appreciation of God or a higher moral force. A second notion is that of belongingness and suggests that Black family life must meet the pragmatic (or economic) and psychological (or emotional) demands on the individual.

Another notion is what Nobles calls the continual flexibility in circularity, which suggests that Black family life is continuous, not fixed or understood based on roles and functions of individual members, and each element of family life is interrelated—not separable. As these notions are observed in Black families, one is likely to see interchangeable and egalitarian family roles, an emphasis on the wealth of interpersonal relationships rather than on the wealth of material possessions, and interdependence between the elderly and the family. In contrast, these aspects allow for the critique of dysfunctional Black family life and amelioration of the same.

Table 1.1
Categories of Black Cultural Expressions and Styles

Extended Self-Knowledge Arenas	Dixon & Foster, 1971 Beyond Black or White	Pasteur & Toldson,1982, The Roots of Soul	Rose, 1982 Cultural Values	Boykin, 1983 Characteristics of Culture	White & Parham 1990, Psychological Themes	Jones, 1991 TRIOS	Hecht, Collier, & Ribeau, 1993 Communication
Divine				Spirituality		Spirituality	
Worldview	Humanism		Diunital Orientation	Social Time Perspective	Value of Direct Experience	Time	Realism
Affect	Empathetic Understanding	Depth of Feeling	Affective Humanism	Affect	Emotional Vitality		Positivity
Self-Other	Rhythm	Naturalistic Orientation		Harmony	Interrelatedness	Rhythm	
	Communalism		Sharing	Communalism			Sharing
	Attribute of Oppression/ Paranoia				Distrust and Deception		Assertiveness
	Value of Limited Reward				Resilience		
Personal Style	Styling	Stylistic Renderings	Uniqueness	Expressive Individualism	Realness	Improvisation	Uniqueness
				Verve			
		Poetic & Prosaic Vernacular		Orality		Oral Expression	
		Expressive Movement		Movement			

(continued)

Table 1.1
Continued

Extended Self-Knowledge Arenas	Asante, 1985, Seven Senses of African Aesthetic	Asante, 1987, The Afrocentric Idea	Myers, 1988 Optimal Psychology Themes	Karenga, 1993 Nguzo Saba
Divine			Ontology	Mythology
			Life-Space	
			Process	
Worldview		Nommo	Axiology	Creative Motif
			Epistemology	Ethos
Affect			Behavioral Values	
Self-Other		Rhetoric	Sense of Well Being	Economic
				Social
				Political
				History
				Umoja
				Kujichagulia
			Logic	Ujima
				Kuumba
			Self-Worth	Imani
				Ujamaa
				Nia
Personal Style	Polyrhythm Polycentrism	Improvisation	Identity	
	Dimensional			
	Repetition	Lyrical Quality		
	Curvilinear	Vocal Artifact		
	Epic Memory	Indirection		
	Wholism			

AFRICAN-CENTERED PSYCHOLOGY: REVOLUTIONARY, EVOLUTIONARY, OR REACTIVE?

If there are no appreciable differences between persons of varying racial backgrounds, then the search for culturally diverse interventions may be futile. Yet, if there are some reasons to support different world views and the impact of these views on perception and behavior, and the implications for novel psychological assessment and intervention tactics, then the search is hampered only by the finding of an adequate methodology with which to prove these points.

Most of the discussion on the African American communities has been to justify or explain its anger and resistance toward the majority culture. Yet even this view forgets the multiplicity of expressions evident in the African American community since the early 1600s. Jones and Block (1984) make a distinction between a reactionary cultural view of African Americans and an evolutionary view. The reactive cultural view of blacks is used to describe the African American community's approach to living in a racially hostile environment. The evolutionary view is less well-known and suggests that there are expressions that are culturally generated and socialized rather than developed through resistance of outer-culture forces (i.e., racism) (Boykin & Toms, 1985). This view high-lights the development of symbols, behaviors, and rituals that exist and have existed over millennia, without the influence of oppressive forces. Jones and Block (1984) continue by stating that

If black Americans are attuned to a set of beliefs, predilections, perceptions, values and so on that diverge from those of the majority culture, it would be important to understand what differences exist and what their implications are for the model, practice and goals of psychotherapy. (p. 59)

Alternate views of African American behavior and functioning have been opposites or points along a continuum and have been helpful in demonstrating that the model theoreticians use to interpret behavior also drives the solutions to the problems that are identified. The culturally defi-cient versus the culturally different versus the social-structural scheme has been proposed (Boykin, 1986). There are also the blocked opportunity vs. the underclass approaches (Boykin, 1986).

All of these schemes relate to behaviors that are viewed in reference to majority culture or American middle-class standards. Blocked opportu-nity models assume that other members in society have opportunity. Cul-tural deficiency models assume the lack of some attribute within a cultural group. In other words, the burning question behind these models seems to be asking, "Why is it that black people behave different from whites?" Instead there is a better question posed by African American theorists in order for African American culture to be identified as distinctive. That question is, "How can we understand African American or Afro-Caribbean or African behavior in its own context, based on its own rules, and with its own paradigms of understanding?"

Worldview differences do exist. They exist in perception of values, per-ception of therapy, and in affective experience (Jones & Block, 1984; Stevenson & Renard, 1993) and will continue to exist despite societal change. The denial of affect as an essential ingredient in healthy human intellectual functioning is quite prevalent in Euro-American psychology and education (Akbar, 1985; Jones & Block, 1984). While its definition with respect to education has been variable and we are cautioned to illuminate affect's relationship with other dimensions of humanness (Beane, 1990), honesty of emotional expression still reigns as one key aspect that many African Americans tend to integrate in their knowledge-gathering styles.

Beane views affective education differently as related to the socialization of morals, values, and ethics. School contexts need to have a broader understanding of affect—also related to self-esteem and social change; "it includes the self-perceptions, values, morals, and ethics that adults, both inside and outside the school, desire and/or consider desirable and delib-erately attempt to promote in young people" (p. 14–15, Beane, 1990). Beane also defines affect as "a dimension of human thought and behavior that is based on preferences and choices tied to beliefs, aspiration, attitudes and appreciations found in both personal and social activity" (p. 14, Beane, 1990). In many respects affective education is akin to racial socialization, a process evident in African American family communication for centuries.

But what can we use to guide us in the assessment and legitimate development of these cultural African-centered differences specifically if they can increase one's investment in and benefit from an educational or psychological intervention without suggesting that differences mean problematic, less smart, less effective? The concept of the both-and is what is most important here. That African Americans are both different and the same requires a worldview that does not minimize either of these aspects for understanding the psychology of behavior and its implications for education of African American youth. Before we isolate the various components of human nature that African-centered psychology would attempt to integrate and develop, let's consider the implications of these ideas for traditional education and psychotherapy.

BRINGING CULTURAL RELEVANCE TO EDUCATION AND PSYCHOLOGY

Many authors have written volumes of literature on Africanisms and culturally different values over several decades, only to find their information discounted and ignored by mainstream anthropology, psychology, and education (Boyd-Franklin, 1989; Herskovits, 1945; Spencer, 1987). For example, Spencer (1987) points out that a major problem with research on Black child identity is that "minority focused research offered from the perspective of minority scholars is seldom cited by academic psychologists" (p. 105). So, while there are many evils to face when one sets out along an African-centered path, there is none more deadly than forgetting the historical contributions of wise and adventurous heroes and heroines who doggedly proclaimed the importance of recognizing a unique African American ethos.

As we recognize authors who have heralded the importance of cultural values in scholarship, the cultural relevance of American education to African American youth has been called into question (Boykin, 1986; Ferguson, 2000; Ogbu, 1985; Tobias, 1989). One possible reason for its irrelevance is that the rhythm and style of teaching and socializing in public schools are incongruent with the home and community environments of African American children (Hale-Benson, 1985). Another is the lack of applicability of content to the harsh ecological conditions many urban Black adolescents endure (Tobias, 1989). In discussing the plight of poor children in the primary grades, Goldhammer (in Tobias) emphatically makes this point.

Unless he is downright dull, it is almost impossible to imagine that at some level of experience the child is not aware of the thundering disparity between the real world and the school's priggish, distorted, emasculated representation of that world (p. 3).

African American youth are aware that the principles of the current educational system do not match the cultural imperatives of their community, families, or peer group. According to Tobias (1989),

Curriculum relevancy then is an attempt to make subject matter come alive by presenting concrete examples and making references to real life experiences of students. It is also an attempt to give students the tools needed to survive in a super technological age. For Black students, nothing could be more essential. (p. 215)

There are still some students who attempt to exercise biculturalism as a way to survive in two different environments. Some do not fare as well. One might envision what many children go through, that is, the daily occurrence of many African American boys and girls undergoing cognitive dissonance and linguistic manipulation as they enter a school classroom, simply to survive the day. On leaving the school grounds, a return to a Black English vernacular allows the children to make it through the night. Often, the very completion of a homework assignment becomes a statement of disloyalty to one's cultural peer network. The cultural mismatch of content and style of the American education system to the lives and experiences of these children stand out as two critiques that have to be addressed. It is inclusive of but broader than a "family values" framework.

Calls for educational reform come from all quarters (Fine & Weis, 1998), but to say that education is culturally irrelevant requires empirical support and specific recommendations. In fact, the strengths and weaknesses of this position of cultural irrelevancy have been elucidated (Ogbu, 1985). Finding quick answers to sweeping social problems is not the focus of this chapter, however. Identifying key therapeutic and educational emphases of an African-centered psychology as applied to particular social problems is the focus. It is proposed that cultural relevancy must be broadened, but in an African-centered framework. This will invariably include the recognition of alternate ways of learning and the reintegration of these learning styles into the current educational system (Hale-Benson, 1985). Perhaps the pearls of wisdom generated by African-American thinkers over the decades can be included into an African-centered psychological and educational agenda in a manner that is investigative rather than definitive. The implications for sensitivity to other cultural groups and to girls and women are equally important.

IMPLICATIONS FOR COMMUNITY PSYCHOLOGY INTERVENTION

We believe isolating any one dynamic of African American perception and behavior from its context in order to understand it means to eventually destroy the knowledge of the entity being studied. It is disjointed thinking to surmise about African American youth dropping out of school and exclude their views of the educational system's inability to help them. Many believe that educational leaders are losing the vision and ability to help all youth achieve a better life, develop self-esteem, apply basic cultural learning styles, and stimulate creative ideas springing forth from that cultural worldview (Fine, 1991).

Perhaps inner-city black youth are learning to look elsewhere to find knowledge about how to survive the world. The fact that there are other ways of knowing the world means that there are other definitions of what constitutes a method of survival as well as what constitutes success. Role models of drug dealers may not fit university views of successful business administration, but young children from the inner city who are exposed to these role models may see a different picture (Anderson, 1990). In fact, basic values of capitalism can be said to flourish in some drug-dealing networks if the presence of organizational productivity, reinvestment of capital, high capital yield, and high employee turnover are acknowledged.

The tenets of an African-centered education would further the use of the notions of uniqueness, wholeness, and multiple knowledge venues. Boateng (1990) states that "traditional African education, unlike the formal systems introduced by the colonialists, was inseparable from other segments of life. Traditional African education was there not only to be acquired but also to be lived" (p. 110). In this framework, the process of communicating the values and traditions of a cultural society across generations made it much easier to move children from stages of infancy to childhood through puberty and adolescence to eventual adulthood. There was no separation of education from personal growth and responsibility or commitment to the community. The notion of extended self has importance here because in many traditional African philosophies membership in a family or community implied much more than "showing up"; no, it implied the communal recognition of ontology, or that one's existence was connected to a spiritual and material past of traditions, values, and people (Myers, 1988; Nobles, 1991). A person's behavior and attitude were related to "being" and to be out of step or mis- "be-(hav)-ing" would require a response from the community. Solutions and problems are a communal affair. It was a problem of the educational system and the entire tribal community for a child not to be learning, not the child's problem alone. Moreover, education has the function of preparing youth for adulthood in a holistic fashion (Boateng, 1990), without the minimally successful disjointed paradigm shifting that invariably occurs every day that African American children leave their homes to go to school.

Boateng (1990) goes further to suggest that one strong approach for educating youth was through oral literature that included fables, folktales, legends, myths, and proverbs. These are contextually based modes of teaching that integrates rhythm, improvisation, oral expression, spirituality, and time orientations (Jones, 1991; Murrell, 2002). We challenge the zeitgeist of negativity that fosters the superficial view of African-centered epistemology as a hate-mongering. Such a nonintellectual attack on African-centered philosophy without investigating the writings of its most prolific authors is akin to calling "all whites racist."

The identification of components that African-centered philosophy might apply to psychological and educational problems is not a new phenomenon, just a forgettable one. Cultural socialization is resurging as a potentially creative phenomenon that integrates many, if not all, of the key elements of African-centered psychology and balances both the socially oppressive and culturally empowering variants of African American cultural expression. So how is this psychology applied to addressing the health of the Black male teen?

WHY FOCUS ON VIOLENCE AND BLACK MALES?

Aggression and exposure to aggression constitute the most stressful and life-threatening health risks for African American youth (Cornwell, 1994; Cotten, Resnick, Browne, & Martin, 1994; Durant, Cadenhead, Pendergrast, & Slavens, 1994; Durant, Pendergrast & Cadenhead, 1994; Garbarino, Dubrow, Kostelny, & Pardo, 1992; Greenberg & Schneider, 1994; Price, Kandakai, Casler, & Everett, 1994; Rosella & Albrecht, 1993; Wilson, 1990). Violence is both real and exaggerated in Black urban communities. Homicide remains the leading cause of death for Black men ages 15 to 44 years and approximately 33 percent of all Black men are incarcerated, on parole, or on probation (U.S. Department of of Health and Human Services, 2001b, 1999). Youth between the ages of 12 and 19 are twice as likely to be the victims of violent crime compared with adults (aged 25 years and over) (U.S. Department of Health and Human Services, 1999) and the vast majority of Black adults between the ages of 20 and 75 know someone who has been shot (Price et al., 1994). An unknown but disturbing consequence of violence is the physical injury of urban teenagers reported by the Bureau of Justice Statistics. Some very serious injuries, about 20 percent of all injuries to older adolescents, include broken bones, internal injuries, loss of consciousness, and moderate hospital-stay injuries (Fitzpatrick & Boldizar, 1993; U.S. Department of Health and Human Services, 1999).

Males are more likely to witness or be the victims of physical violence than females (Fitzpatrick & Boldizar, 1993; Shakoor & Chalmers, 1991).

Shakoor and Chalmers (1991) found that 75 percent of the participating boys and 10 percent of the participating girls in their sample of 1,035 school children ages 10 to 19 years had witnessed the shooting, stabbing, robbing, or killing of another person. The frustrated nature of aggression, anger, and fear of attack makes many bystanders (other youth) vulnerable in a given dispute (Brice-Baker, 1994; Hammond & Yung, 1991; 1993). Exaggerated images of Black violence promote detrimental psychological consequences for youth (Jones, 1991; Stevenson, 1992) despite the decrease in the rate of violent crime in our society and the fact that only 15 percent of "high-risk youth are responsible for 75 percent of juvenile offenses committed" (Becker & Rickel, 1998, p. 245; Howell, 1995). The image of the Black teen is portrayed as aggressive and criminal and that image influences the way in which these youth develop gender identities. These images are rebelled against and appropriated to demonstrate power in powerless neighborhood and family contexts (Anderson, 1990).

A major tragedy of adolescence in some high-risk urban contexts is the exposure to and witnessing of violence, the fear of it, and the necessity of appropriating violent behaviors as a means of self-protection (Bell & Jenkins, 1991; Durant, Pendergrast & Cadenhead, 1994; Murata, 1994; Cotten et al., 1994; Shakoor & Chalmers, 1991). Witnessing violence inflicted on loved ones, or "covictimization," is as psychologically damaging as being the victim of physical violence (Durant et al., 1994; Shakoor & Chalmers, 1991). Conversely, Fitzpatrick (1993) found that an experience with violence results in increased depression, whereas witnessing of violence does not.

Nevertheless, exposure to violence in any form tends to influence the development of anger and violence in young people. Stress-coping and cognitive restructuring strategies can reduce negative psychological outcomes to violence exposure and promote resilient outcomes (Fitzpatrick, 1993; Rosella & Albrecht, 1993). We expect to identify anger coping strategies and the mediators that prevent or trigger the interpersonal violence.

Anger expression has been the topic of clinical intervention research for over two decades (Gibbs, 1988, 1993; Grier & Cobbs, 1992; Johnson, 1990; Kassinove, 1995). In a positive way, anger can be motivation to support creative, competent, and productive activity. Anger toward institutions of discrimination is an appropriate response (Balcazar, et al., 1994; Freeman, 1994; Greenberg & Schneider, 1994; Russell, 1983). Gibbs (1993) states that there are detrimental aspects to anger for Black youth that include debilitating physical and psychological symptoms, negative and self-defeating attitudes, poor job performance, self-destructive behaviors, and loss of hope for the future. The deleterious emotional effects of the expression and suppression of anger for African American males have been researched (Johnson, 1988, 1990; Johnson, Spielberger, Worden & Jacobs,

1987). The findings suggest that anger suppression in males and females contributes to greater health risks.

To be sure, there are objective and subjective meanings of danger. Objective meanings reflect the likelihood that "an individual will suffer injury in a particular situation." Subjective meanings reflect the feeling of impending harm. What is subjectively dangerous for some is not dangerous for others (Garbarino et al., 1992). African American youth trials with aggression are also based on a real fear of attack. Results from the 1987–1989 National Crime Surveys showed that young Black urban males were most likely to be the victims of a handgun attack and the rate of attack was over twice the rate of same-age urban white men or black women (Greenwood, Model, Rydell, & Chiesa, 1996). The portrayal of Black young men as victims is a rare image in the American media landscape.

Unfortunately, the literature on youth aggression also lacks consideration of the cultural and ecological realities in the social contexts of Black youth, who make up a disproportionate percent of students at risk for school failure and social ostracism. PLAAY attempts to look for resilience of youth with disabilities in their historical, cultural and ecological experiences.

HISTORICAL SOCIETAL IMAGING OF AFRICAN AMERICAN MALE AGGRESSION

The history of intervention with the anger and aggression of African American youth can be subsumed under the rubric of "control" (Sampson & Laub, 1993). Historically, enslavement in America was more than an economic enterprise in which Africans were expected to perform insurmountable labor without pay, under daily threat of rape, injury, and murder, and separated from loved ones and family sometimes with no chance of seeing them again. Enslavement involved psychological as well as physical torture and over centuries while America struggled and experimented with developing a free and democratic society.

More than guinea pigs in the American democratic experiment, Africans were believed to be threats to the American value system of Social Darwinism, which posited evolutionary hierarchy among various racial groups. The dehumanization of African Americans as enslavable animals and creatures not human led to social values and ethics that could justify severe dissociative and bizarre treatment of Blacks, such as lynching, sterilization, and institutionalization (Finkelman, 1992).

These unconscionable acts were justifiable if several assumptions are taken as givens. One is the belief that the African is not human. A second assumption is that men, particularly white men in power, could be sanctioned to engage in any form of aggression to protect what they deemed to be within their possession. This could include their property (including land or slaves, however acquired), their families (including wife and children), and their dignity (however defined, but primarily defined with maintaining power, control, and dominance among persons, place, and social status). And the third assumption for the justification of unconscionable violence against Africans is if their different behaviors, culture, and looks could be portrayed as extremely life-threatening to those men and their possessions. In the least, the level of dissociation required to commit acts of violence upon the psychological and physical bodies of Africans can be explained if the level of fear and threat to possession is deemed to be extreme (Finkelman, 1992).

Nisbett & Cohen (1996) discuss the mentality and ethos of southern justice that reveals that the lack of proximity of legal authority, the spread-out nature of the geography, and the social dominance needs of White hypermasculinity contributed to the flagrant and widespread application of violence and aggression towards others in order to maintain honor and dignity. It must be noted that Nisbett & Cohen are clear that "honor" here is defined as unrelated to a system of morality or character building but to the maintenance of power and status. Again, the implications of these strands of historical reality are multiple. They suggest that the level of threat that often a society or local citizenry experiences dictates the development of social policy that governs the management and control of "deviant groups."

More frequently, we see the familiar Western societal image that men are not real men until they can tame their surroundings and the people they "own" in those surroundings. Weapon-carrying and related attitudes of violence are often intertwined with gender identity and must be addressed in culturally relevant programs (Cotten et al., 1994; Spencer, 1985). Black young men are no different from most youth today who discern that these images are avenues to prominence and status. The connection between the history of American violence, the proliferation of gun making, and the enslavement of African Americans has received some attention lately. Lane, Johnson, & Adler (1998) quite eloquently illuminate this connection in their book, *Murder in America: A History* and state clearly that violence is "built into our culture." Lane, Adler, & Johnson said that: "It all seems to go back to slavery." In discussing the country's earliest slave plantations, they said they were "particularly savage.... It was a system that had to be enforced by the 'master' himself—there was no law enforcement, he was the law."

The proliferation and fascination with guns has a long history but psychologically it masks a fear of annihilation dynamics prevalent during slavery. Guns make their owners feel in control and as if they single-handedly can conquer any threat that they are faced with. Some young African American men feel that carrying weapons will help them survive. Our cultural socialization intervention attempts to address the impact of negative images on gender identity, anger and racial socialization, and on violent behaviors among African American youth.

Some researchers and social critics contend that the intensity of the fear of Blacks, and particularly boys and men, has not subsided during the past four centuries and can be traced to continued disproportionate treatment of individuals not accused of criminal behavior as well as inhumane punishment of individuals thought to behave in an angry or aggressive manner (Finkelman, 1992; Sampson & Laub, 1993). The trend of placing young teens on trial as adults and the misapplication of the death penalty to the poor are just two examples cited to make the point of disproportionate treatment. Investigation into the current responses of the juvenile justice system to the aggressive behaviors of youth also reveal differential treatment across varying levels of disposition (Frazier & Bishop, 1995). Intervention development in the future must consider these larger systemic dynamics if researchers can expect to address the problem of Black male anger and aggression.

There is evidence to suggest that using long-term culturally relevant interventions that consider the historical, contemporary sociopolitical dynamics of American society as well as the intrapsychic, interpersonal, and familial struggles and strengths of the African American male can be more cost-effective and preventative than a multitude of state-controlled strategies (including probation, detention, incarceration and infrequent murder at the hands of police) (Frazier & Bishop, 1995; Greenwood, Model, Rydell, & Chiesa, 1996). It can be said that the fact that serious injustices against the Black populace caused by authorities like police occur sporadically only solidifies the psychologically damaging and horrific impact. Behavior modification theorists and researchers have long held the importance of variable-ratio schedules on the maintenance of certain behaviors (e.g., in this case, fear and distrust of social authority). The theoretical foundation for the development of culturally relevant interventions must consider historical and ecological as well as cultural contexts that influence individual behaviors and perceptions of Black youth.

WHAT IS CULTURAL SOCIALIZATION AND WHY USE A CULTURAL SOCIALIZATION MODEL?

Racial socialization represents different processes whereby families, peers, and caring communities prepare youth to survive in a world hostile to racial difference. We believe that interventions must integrate racial and cultural socialization strategies if they are to meet the cultural and emotional needs of African American youth (Stevenson & Davis, 2003; Stevenson, Davis, & Abdul-Kabir, 2001; Stevenson, Hassan, Lassiter, Davis, Abdul-Kabir, Cassidy, Fry, Mendoza-Denton, Yancy, Purdie, & Best, 2001). The intervention strategies that flow from the theoretical frameworks mentioned early in this chapter can be found in Figure 1.1 in which a composite theory of cultural socialization is proposed.

Figure 1.1
Composite Theory of Cultural Socialization

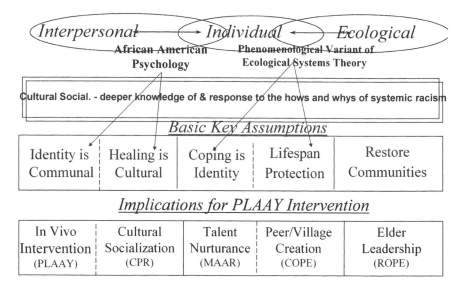

We believe that cultural and racial socialization are necessary as buffers to protect African American youth from the onslaught of subtle and blatant racial violence. It is assumed that these forces are systemic and operate apart from any identifiable institutional support. It is assumed that without protection, youth are at risk for psychological maladjustment. Active cultural socialization is necessary because youth are unaware of these onslaughts. It is equally true that these onslaughts can be exaggerated and thus leave many hypervigilant youth at risk for seeing danger where little exists, thus taking them out of the opportunity loops that society has available.

Research on racial socialization has increased over the last two decades. Scholars have begun to acknowledge the importance of childrearing in a racially hostile world and measure its frequency and psychological impact (Bowman & Howard, 1985; Boykin & Toms, 1985; Demo & Hughes, 1990; Hale-Benson, 1985; Harrison, 1985; Hughes & Chen, 1997; 1999; Johnson, 1988; McAdoo, 1985; McAdoo, 1988; Marshall, 1995; Peters, 1985; Powell-Hopson & Hopson, 1992; Spencer, 1983; Stevenson, 1994; Thornton, Chatters, Taylor, & Allen, 1990; Thornton, 1997, 1998). Most of the work on racial socialization takes the perspective that families are the primary agents of communication and if they don't discuss racial coping strategies directly, it's highly likely that youth will not receive it.

Stevenson and colleagues have found that a unique and often forgotten perspective in the field of racial socialization research is the adolescents'

Table 1.2

Protective, Proactive, & Adaptive Types of Selective Racial Socialization Strategies

Categories of Black Cultural Expression (Stevenson, 1998; Jones, 1991; Boykin, 1983)	Spencer (1983)	Bowman & Howard (1985)	Peters (1985)	Sampson & Groves, 1989, Community Social Organization	Jarrett, 1995, Growing Up Poor	Stevenson, & Abdul-Kabir, 1996, Parenting from the Bottom	Hughes & Chen, 1997	Stevenson et al, 2001, 2002, Parental and Adolescent Racial Socialization
Protective (Reactionary) (Mainstream)	Knowledge of Black history for child and parent	Racial barriers	Teaching children to survive;		Stringent Parent Monitoring	Addressing School Alienation	Promotion of Mistrust	Discrimination Alertness/ Racism Awareness
	Childrearing about race, racism and discrimination		Non-reciprocality of fair play		Restricted Family-Community Relations	Parental Isolation and Parenting for Violent Contexts	Preparation for Bias	Antagonism Coping
	Childrearing about gender concerns		Getting a good education			Colorism		Mainstream Fit
Proactive (Evolutionary) (Minority)		Ethnic pride	Self-respect and pride	Quality/Quantity of Local Friend and Kin Networks	Supportive Adult Network Structure	Metaphorical Parenting		Cultural Pride Reinforcement/ Extended Family Caring
					Joins w/Mobility-Enhancing Institutions	Rhetorical Wit		Cultural Legacy Appreciation
Adaptive (Bicultural) (Cultural)	Concerns about the educational success	Self-development	Love	Participation in Formal/Voluntary Organizations	Adult-Sponsored Youth Development	Cultural Style Parenting	Egalitarianism	Spiritual Coping
	Childrearing about civil rights	Egalitarianism		Supervising and Controlling Youth		Parent Involvement	Cultural Socialization	Life Achievement Struggling
						Multi-tasking		

view of the socialization they've received from their families. Several research endeavors with this adolescent perspective have focused on two types of racial socialization: beliefs and experiences. Racial socialization beliefs reflect how much adolescents agree with the importance of racism awareness, extended and family caring, spiritual and religious coping, and cultural pride reinforcement (Stevenson, 1994). Racial socialization experiences represent how often adolescents report that their families talk to them about coping with antagonism, being alert to discrimination, reinforcing cultural pride, appreciating their cultural heritage, and coping in mainstream society (Stevenson, Herrero-Taylor, & Cameron, in press). (These are proactive and protective messages and interactions that arise in family conversations about race.) Adaptive messages represent an integration or combination of proactive and protective intentions. These three types of racial socialization communications are discussed more fully in chapter 2. Table 1.2 includes selected examples of authors who have studied racial socialization practices and provides examples of racial socialization strategies that fit within protective, proactive, and adaptive categories. These strategies still require more research to determine their relationship to emotional functioning and well-being.

WHAT IS THE RELATIONSHIP BETWEEN RACIAL SOCIALIZATION AND ANGER EXPRESSION?

Our research has found a link between racial socialization (RS) beliefs and experiences about RS and anger expression in Black youth. Black adolescent boys who believe strongly in family RS show increased anger control and lower levels of anger acting-out and internal anger experience. Conversely, Black adolescent girls who endorse high levels of RS show decreased anger control and greater internal anger experience, with no change in anger acting-out (Stevenson, et al., 1997). For RS experiences, all adolescents demonstrate higher levels of anger control if they report receiving coping with antagonism and cultural legacy socialization whereas teenagers who report receiving high levels of alertness to discrimination socialization show high levels of anger expression (Herrero-Taylor, Mitchell, & Stevenson, in press; Stevenson, et al., 2002; Stevenson, Herrero-Taylor, & Cameron, in press).

The journey toward culturally socializing psychological interventions must make several stops along the way. One stop must include an appreciation and embracing of the cultural history of the people under study. The good, bad, and the ugly of a person's history must be identified and recognized if psychological healing can take place and long before reconciling of these disparate aspects of the extended self can be expected. Another stop should include an integration of the cultural style and language of the people who are under investigation. A third stop must include the recognition that the dynamics of mental health are intertwined with the need for intellectual and psychological liberation as well as economic and political power. A fourth stop must somehow integrate ways to manage the subtle and the blatant statements of symbolic racism in the lives of the participants/clients as they pertain to their unique experiences (i.e., Black males). Finally, in our research endeavors novel and creative methods must accompany this journey from beginning to end where the "usual suspects" of methodology and interpretation in the Western psychological canon are questioned and critiqued for their lack of knowledge about people of African descent. The PLAAY project seeks to integrate multiple theoretical perspectives that entertain the relevance of culture and ecologies while simultaneously appreciating the daily experiences that Black male youth endure. We think that, while paradoxical in nature, playing with anger has the potential to match the "myriad subtleties" and "obtuse ironies" of American justice and freedom for Black boys who live in a world expecting them to be something else.

GETTING AND KEEPING THE ATTENTION OF BLACK MALE TEENS

Trying to keep the attention of Black males in an educational setting requires a lot of heart, persistence, and creativity. The reasons have little to do with the educational challenges and most to do with their demand for authenticity and cultural relevance. That is, "keeping it real, keeping it real, keepin' it real." Educators have to pay attention to this cultural worldview to gain and keep the attention of youth. Boys need to know that the world they live in during off-school hours is translatable to the world during school hours. Treatment interventions to ameliorate the educational and psychological health of Black male teens have to "get with it" as well. Sometimes this means that very old and useful strategies can be remodeled and repackaged to include the cultural elements of a popular urban culture. Other times, however, cultural relevance can be possible only if an in-depth integration of urban popular culture with the educational and psychological institutions occurs such that these institutions will be forced to adjust and repackage curricula.

So we targeted basketball, martial arts, street corner and barber shop debate, rap and hip-hop, Ebonics, racism awareness, and cultural style and socialization with individual and group psychotherapy, family systems intervention, in vivo anger management, and teacher consultation. Several themes undergird this integration of cultural relevance and intervention. One theme behind this integration is that the emotional life of the child must be central to all that we do and if cultural relevance is an expectation for intellectual engagement, then so be it. A second theme is that cultural socialization is a required protective, creative, and proactive process that Black youth require to identify, and psychologically manage racism, sexism, and discrimination. We have to be explicit when teaching youth how to cope with and identify socially oppressive and culturally empowering dynamics. A third theme is that Black psychological theories and principles must frame the psychological interventions that seek to improve the health conditions of African Americans. Using the cultural experiences of Western middle to upper class white males as role models for effective treatment respondents must end. A final theme is that movement is one key but often untapped arena to address the mental health orientations of Black youth. The psychology of movement lends itself to novel and creative methods for assessment and improvement of psychological well-being.

IS PLAY A RELEVANT ARENA FOR UNDERSTANDING AGGRESSION IN TEENAGE MALES?

When trying to understand the rhythm of anger and aggression in young Black males, we need to watch them before, during, and after the fights they get into; and sometimes we have to get between them. How does the desire to fight get into little boys who need hugs, kisses, and playtime? Play is considered to be the one time children can receive therapy without therapists. Play is usually thought to be the work of children, but mostly that of young children. Rarely do we consider playtime as necessary for junior and senior high school students. Such a perspective can be found in the decreasing use of gym time for developmentally appropriate play and the increasing use of gym time for learning athletic sports, which may or may not address the human need to work out character or social development through play. So we try to use play for older children and young teens to understand their psychological strengths and challenges and to intervene with them during the play process. We also rely on African-centered philosophical system concepts and values to buttress the varied intervention strategies. So movement, spirituality, expressive individualism, communalism, rhythm, harmony, verve, and orality all play key roles in the development of the culturally relevant strategies we are calling PLAAY.

PLAAY stands for preventing long-term anger and aggression in youth. The PLAAY project is a multicomponent program that seeks to reduce the anger and aggression of youth with a history of interpersonal conflict. The PLAAY project is an NIMH-sponsored, cultural socialization endeavor that seeks to reduce the anger and aggression of youth with a history of interpersonal conflict. So far, we have worked with more than 260 boys in an alternative discipline school for students who have a history of physical assault toward teachers and/or other students. The program components include escapist martial arts (MAAR—martial arts anger reduction), in vivo intervention during basketball play (TEAM—teaching emotional empowerment through athletic movement), cultural socialization therapy classes (CPR—cultural pride reinforcement), parent empowerment groups (COPE—community outreach through parent empowerment), and monthly rites of passage groups (ROPE—rites of passage empowerment). In the martial arts and basketball intervention components, the role of movement is essential to understanding how the boys express their confidence and frustration. The martial arts component is devised to teach boys how to manage their emotions internally through exercises that stimulate minor frustrations (what we call "Disco-ordination").

These same frustrations can be found in the multiple physical contacts in basketball play in which the focus is on external expression of anger. Over time we teach the boys how to manage their emotions in these active athletic contexts that pull at their identities. We believe that the process of simultaneously becoming frustrated and successfully managing these frustrations is key to the prevention of long-term aggression. Also, we want to be there when the boys are frustrated, angry, and aggressive so that we can understand more deeply how this aggression occurs and why it makes sense to the boys.

In the culturally relevant group therapy we call CPR, we try to engage the boys in debate and discussion about topics ranging from racism, black-on-black violence, fear, how to manage policemen, to surviving family abuse and future goals and aspirations. Virtually any topic of concern can be talked about in the groups even though we have a curriculum that identifies ways to reduce violence among Black teens.

What is culturally relevant about CPR besides the sharing of information regarding the racism and discrimination that Black males face, and the encouragement of their untapped strengths and gifts, is the process by which we engage them to talk about these and other issues. We often find that it is important to bring to light their exaggerated sense of bravado and their belief that they are fooling most people through supportive but combative debate, in much the same way that "barber shop" or "street corner" conversations take place. They often take place when participants lay out their thoughts and make a case for it in front of everybody else. This work follows the frameworks of many Black psychologists including Roderick Watts and colleagues on developing critical consciousness in Black boys (Watts, Abdul-Adil, & Pratt, 2002; Wilson, 1990).

Of course, we try to encourage discussions that are not always lively and combative, but the combativeness is meant to stimulate passion and motivation, rather than to stir up anger and hostility. We feel that this type of debate is familiar and reveals character and while in other contexts, it may end up in aggression, it does not have to, especially if a person is heard and listened to. There are some learning processes that are possible only when debate and passion are stimulated. Some educational learning theorists and researchers actually criticize lecture-like and "broadcast" methods of disseminating information as inferior to the types of interactive strategies we have adopted in PLAAY.

Passion is not too far a cry from anger and aggression but that is exactly what professionals will need if they are ever going to understand the boys and avoid "missing," "dissing," and "pissing" them off. This passion mirrors the coping strategies of managing the "street life" (Payne, 2001). Experiencing something emotional about their lives is a requirement in our opinion before we can learn how their experiences can inform interventions. By "talking out" and "acting out" the issues they are passionate about, boys can see these issues differently rather than simply react to them. We all need time for reflection on what we do, or else we are destined to repeat what we know (or barely know). We, as guides with the CPR group, can interject challenge and support without calling it that. We can propose alternative strategies or options in role-played dilemmas that bring contemplation to their one-way tactics such that other choices are possible. We can identify and challenge non sequiturs in the boys' arguments and we can debate just as vociferously while still communicating their worth and our caring for them. And all this without letting the situation spiral into aggression. We can have high expectations of them. We can let them win the arguments but the goal is to keep them talking, feeling, reflecting, choosing, not winning, not mind-controlling, and not criticizing each other.

In the PLAAY project, we have many principles underlying the work that we do, but one in particular stands out as critical in reminding us that we are working with boys. It is the principle of touching. It is important to touch the boys in some way. By touch, we mean both physically and emotionally, perhaps spiritually or existentially. Many of the boys expect the adults and youth in their world to reject them. So we believe it is important to greet the boys whenever we see them and to let them know, often by touch (handshake, hug, some form of affectionate engagement), that we acknowledge them. Over time, they do as we all do, as all humans do—respond. They expect to be touched. They expect to be protected. Most expect to be corrected. Now, the boys can tell us the parameters of that touch (i.e., how close, how much, when?), but they *will* receive acknowledgement. In a relationship in which touching is a key component, we believe anything can happen.

Before the data are collected and analyzed and before the writing of the dynamics has been stored in volumes on library bookshelves across the country, we would like to believe that the knowledge gained from the PLAAY project would extend at least the simple prescription that African American boys should be nurtured as such. This book is about that project and the myriad processes that led to that kind of nurturing.

CONCLUSION

While the revival of interest in African-centered ideas could be ignored again—should mainstream psychology and education seek not to give it due respect or participate in inauthentic bastardization of it—the attempts to understand its implications for influence in education and to remember its potential strengths are nonetheless worthwhile. To remember African ideas and ethos to recreate psychology and education does not have to mean to walk blindly into some romanticized notion of Africa. It does not have to suggest a removal of all things non-African from our presence. (In fact, what exactly is non-African, anyway?) It is to weigh the advantages and disadvantages of breathing life into values, principles, and world-views that appreciate human diversity, that accentuate strength, that encourage empowerment, that promote integration of opposites, and that foster spirituality. The PLAAY project attempts to integrate many of those realities. They reflect in essence the soul of remembering, of reattaching aspects of an African ethos that, while threatening to other paradigms, is primarily liberating—liberating in the Bob Marley understanding of "freeing ourselves from mental slavery." We are not proposing the adoption of an African way of life here because there are diverse views about exactly what that means, but there are virtuous benefits for socialization and health in the principles we've discussed. Scholars, researchers, clinicians, social workers, and community leaders from every racial and ethnic background cannot afford to forget this. Our ancestors' memories and our children's lives depend on it.

Before we discuss the components of the PLAAY project in detail, we have to integrate our understanding of African philosophy and psychology with a theory of cultural socialization. In the next chapter, we will discuss how and why cultural socialization is necessary to combat the persistent negative but systematic perceptions of African American youth that we call the Catch-33.

REFERENCES

Akbar, N. (1981). Mental Disorder among African Americans, *Black Books Bulletin, 7(2)*, 18–25.

Akbar, N. (1985). Our Destiny: Authors of a scientific revolution. In H. P. McAdoo (Ed.) and J. L. McAdoo. *Black children: Social, educational, and parental environments. Sage focus editions, 72.* (pp. 17–31).

Anderson, E. (1990). *Streetwise.* Chicago: University of Chicago Press.

Asante, K. W. (1985). Commonalities in African dance: An aesthetic foundation. In M. Asante (Ed.) and K. W. Asante (Ed.), *African culture: The rhythms of unity.* Westport, Conn: Greenwood Press.

Asante, M. (1987). *The Afrocentric idea.* Philadelphia: Temple University Press.

Asante, M. K. & Asante, K. W. (1992). *African culture: The rhythms of unity.* Trenton: African World Press.

Balcazar, F.E., Suarez-Balcazar, Y., & Fawcett, S.B. (1994). Intervention research methods and the empowerment of Black males. In R.G. Majors & J.U. Gordon (Eds.), *The American Black Male: His present status and future.* Chicago: Nelson-Hall.

Beane, J.A. (1990). Affect in the curriculum: Toward democracy, dignity, and diversity. New York: Teacher College Press.

Becker, E. & Rickel, A.U. (1998). Incarcerated juvenile offenders: Integrating trauma-oriented treatment with state-of-the-art delinquency interventions. In T.P. Gullotta, G.R. Adams, & R. Montemayor (Eds.), *Delinquent Violent Youth: Theory and Interventions.* Thousand Oaks, CA: Sage Press.

Bell, C.C. & Jenkins, E.J. (1991). Traumatic stress and children. *Journal of Health Care for the Poor and Underserved, 2(1),* 175–185.

Blackwell, J.E. (1991). *The Black community: Diversity and unity.* New York: Harper-Collins.

Boateng, F. (1990). Combatting deculturalization of the African-American child in the public school system: A multicultural approach. In K. Lomotey (Ed.), *Going to school: The African-American experience. SUNY series, frontiers in education.* (pp. 73–84).

Bowman, P. & Howard, C. (1985). Race related socialization, motivation, and academic achievement: A study of Black youths in three-generation families. *Journal of American Academy of Child Psychiatry, 24,* 134–141.

Boyd-Franklin, N. (1989). *Black families in therapy: A multi-systemic approach.* New York: Guilford Press.

Boykin, A.W. (1986). The triple quandary and the schooling of Afro-American children. In U. Neisser (Ed.), *The school achievement of minority children: New Perspectives.* Hillsdale, NJ: Lawrence Erlbaum.

Boykin, A.W. (1991). Black psychology and experimental psychology: A functional confluence. In R.L. Jones (Ed.), *Black Psychology.* Hampton, VA: Cobb & Henry Publishers.

Boykin, A.W. & Toms, F.D. (1985). Black child socialization: A conceptual framework. In H.P. McAdoo & J.L. McAdoo, (Eds.), *Black children: Social, Educational, and Parental Environments.* Newbury Park: Sage.

Brice-Baker, J.R. (1994). Domestic violence in African-American and African-Caribbean families. *Journal of Social Distress and the Homeless, 3,* 23–38.

Burke, P.J. (1980). The self: Measurement requirements from an interactionist perspective. *Social Psychology Quarterly, 43,* 18–29.

Bursik, R.J. Jr., & Grasmick, H.G. (1993). Economic deprivation and neighborhood crime rates, 1960–1980. *Law & Society Review, 27,* 263–283.

Coie, J.D. & Jacobs, M.R. (1993) The role of social context in the prevention of conduct disorder. *Development & Psychopathology. 5(1–2)* 263–275.

Cornwell, E.E. (1994). Violence, guns, and race: Health-care professionals must speak out. *Journal of the National Medical Association, 86,* 333–334.

Courlander, H. & Herzog, G. (1947). *The cow-tail switch and other West African stories.* New York: Henry Holt and Company.

Cotten, N.U., Resnick, J., Browne, D.C., & Martin, S.L. (1994). Aggression and fighting behavior among African-American adolescents: Individual and family factors. *American Journal of Public Health, 84,* 618–622.

Demo, D.H. & Hughes, M. (1990). Socialization and racial identity among Black Americans. *Social Psychology Quarterly, 53(4),* 364–374.

Dixon, V. (1976). Worldviews and research methodology. In L. King (Ed.) *African philosophy: Assumptions and paradigms for research on black persons*. Los Angeles, CA: Fanon R & D Center.

Dixon, V. & Foster, B. (1971). *Beyond black or white*. Boston: Little-Brown.

DuBois, W. E. B. (1903). *The souls of Black folk*. Kraus International Publications.

———. (1928). The possibility of democracy in America. *Crisis: Journal of Crisis Intervention & Suicide, 53*, 353–355.

———. (1944). Prospect of a world without race conflict. *American Journal of Sociology, 49*, 450–456.

Durant, R. H., Cadenhead, C., Pendergrast, R. A., & Slavens, G. (1994). Factors associated with the use of violence among urban Black adolescents. *American Journal of Public Health, 84*, 612–617.

Durant, R. H., Pendergrast, R. A., & Cadenhead, C. (1994). Exposure to violence and victimization and fighting behavior by urban Black adolescents. *Journal of Adolescent Health, 15*, 311–318.

Ferguson, A. A. (2000). *Bad boys: Public schools in the making of black masculinity*. Ann Arbor: University of Michigan Press.

Fine, M. (1991). *Framing dropouts: Notes on the politics of an urban high school*. New York: State University of New York Press.

Fine, M. & Weis, L. (1998). Crime stories: A critical look through race, ethnicity, and gender. *Qualitative Studies in Education, 11(3)*, 435–459.

Finkelman, P. (1992). *Lynching, racial violence, and law*. New York: Garland Publishing.

Fitzpatrick, K. M. (1993). Exposure to violence and presence of depression among low-income, African-American youth. *Journal of Consulting and Clinical Psychology, 61*, 528–531.

Fitzpatrick, K. M. & Boldizar, J. P. (1993). The prevalence and consequences of exposure to violence among African-American youth. *Journal of the American Academy of Child and Adolescent Psychiatry, 32*, 424–430.

Franklin, V. P. (1992). *Black self-determination: A cultural history of African American resistance*. Brooklyn, NY: Lawrence Hill Books.

Frazier, C. E. & Bishop, D. M. (1995). Reflections on race effects in juvenile justice. In K. K. Leonard, C. E. Pope, & W. H. Feyerherm (Eds.), *Minorities in Juvenile Justice*.

Freeman, E. M. (1994). Empowerment opportunities for Black adolescent fathers and their nonparenting peers. In R. G. Majors & J. U. Gordon (Eds.), *The American Black Male: His present status and future*. Chicago: Nelson-Hall.

Garbarino, J., Dubrow, N., Kostelny, K., & Pardo, C. (1992). *Children in Danger: Coping with the consequences of community violence*. San Francisco, CA: Jossey-Bass.

Gibbs, J. R. (1988). *Young, Black and male in America: An endangered species*. Dover, MA: Auburn House.

Gibbs, J. R. (1993). Anger in young Black males: Victims or victimizers? In R. G. Majors & J. U. Gordon (Eds.), *The American Black male: His present status and his future*. Chicago: Nelson/Hall.

Gorman-Smith, D., Tolan, P., Zelli, A., & Huesmann, L. (1996). The relation of family functioning to violence among inner-city minority youth. *Journal of Family Psychology, 10*, 115–129.

Greenberg, M. R., & Schneider, D. (1994). Violence in American cities: Young Black males is the answer, but what was the question? *Social Science and Medicine, 39*, 179–187.

Greenwood, P. W., Model, K. E., Rydell, C. P., & Chiesa, J. (1996). Diverting children from a life of crime: Measuring costs and benefits. *Rand Corporation Bulletin, MR-699.0-UBC/RC/IF.*

Grier, W. & Cobbs, P. (1992). *Black rage.* (2nd edition). New York: Basic Books.

Hale, J. (1991). The transmission of cultural values to young African American children. *Young Children, 46(6),* 7–15.

Hale-Benson, J. (1985). *Black children: Their roots, culture and learning styles.* Provo, UT: Brigham Young University Press.

Hammond, W. R. & Yung, B. R. (1991). Preventing violence in at-risk African-American Youth. *Journal of Health Care for the Poor and Underserved, 2(3),* 359–373.

Hammond, W. R. & Yung, B. R. (1993). Psychology's role in the public health response to assaultive violence among young African-American men. *American Psychologist, 48(2),* 142–154.

Harrison, A. O. (1985). The black family's socializing environment: Self-esteem and ethnic attitude among black children. In H. P. McAdoo and J. L. McAdoo (Eds.), *Black children: Social, educational, and parental environments* (pp. 174–193). Beverly Hills, CA: Sage.

Hecht, M., Collier, M. J., & Ribeu, S. (1993). *African American communication. Ethnic identity and cultural interpretation.* Newbury Park, CA: Sage.

Herrero-Taylor, T., Mitchell, E. R., & Stevenson, H. C. (In press). Extending the Buffer Zone: Further Examination of Racial Socialization, Neighborhood Risk, and Anger Expression in African American Adolescents. In M. Spencer (Ed.), *Identity in Context.* Hillsdale, NJ: L. Erlbaum Associates.

Herskovits, M. J. (1945). Problem, method and theory in Afroamerican studies. *Afroamerica, 1,* 5–24.

Hilliard, A. G. (1983). Psychological factors associated with language in the education of the African American child. *Journal of Negro Education, 52(1),* 24–34.

Hoshmand, L. (1987). Alternate research methodologies in counseling psychology. *The Counseling Psychologist, 17(1),* 37–98.

Howell, J. C. (Ed.). (1995). *Guide for implementing the comprehensive strategy for serious, violent, and chronic juvenile offenders.* Claremont, CA: Hunter House.

Hughes, D., & Chen, L. (1997). When and what parents tell children about race: An examination of race-related socialization among African American families. *Applied Developmental Science, 1,* 200–214.

Hughes, D., & Chen, L. (1999). The nature of parents' race-related communication to children: A developmental perspective. In L. Balter & C. Tamis-LeMonda (Eds.), *Child psychology: A handbook of contemporary issues.* Philadelphia: Taylor & Francis.

Jenson, G. F. (1972). Parents, peers, and delinquent action: A test of the differential association perspective. *American Journal of Sociology, 78,* 562–575.

Johnson, D. J. (1988). Racial socialization strategies of parents in three Black private schools. In D. T. Slaughter & D. J. Johnson (Eds.), *Visible now: Blacks in private schools.* New York: Greenwood Press.

Johnson, E. H. (1990). Interrelationships between psychological factors, overweight, and blood pressure in adolescents. *Journal of Adolescent Health Care, 11,* 310–318.

Johnson, E. H., Spielberger, C., Worden, T. J., & Jacobs, G. A. (1987). Emotional and familial determinants of elevated blood pressure in Black and White adolescent males. *Journal of Psychosomatic Research, 31,* 287–300.

Jones, J. (1991). The politics of personality: Being Black in America. In R. L. Jones, (Ed.), *Black Psychology.* Hampton, VA: Cobb & Henry Publishers.

Jones, J. M. & Block, C. B. (1984). Black cultural perspectives. *Clinical Psychologist. Vol 37(2),* 58–62.

Kaminoff, R. D., & Proshansky, H. M. (1982). Stress as a consequence of the urban physical environment. In L. Goldberger & S. Breznitz (Eds.), *Handbook of stress: Theoretical and Clinical Aspects.* New York: Free Press.

Karenga, M. (1993). *Introduction to Black Studies.* Los Angeles, CA: University of Sankore Press.

Kassinove, H. (1995). *Anger disorders: Definition, diagnosis, and treatment.* Washington, DC: Taylor & Francis.

Kuperminc, G. & Reppucci, N. (1996). Contributions of new research on juvenile delinquency to the prevention and treatment of antisocial behavior, comment on Gorman-Smith et al. (1996). *Journal of Family Psychology, 10,* 130–136.

Kupersmidt, J. B., Griesler, P. C., DeRosier, M. E, & Patterson, C. J., et al. (1995). Childhood aggression and peer relations in the context of family and neighborhood factors. *Child Development, 66(2),* 360–375

Lal, B. B. (1995). Symbolic interaction theories. *American Behavioral Scientist, 38,* 421–441.

Lane, R., Johnson, D. R., & Adler, J. S. (1998) *Murder in America: A History.* Chicago, IL: Ohio State University Press.

Marshall, S. (1995). Ethnic socialization of African American children: Implications for parenting, identity development and academic achievement. *Journal of Youth and Adolescence, 24,* 377–396.

Massey, D. S. (1990). American apartheid: Segregation and the making of the underclass. *American Journal of Sociology, 96,* 329–357.

Matseuda, R. L. & Heimer, K. (1987). Race, family structure, and delinquency: A test of differential association and social control theories. *American Sociological Review, 52,* 826–840.

McAdoo, H. P. (1985). Racial attitude and self-concept of young Black children over time. In H. P. McAdoo & J. L. McAdoo (Eds.), *Black children: Social, Educational, and Parental Environments.* Newbury Park, CA: Sage.

McAdoo, J. L. (1988). The roles of black fathers in the socialization of black children. In H. P. McAdoo (Ed.), *Black Families.* Newbury Park, CA: Sage.

Mead, G. H. (1956). Play, the game, and the generalized other. In A. Strauss (Ed.), *The Social Psychology of George Herbert Mead.* Chicago: University of Chicago Press.

Murata, J. (1994). Family stress, social support, violence, and sons' behavior. *Western Journal of Nursing Research, 16,* 154–168.

Murrell, P. C. (2002). *African-Centered Pedagogy: Developing Schools of Achievement for African American Children (The Social Context of Education).* Albany, NY: State University of New York.

Myers, H. F. (1982). Research on the Afro-American family: A critical review. In B. A. Bass, G. E. Wyatt, & G. J. Powell (Eds.), *The Afro-American Family.* New York: Grune & Stratton.

Myers, L. J. (1988). *Understanding an African-centered world view: Introduction to an optimial psychology.* Dubuque, IA: Kendall/Hunt.

Nisbett, R. E., & Cohen, D. (1996). *Culture of Honor: The psychology of violence in the south.* Boulder, CO: Westview Press.

Nobles, W. (1974). Africanity: Its role in Black families. *The Black Scholar, 5,* 9.

Nobles, W. (1989). Psychological nigrescence: An African-centered view. *The Counseling Psychologist, 17,* 253–257.

Nobles, W. (1991). African philosophy: Foundations for Black psychology. In R. L. Jones (Ed.), *Black Psychology.* Hampton, VA: Cobb & Henry Publishers.

Ogbu, J. U. (1985). A cultural ecology of competence among inner-city Blacks. In M. Spencer, G. Brookins, & W. Allen (Eds.), *Beginnings: The Social and Affective Development of Black Children.* Hillsdale, NJ: Erlbaum.

Outlaw, F. H. (1993). Stress and coping: The influence of racism of the cognitive appraisal processing of African Americans. *Issues in mental health nursing, 14,* 399–409.

Overstreet, S., Dempsey, M., Graham, D. & Moely, B. (1999). Availability of family support as a moderator of exposure to community violence. *Journal of Clinical Psychology, 28,* 151–159.

Payne, Y. A. (2001). Black men and Street Life as a Site of Resiliency: A Counter Story for Black Scholars. Special Issues: Under Covers: Theorizing the Politics of Counter Stories. *International Journal of Critical Psychology, 4,* 109–122.

Pearlin, L. I. (1982). The social contexts of stress. In L. Goldberger & S. Breznitz (Eds.), *Handbook of stress: Theoretical and Clinical Aspects.* New York: Free Press.

Peters, M. F. (1985). Racial socialization of young Black children. In H. P. McAdoo & J. L. McAdoo (Eds.), *Black children: Social, educational, and parental environments.* Newbury Park: Sage.

Powell-Hopson, D. & Hopson, D. S. (1992). Implications of doll color preferences among Black preschool children and White preschool children. In A. K. H. Burlew, W. C. Banks, H. P. McAdoo, and D. A. Y. Azibo (Eds.), *African American Pyschology: Theory, research, and practice* (pp. 183–189). Newbury Park, CA: Sage.

Price, J. H., Kandakai, T. L., Casler, S., & Everett, S. (1994). African-American adults' perceptions of guns and violence. *Journal of the National Medical Association, 86,* 426–432.

Potts, R. G. & Watts, R. J. (2003). Conceptualization and models: The meanings of difference in racial and ethnic minority psychology. In G. Bernal, J. E. Trimble, A. K. Burlew, & F. T. L. Leong (Eds.), *Handbook of racial and ethnic minority psychology.* Thousand Oaks: Sage Publications.

Ridley, C. R. (1984). Clinical treatment of the nondisclosing Black client: A therapeutic paradox. *American Psychologist, 39,* 1234–1244.

Rosella, J. D. & Albrecht, S. A. (1993). Toward an understanding of the health status of Black adolescents: An application of the stress-coping framework. *Issues in Comprehensive Pediatric Nursing, 16,* 193–205.

Russell, G. W. (1983). Crowd size and density in relation to athletic aggression and performance. *Social Behavior and Personality, 11,* 9–15.

Sampson, R. J. (1992). Family management and child development: Insights from social disorganization theory. In J. McCord (Ed.), *Facts, Frameworks, and*

Forecasts, Volume 3 of *Advances in Criminological Theory.* New Brunswick, NJ: Transaction Publishers.

Sampson, R. J. & Lamb, J. H. (1993) Structural variations in juvenile court processing: Inequality, the underclass, and social control. *Law & Society Review, 27*, 285–311.

Semaj, L. T. (1985). Afrikanity, cognition, and extended self-identity. In M. Spencer, G. Brookins, & W. Allen (Eds.), *Beginnings: The Social and Affective Development of Black Children.* Hillsdale, NJ: Erlbaum.

Shade, B. J. (1991). African American patterns of cognition. R. L. Jones (Ed.), *Black psychology* (3rd ed.).

Shakoor, B. H. & Chalmers, D. (1991). Co-victimization of African-American children who witness violence: Effects on cognitive, emotional, and behavioral development. *Journal of the National Medical Association, 83*, 233–239.

Simons, R. L., Murry, V., McLoyd, V., Lin, K., Cutrona, C., & Conger, R. D. (2002). Discrimination, crime, ethnic identity, and parenting as correlates of depressive symptoms among African American children: A multilevel analysis. *Development and Psychopathology, 14*, 371–393.

Spencer, M. B. (1983). Children's cultural values and parental child rearing strategies. *Developmental Review, 3(4)*, 351–370.

Spencer, M. B. (1985). Cultural cognition and social cognition as identity correlates of Black children's personal-social development. In M. Spencer, G. Brookins, & W. Allen (Eds.), *Beginnings: The Social and Affective Development of Black Children.* Hillsdale, NJ: Erlbaum.

Spencer, M. B. (1987). Black children's ethnic identity formation: Risk and resilience of castelike minorities. In J. S. Phinney & M. J. Rotheram (Eds.), *Children's Ethnic Socialization: Pluralism and Development.* Newbury Park, CA: Sage.

Spencer, M. B. (1990). Parental values transmission: Implications for the development of African American children. In J. B. Stewart & H. Cheatham (Eds.), *Interdisciplinary Perspectives on Black Families.* Atlanta: Transactions.

Spencer, M. B. & Markstrom-Adams, C. (1990). Identity processes among racial and ethnic minority children in America. *Child Development, 61*, 290–310.

Stevenson, H. C. (1992). Invisibility revisited: Challenging the negative images of black males. *AFTA Newsletter,* American Family Therapy Association, *48*, 15–19.

Stevenson, H. C. (1994). Validation of the scale of racial socialization for adolescents. Steps toward multidimensionality. *Journal of Black Psychology, 20, 4*, 445–468.

Stevenson, H. C. (1998). Raising Safe Villages: Cultural-ecological factors that influence the emotional adjustment of adolescents. *Journal of Black Psychology, 24*, 44–59.

Stevenson, H. C. & Abdul-Kabir, S. (1996). Reflections of hope from the "Bottom": Cultural strengths and coping of low-income African American mothers. *Proceedings of the Roundtable on Cross-Cultural Psychotherapy,* Teachers College, Columbia University, New York.

Stevenson, H. C. & Davis, G. Y. (2003). Racial Socialization. In R. Jones (Ed.), *Black Psychology,* 4th Edition. Hampton, VA: Cobb & Henry.

Stevenson, H. C., Herrero-Taylor, T., & Cameron, R. (In press). Buffer zone: Impact of racial socialization experiences and neighborhood dangers and resources on anger expression in African American adolescents. In D. Johnson & A. Hunter (Eds.), *Racial Socialization: Ecologies of Child and Adolescent Development*, part of a Series in Advances in African American Psychology (R. Jones, Series Editor). Hampton, VA: Cobb & Henry.

Stevenson, H. C. & Renard, G. (1993). Trusting ole' wise owls: Therapeutic utilization of cultural strengths in African American families. *Professional Psychology: Research and Practice, 24(4),* 433–442.

Stevenson, H. C., Cameron, R., Herrero-Taylor, T. & Davis, G. (2002). Mitigating Instigation: Cultural Phenomenological Influences of Anger and Fighting among "Big-Boned and Baby-Faced" African American Youth. *Journal of Youth and Adolescence, 31,* 473–485.

Stevenson, H. C., Davis, G. Y., & Abdul-Kabir, S. (2001). *Stickin' To, Watchin' Over, and Gettin' With: An African American Parent's Guide to Discipline.* San Francisco: Jossey-Bass.

Stevenson, H. C., Cameron, R., Herrero-Taylor, T., & Davis, G. Y. (2002). Development of the Teenage Experience of Racial Socialization Scale: Correlates of race-related socialization from the perspective of Black Youth. *Journal of Black Psychology, 28,* 84–106.

Stevenson, H. C., Hassan, N., Lassiter, C., Davis, G., Abdul-Kabir, S., Cassidy, E., Fry, D., Mendoza-Denton, R., Yancy, R., Purdie, V., Best, G. (2001). *The PLAAY Project: Preventing Long-term Anger and Aggression in Youth.* In the Conference Proceedings of the National Men's Health and Fitness Conference, June, 1999, Sponsored by the Philadelphia Department of Public Health.

Stevenson, H. C., Reed, J., Bodison, P. & Bishop, A. (1997). Racism stress management: Racial socialization beliefs and the experience of depression and anger for African American adolescents. *Youth and Society, 29,* 197–222.

Terrell, F. & Taylor, J. (1980). Self concept of juveniles who commit Black on Black crimes. *Corrective and social psychiatry and Journal of Behavior Technology Methods and Therapy, 26,* 107–109.

Thornton, M. C. (1997). Strategies of racial socialization among Black parents: Mainstream, minority, and cultural messages. In R. J. Taylor, J. S. Jackson, & L. M. Chatters (Eds.), *Family life in Black America.* Thousand Oaks, CA: Sage.

Thornton, M. C. (1998). Indigenous resources and strategies of resistance: Informal caregiving and racial socialization in Black communities. In H. I. McCubbin, E. A. Thompson, A. I. Thompson, & J. A. Futrell (Eds.), *Resiliency in African-American families.* Thousand Oaks, CA: Sage.

Thornton, M. C., Chatters, L. M., Taylor, R. J., & Allen, W. R. (1990). Sociodemographic and environmental correlates of racial socialization by Black parents. *Child Development, 61,* 401–409.

Tobias, S. (1989). Another look at research on adaptation of instruction to student characteristics. *Educational Psychiatrist, 24,* 213–227.

Toldson, I. L. & Pasteur, A. B., (1982). *Roots of soul: The psychology of Black expressiveness.* New York: Anchor Press, Doubleday.

U.S. Department of Health and Human Services (1999). *Youth violence: A report of the surgeon general.* Rockville, MD: Office of the Surgeon General, Substance Abuse and Mental Health Administration, and Public Health Service.

U.S. Department of Health and Human Services (2001a). Mental Health: A report of the surgeon general. Rockville, MD: U.S. Department of Health and Human Services, Substance Abuse and Mental Health Administration, Center for Mental Health Services, National Institutes of Health, National Institute of Mental Health.

U.S. Department of Health and Human Services (2001b). Mental Health: Culture, race, and ethnicity: A supplement to mental health: A report of the surgeon general. Rockville, MD: U.S. Department of Health and Human Services, Substance Abuse and Mental Health Administration, Center for Mental Health Services, National Institutes of Health, National Institute of Mental Health.

Watts, R. J., Abdul-Adil, J. K., & Pratt, T. (2002). Enhancing critical consciousness in African American young men: A psychoeducational approach. *Journal of Men and Masculinity, 3,* 41–50.

White, J. L. & Cones, J. H. (2000). *Black man emerging: Facing the past and seizing a future in America.* New York: Routledge.

White, J. L. & Parham, T. A. (1990). *The psychology of Blacks: An African American perspective.* New York: Prentice Hall.

Wilson, M. N. (1986). The Black extended family: An analytical consideration. *Developmental Psychology, 22,* 246–258.

Wilson, A. N. (1990). *Black-on-Black Violence.* Bronx, NY.: African World InfoSystems.

Zimmerman, M. A., Israel, B. A., Schulz, A., & Checkoway, B. (1992). Further explorations in empowerment theory: An empirical analysis of psychological empowerment. *American Journal of Community Psychology, 20,* 707–727.

CHAPTER 2

Why Black Males Need Cultural Socialization

Howard C. Stevenson Jr., Gwendolyn Y. Davis,
Robert Carter, and Sonia Elliott

Between me and the other world there is ever an unasked question; unasked by some through feelings of delicacy; by others through the difficulty of rightly framing it. All, nevertheless, flutter round it. They approach me in a half-hesitant way, eye me curiously or compassionately, and then, instead of saying directly, How does it feel to be a problem? They say, I know an excellent colored man in my town; or, I fought at Mechanicsville; or, Do not these Southern outrages make your blood boil? At these I smile, or am interested, or reduce the boiling to a simmer, as the occasion may require. To the real question, How does it feel to be a problem? I answer seldom a word.

—W. E. B. DuBois, 1903

Daunted by negative evil image after negative evil image, Black boys and young men are forced to choose repeatedly whether or not to "let someone have it." Whether they are poor or rich, short or tall, handsome or ugly, "phat" (People Having Awesome Traits) and living large or broken and torn up, Black males must daily ask themselves that infamous Clint Eastwood as Dirty Harry question, "Do you feel lucky?" And more times than not, they react angrily based on centuries of unbridled emotional injury from a society that daily asks the same question (Majors & Gordon, 1994). Subsequently, in the process of reactive self-defense (Spencer, Cunningham and Swanson, 1995), assertive intelligence or simply walking down the street, they scare the "hell" out of everyone around them (including themselves) and are at risk for further physical and emotional injury. Claude McKay's poem "Outcast" is telling in that it describes how America's image-making frames the past, present, and future of African American manhood. McKay (1953) targets the stigma of living in America as a Black man when he writes,

Something in me is lost, forever lost,
Some vital thing has gone out of my heart,
And I must walk the way of life a ghost
Among the sons of earth, a thing apart.

Like ghosts, Black men are conspicuous by the fear they generate (or are perceived to generate), yet they are unseen in so many elegant ways, under what McKay calls "the White man's menace," a tragedy destined to keep them "a thing apart." What Black men really think, feel, and struggle with is invisible to the American media, psychology, and social science landscape (Majors & Gordon, 1994). On the other hand, some images of Black manhood are very stark in the minds of Americans (Stevenson, 1992). The images depict him as a person who is physically and sexually aggressive and wanton, irresponsible toward his children, homicidal and unrepentant in nature and potential, and as a person who can get away with murder. These images are conspicuous and are maintained so by their systematic repetition within and across the various institutions in our society—and by their persistence over decades, even centuries—despite the changing of the times and positive images (Majors & Gordon, 1994).

The very fact that these images are persistent, pervasive, and perpetual is more than a sign, it is a symbol of systematic processes, so much so that it would be futile to find these images mutable simply by raising awareness of them. And even if an exception to the rule could be found, the resolution of the dilemma for that individual, excellent colored man will not come from a processing of stereotypes. The systematic nature of these images represents a severe form of psychological violence but one would be hard-pressed to remember when they didn't exist. This violence is not just psychological, but it is mostly so, and while it leads to physical consequences (e.g., the disproportionate beating and killing of Black men by police), it is immutable and we would be surprised at how difficult it would be to remove it from the American image landscape. Thus, what we are calling *conspicuous invisibility* is the persistent, pervasive, and perpetual systematic imaging of Black men as problematic and the systematic blindness or refusal to acknowledge and remember African American male talent and potential. This struggle is what DuBois referred to when he revealed the brilliant but revealing rhetorical American question to the Negro that underlies most if not all American social interactions and evaluations, "How does it feel to be a problem?"

Dr. Anderson Franklin (1999) wrote an excellent treatise on the psychological dilemmas of Black manhood in America. By developing the concept of the "invisibility syndrome," he has opened multiple research and clinical avenues. Franklin makes clear the point that Black male psychological survival is unique and that there is little precedence for it despite the number of similar experiences that other racial/gender groups have survived. America has a long history with its negation, rejection, and dehumanization of African American men and in the "invisibility syndrome," Franklin provides strategies for understanding and amelioration. Ralph Ellison's classic *Invisible Man* (1951) is part of the tradition of writings on this topic, and we find a variety of experiences that describe this phenomenon in African American literature.

Franklin's work is timely given the lack of critical understanding in the counseling profession about how African American men and boys experience the world and psychotherapy (Franklin, 1999). The invisibility syndrome accurately describes what African American males experience. His work is ultimately phenomenological in a respectful manner, yet it is also very instructive for mental health professionals in explaining what to do about intervention. Dr. Franklin raises the standard of complexity to the psychological dynamics and cognitive machinations that African American men experience. If his ideas go unaddressed, our profession will continue to ignore ineffective mental health care services for African American men.

While reading Franklin (1999), I (Stevenson) could not help but reflect upon my own experiences as an African American man. I could not stop myself from shouting an exuberant "Amen" when certain points were made. These points, which I see as so basic to my psychological existence are very hard to explain to anyone who is not African American. That most of the world is unaware of these dynamics is remarkable. That the world does not care is expected. This is essential to this work—that the readers understand that my own emotional phenomenological responses sit alongside my critical analyses of this work. The result was to feel empowered by Franklin's words as well as to make a feeble attempt to extend and communicate the meaning of these psychological dynamics for Black men. So, thanks to Dr. Franklin, my responses are couched in the old Black church idiom of "He gave me legs to run on," a phrase that reflects the process that takes place when people receive support to survive daily when they are weary and when life looks bleak. What Dr. Franklin has done is the equivalent of empowering others to speak about age-old secrets and unfinished psychological ideas.

PSEUDO-OBJECTIVITY OF MAINSTREAM SOCIAL SCIENCE

Too often psychologists mistake social science as an objective institution when in reality scientists are men and women with subjective biases (Morowitz, 1997). Scientists often interpret difficult social circumstances to represent random occurrences instead of systemic expectation and routine. Such is the challenge of accepting the notion of objectivity implicit in American social science when history has shown that science often surmises negatively about the talents and challenges of African American people. This reality is reflective in what William James, the father of philosophical psychology once wrote, "A great many people think they are thinking, when they are merely rearranging their prejudices."

The violence and hostility inflicted on Black boys by established institutions is more than coincidence. We believe America would lead us to think that racism follows a variable ratio schedule with rare spikes, one in which predicting the occurrence of racism would be impossible. The trouble with validating the variable ratio schedule of racism in the individual life of Black boys and young men is that it belies a belief in the random nature of violence. (The exception here is when violence is believed to be committed or expected from Black men. Then it's commonplace, happenstance, epidemic, and "predictable.") Black folk can expect to be "dissed" in the common discourse of television news. They may not be able to predict when, but the systemic nature of the beast is not being able to predict when but how many times when. What is harder than predictability to understand is the verifiable, undeniable experience of being Black and male and different in this world and then seeing the world ignore it.

While invisibility as a psychological challenge for Black men is not new, it has rarely been applied to intervention. Franklin should be applauded for addressing invisibility directly while simultaneously illuminating what Asante (1987) calls the "peculiar arrogance" of Western scientific inquiry and also "White" American society. This arrogance, which is unique and buttresses the racism that Black men experience leads to peculiar and bizarre forms of inhumanity. Peculiar arrogance is "the arrogance of not knowing what it is that they do not know, yet they speak as if they know what all of us need to know" (Asante, 1987). It is this peculiar arrogance that reflects how American majority culture continues to denigrate the strivings of African American men and to apply a consistent cultural racism (Jones, 1997) toward these strivings, while simultaneously behaving compassionately, politely and nicely toward Black plight.

After reflecting on this peculiar arrogance, applying our professional experience in conducting clinical and research work with African American men, and integrating Franklin's notion of "invisibility syndrome," we would like to propose the idea that this invisibility is both hidden *and* visible, not just either. A both-and reality perspective is discussed in chapter 1. An example of how a "both-and" view might reframe a particular discussion is shown in Figure 2.1 in which Maslow's Hierarchy of Needs can be seen as linear (traditional view) or both linear and circular. This shift also presents a different evaluation of a person's life experiences, especially if self-actualization needs and belonging needs have to be considered simultaneously. We also want to propose that the application of the African American psychological theoretical contribution of a "both-and" reality adds a novel twist to this discussion and can extend the understanding of the psychological dilemmas of being Black in America.

Figure 2.1
Maslow's Hierarchy of Needs: Traditional and Revised View

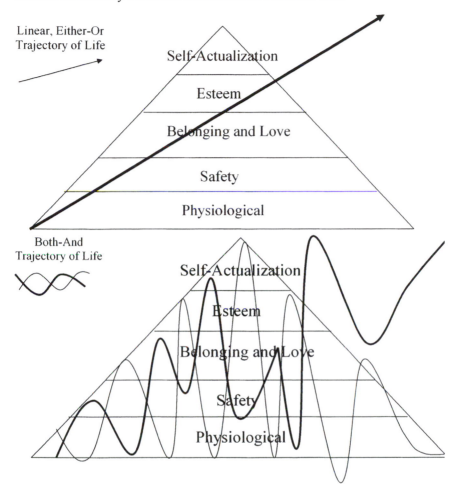

CONSPICUOUSNESS OF PSYCHOLOGICAL INVISIBILITY

This chapter also presupposes and proposes a basic tenet of African American psychological functioning and that is that effective survival and self-actualization hangs on the balance of understanding "both-and" processes. That is, instead of interpreting human behavior and functioning from a perspective of either normal *or* abnormal, smart or intellectually challenged, slow or fast, it should be interpreted as a combination or synthesization of opposites, often taking place simultaneously. We are indebted to several Black psychology authors who have challenged Western inquiry and the psychopathological interpretations of Black behavior (Akbar, 1985; Asante, 1987; Myers, 1988; Myers et al., 1991; Nobles, 1989, 1991). So, we are proposing that life for Black males involves both visible and invisible processes that identify extreme behaviors as conspicuously salient, and everyday commonplace human behaviors as invisible and unexpected.

Franklin's paper describes an African American male client named Sam. For example, when Franklin describes Sam's encounters with the attitudes of White women and the Black male vigilance about the danger of White female misinterpretation, he ventures into an arena that is rarely discussed. He writes about the way Black men must tiptoe around the threat and fear that White women or society may imagine, exaggerate, and project upon them. The consequential phenomenon in some Black men is to react first to these confusing messages and ask questions later. Despite the fact that we identify with this phenomenon emotionally, it supports what Spencer, Cunningham, and Swanson (1995) and others have found when Black adolescent males are using exaggerated macho identity stances, they are in fact, coping. Spencer, Cunningham, and Swanson's work on reactive coping defines this reactivity as a way to deal with the complications of a racially ambivalent world. Moreover, this reacting is a reflection of a person's identity striving.

In Spencer's work, the identity striving of Black males *is* coping. The social interactions they experience push them to *be* not *become*, to *do*, not just plan what to do. As adolescents and adults, Black men must often struggle with presenting a clarified identity with specific masculine actions, not an ambiguous or multidimensional identity, because the social interactions and context often demand it. Too many fall prey to trying to fit into the images that are set for them to walk into like the blind into oncoming traffic or like lemmings into the sea. Some Black men would rather "fight than switch," with "switch" representing a weak "lukewarm," unassertive identity presentation without a clue that they are playing to the only roles afforded Black males through centuries of racism. Therefore, to tiptoe is no small thing. To tiptoe is to be at psychological risk or fear being at psychological risk of falling into the stereotypic threat (Steele & Aronson, 1998) of the hostile, angry, aggressive, promiscuous Black male, while simultaneously backing into the stereotype. Ironically, many Black men tiptoe to avoid the traps and back step into them anyway. As one angry African American male academic at an Ivy-league psychology program can attest, swallowing one's anger eventually leads to "cussing somebody out" sooner or later (Stevenson, 2002).

Gwendolyn Brooks' poem, "We Real Cool" (1968), is telling in that it describes how America's image making frames the past, present, and future

of African American manhood. Black boys and men die soon by appropriating, internalizing, and regurgitating the images that the world sets up for
them (Canada, 1998). So to tiptoe, for some, is to be without existence.

What is this tiptoe dynamic? It is the feeling or pressure to fight and
adopt the world's perceptions of uncontrollable Black boys and men.
Sometimes, Black boys and men feel as though the tiptoe dynamic is protective because to be so vigilant is to be aware of their special albeit sometimes tragic circumstance. Yet when they lapse out of denial and venture
into a blind sense of comfort, they hate themselves for being so gullible. To
trust others is a natural response in a world in which they want to live
unencumbered by the world's pain or racism. This dilemma is often
framed (fairly or unfairly) as the stupidity of trusting White people. It is
human to want to live without a constant vigilance. Yet, Black men often
feel like the moment they have opened their hearts and minds toward the
view that "life is fair" or "not everyone sees me as a problem" or "she can
be trusted," then their trust is trampled on. In the example of Sam, this
phenomenon of being angry with oneself for being comfortable and letting down one's guard is very important and must not be overlooked in
Black male psychology. The words of the song "What Kind of Fool Am I?"
echo loudly after each of these encounters with a world that expects
African American men to be troublesome.

NO NEWS IS GOOD NEWS: MANAGING THE IMAGES
OF BLACK MALES

A review of the PsychInfo database reveals that very little psychological
interpretation has been written about the case of Susan Smith and the
murder of her two sons despite its significance for proving America's
reliance on negative Black images to determine the meaning of justice.
Davis (1997) has reviewed the matter from a psychoanalytic view and
emphasized the "either-or" "good-evil" nature of American views of
motherhood. In October of 1994 for eight whole days, Susan Smith fooled
the world into believing that a Black man had hijacked her car, kidnapped
her two young boys, one 3 years old and the other 14 months old, and was
heading toward an adjoining county. And for weeks, while the southern
South Carolina community and the rest of the nation was searching for
this "brilliant" Black man, the car that Smith dumped into the lake was
found with the bodies of her two boys lodged in the backseat. The irony of
this story is that most Americans around the country found that another
Black man falsely accused was new news.

Adding insult to injury, I (Stevenson) received a call from a local newspaper reporter with whom I had been arguing regarding the lack of accurate coverage of African Americans. The Susan Smith story presented a
unique opportunity in her mind so she called me to tell me that she was

writing a story that I might finally like. It was about the problem of Black men being falsely accused of crimes they didn't commit and the ease with which the American public believes it. She was so excited to finally meet my standard for culturally relevant reporting, she expected more enthusiasm from my voice on the other end of the phone. I was not excited. She was very disappointed, since this story was to put her into territory beyond her own White liberal sensibility and closer to my own radicalism. She was miffed. She asked me why I wasn't happy that a story was finally being written to my satisfaction.

"So why aren't you excited that we are finally writing a story regarding Black men being falsely accused?"

"Well, it's okay, buuuut...."

"I don't understand, I thought this is what you wanted, finally, a story that tells the truth about Black male conspiracy. This is news."

"Well, it's news to you."

"What do you mean? This is as good as news gets. That's a story."

"Well, this isn't news for Black folks because Black men have been falsely accused of crimes for centuries. This isn't new. It's news to you, but it's not news to me. Now if you really want to write a story, you should write a newspaper article about how this story is news to you but not news to me—how this story is news to some racial groups in American society, but not to others. Now, that's a story!"

Her response was a resounding, "Oh!" I went further to tell her of the amazing irony that some stereotypes last forever while others will not last very long at all. In fact, I facetiously bet her that I could start a rumor and she could help by writing a story about it with loosely associated "facts." But the bet was that the rumor or the stereotype would not last very long because the systemic processes of racism in our society can tolerate only specific types of negative stereotypes, and that these are mostly directed away from Whites and toward Blacks and other ethnically different persons in our society. The rumor I suggested was that of young White teenage or young adult women who have a tendency to kill their newly born or young children. Within the past several years and at the time of Susan Smith's child murders, there were a string of not-so-famous White high school girls who had murdered or disposed of their children, some during the prom nights of their senior year in high school. Ironically, two years later, some more famous examples included the University of Delaware freshman, Amy Grossberg and her boyfriend Brian Peterson, who in 1996, dumped their newborn in a trash dumpster outside of a motel. However, I felt in 1994 that the reporter had plenty of examples then to piece together a rumor.

I was joking, but she didn't laugh nor did she understand the lesson. The lesson was that some rumors could never get started and if they did, they wouldn't last in our society. Conversely, there are some stereotypes that we can never get rid of. But knowing that such a rumor or stereotype wouldn't sit too well with the American public, I persisted by "begging" her to write a story that at least raised the complexity bar of the race relations dynamic. I asked her to pose in the story the same questions I had posed to her which were "Why some of us find this to be news and others of us do not?" and "Why is it difficult to start a rumor about infanticide by White women but not about Black male aggression and violence?" That story was never written. She did not get it and such is the concern that many African Americans feel about the problem of race relations resolution. It is so hard to convince the majority culture to take the leap of psychological introspection necessary to begin talking on the same plane. It's way too scary a leap, intellectually and emotionally, and unfortunately, the research and clinical traditions of American psychology reflect that fear.

I am amazed still that I continue to be asked whether Whites can work with Black folks in therapy given the "great divide" of race relations. It's not that the question is ridiculous. It's a natural question and I mean that with all sincerity. Everyone should have the right to inquire about the unknown and given the tortured race relations in our society, worrying about whether Black folks can receive the help of Whites is expected. But my response to the question receives the most confused looks. I have always felt that it is possible for Whites to work with African Americans, but I say that while many can, many are not able to because they cannot handle the pain and fear and helplessness that comes from the experience. Many leave before they work through the self-critique that comes when questioning their experiences and views of race. This is especially true if they believe as I do that an objective distant view of psychotherapy is inefficient in bringing about change in clients.

When you epistemologically raise the idea that subjective perspectives are a part of the psychotherapy experience then the work with African American males will raise some very challenging implications for the way therapists need to prepare themselves. It has implications for how they will need to engage with clients. It presupposes that they will have to get used to being in a "one-down" position and feel comfortable with the uncomfortableness of that (Stevenson & Renard, 1993). Now where do Whites obtain training in dealing with their discomfort with race? Where do any of us? Well, it can be proposed that folks of color get more practice in this because from a very early age many ethnically diverse individuals and families have to consider how their difference has to be modulated in the majority culture. The chances of learning how to negotiate this tension are greater, although they may not be sufficient. As one proverb spoken often by the great family therapist, Jay Lappin, suggests, "The mouse always knows more about the cat than the cat knows about the mouse."

Working with Black folk in culturally competent ways means more than just accumulating one hundred facts about Black boys and men. This process is scary to most. Questions such as "What if he calls me a racist?" or "What if I can't get in the rhythm of his language and demeanor?" are not problematic questions. They are natural. What is very dangerous is when Whites never seek to resolve or address these questions, particularly as their character and competence are being tested. And White therapists must be most prepared and courageous to face this fear of challenge or privilege because they hold psychological power over their Black male clients. The concern that White folks in power will not critique and challenge their own privilege is a concern that haunts many African Americans.

But psychological freedom fighters, folks of color, enlightened and courageous Whites, and African American males cannot wait for the race relations cold war to thaw any more than they should expect or wait for hell to freeze over. The great walls between the majority culture and ethnically diverse cultures exist and are maintained for a variety of systemic and institutional reasons. The infrequent permeability between these walls should not take center stage in the race relations debate. Our distant and recent history has proved that not even Civil and Civil Rights Wars can tear down these walls. Although race relations are improving in some sectors of American society, to expect the entire society "to get it" is somewhat ludicrous. For persons of color to wait until America "gets it" presupposes an ignorance of the past, a denial of the present, and a fear of the future. At best, it reflects an ignorance of the "peculiar arrogance" of the American intellectual tradition.

An understanding of the invisibility syndrome regarding Black manhood is essential but this America has few tools to learn or internalize that knowledge. There are very few examples of the type of education needed to understand or manage the experience of invisibility, so we might be overly optimistic in expecting America's children to learn how to manage racial tension that has invisibility as its primary conduit. Given these conditions, fearful women and men have little reason or motivation or emotional fortitude to tolerate the knowledge or emotional tension about African American men (and other minority groups) in order to improve their practice of mental health or educational services. Some do—but many shrink from the challenge of the tension and although there are perfectly good psychological reasons for it, justifying racial avoidance is not the focus of this chapter or book.

So if the American public is afraid of making the psychological leap to look introspectively regarding the imaging of Black men and Black males are at risk as long as this introspection is avoided, the solution for African Americans cannot be found in waiting for the light bulb of racial awareness to turn on (Bell, 1992). So what are African American boys and men who are stigmatized by constant disillusionment, idolization, and demagoguery left to do? They are left to understand that the process of stigmatization is not inconsequential or benign. It is not accidental or serendipitous. No manner of consolidating or obsequious accommodation will ameliorate their condition. A revival of the human spirit is called for but one that is knowledgeable about the condition, not naïve. Such a revival must include the strategy implicit in Fanon's (1967) wonderful comment, "I find myself suddenly in the world and I recognize that I have one right alone: that of demanding human behavior from the other. One duty alone: that of not renouncing my freedom through my choices" (p. 229).

The systemic tragedy Black men and boys are faced with is as Kunjufu (1985) has so often pragmatically stated, a conspiracy—but it is worse than we thought. Still it is weaker than we have attempted to imagine if we could only face it head-on. It is a fragile conspiracy, a "tension-free hypocrisy" and is primarily about obfuscation and as a system, it relies on inaction and passive cowardice from Black folk as much as any other actions. It's when African Americans turn a deaf ear and a blind eye to their own pain that this monster has its most devastating psychological hold. Yet, looking at this individual and collective Black pain daily may add to the trauma. Noticing and speaking about the pains of racism is tiring. This racism is as entrenched as water, which makes up most of the world's substance but that even under these conditions, it's the fight for spiritual awakening, psychological freedom, and self-knowledge that matters most.

But the tragedy of racism is not some abstract play, or play on words or race card game, as some might frame it. The experience and perception of discrimination yields damaging emotional and physical health consequences which researchers are beginning to document with enlightening ferocity (Biafora et al., 1993; Clark, Anderson, Clark, & Williams, 1999; Darity, 2003; Jones, 1992; Harrell, 2000; Krieger & Sydney, 1996; Landrine & Klonoff, 1996; Nyborg & Curry, 2003; Utsey, 1998; Williams & Williams-Morris, 2000).

One psychological solution, we propose, is found in the processes of racial and cultural socialization. The solutions may need to be derived from a framework that is both-and and looks beyond the behaviors and psychological fear of the "other." Cultural socialization is meant to be meta-analytic and explain the conditions under which some stereotypes stay alive and some die immediately, why such psychological racial introspection is arduous and seemingly impossible, and why waiting for race relations renewal is not a healthy psychological place for Black men or other ethnically diverse individuals to be. This is why we have proposed elsewhere that the conditions of this particular dilemma for Black men is a Catch-33 (Stevenson & Davis, 2003).

One final psychological insult resulting from America's peculiar institution of racism remains. We call it the Catch-33 and it justifies the active use of racial socialization. It implies that self-alienation and self-dehumanization are inevitable without some resocialization (Cross, 1998).

CATCH-33—THE TRAGEDY OF PROLONGED CATCH-22

Preparing young African American children for survival in an environment that may act malevolently toward them requires families to balance explanations of harsh realities with hopeful messages of opportunity. Some suggest that this dilemma of whether or not to discuss race with children is a "Damned if you do, and damned if you don't" situation. It is what most people call the "Catch-22" dilemma. The "Catch-22" is considered to be situational and temporary and represent the singular incidents of psychological assault. So when acts of racism occur, our natural inclination is to judge them based on the particular situation. Unfortunately, we believe there is a third psychological dilemma and that Catch-22 does not fully capture the long-term effects of being in multiple "damned if you do, damned if you don't" situations. Catch-33 represents the struggle to adopt the belief that one or one's people are "just damned."

Catch-33 represents the larger tragedy (in the Greek sense) of facing the reality that this Catch-22 situation is historic and structural and may not change (see Figure 2.2). It is the inability to resolve the continuous "Catch-22" situations. The psychological assault did not occur just once or yesterday. The particular incidents or set of insults to a person's racial identity from the outside world can initially be identified as exceptional and random.

Once we surmise that it is not the particularities of the insults (i.e., a racist and ignorant assailant or hate group) but the larger systemic interworking of routine power dynamics (which "love" and "hate" groups can unwittingly contribute to), it may shock us to learn that the "damned if you do, and damned if you don't" dilemma is not momentary, isolated, and temporary, like the mumps or measles. This then *is* the tragedy, is it not? When a Black person is shot (multiple times) by policemen for no reason (and without having a gun), or shot in the back of the head (and it is described as self-defense), or hung in his cell (with no apparent suicidal ideation or history), it is one thing. But when it happens again and again and again, with no forceful challenge to its absurdity, horror, or repetition, this is something altogether different and tragic (West, 1993). To believe that one's oppression is not simply a result of random acts, of a minority of "bad" or "evil" people, but a system of random acts based on a definable set of assumptions that imply the inferiority of Black humanity, is troubling. This "matrix" of assumptions may present different challenges but the assumptions do not change. Now, imagine the heightened sense of trauma once a person's pain is recognized to be continuous. If the situ-

Figure 2.2
Catch-33

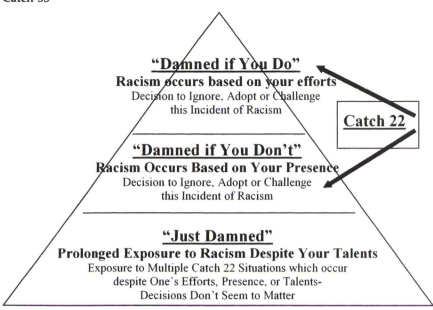

"**Damned if You Do**"
Racism occurs based on your efforts
Decision to Ignore, Adopt or Challenge
this Incident of Racism

Catch 22

"**Damned if You Don't**"
Racism Occurs Based on Your Presence
Decision to Ignore, Adopt or Challenge
this Incident of Racism

"**Just Damned**"
Prolonged Exposure to Racism Despite Your Talents
Exposure to Multiple Catch 22 Situations which occur
despite One's Efforts, Presence, or Talents-
Decisions Don't Seem to Matter

ation is systemic, then the individual cannot simply get out of the particular situation and expect it to be done with. He or she must confront the psychological assault in its larger contextual existence to combat and sidestep the Catch-33.

META-ANALYTIC ADVANTAGES OF RACIAL SOCIALIZATION—COMBATING THE CATCH-33

Facing this "tragedy" constitutes a higher-order sense of anomie that is not remedied by a person's effort; psychological coping talents; skills, or development; or accomplishments. In the same way that influencing or avoiding random acts or "bad" people will not prevent or limit the onslaught of racism trauma, a person's effort becomes inadequate. Such a situation can lead to what West (1993) determines to be "nihilism," the very loss of hope (Stevenson, 1998). The loss of hope that this "tragedy" might end differently or is manageable or not inevitable is the first casualty of acquiescence to Catch-33 dynamics. Tears are probably the healthiest response to these dynamics. We feel that the explicit confrontation of these dynamics is essential and in the form of direct racial socialization strategies involving families and children, peers and siblings, and communities of caring folks (village). By definition, to try to solve this nihilism that we have called "hopelostness" without a different epistemology or village that can carefully resocialize youth is to fail like armies that do not count the cost of war (Stevenson, 1998). Without the proper intellectual and emotional resources, the hope to change the experience of Black dehumanization is not just limited or low—it is lost. In this chapter we propose that racial socialization is an important set of proactive and protective strategies to counteract the dehumanization of Black boys and men that is central to the current tragedy.

That is, the way to challenge the dehumanization of existing paradigms in psychology that do not validate African American behaviors and expressions (Akbar, 1985) is to learn skills in meta-analytic processing. We believe racial socialization can help to develop those skills. Meta-analytic thinking presupposes that to side-step the systemic dynamics of Catch-33, people must have access to ways of thinking above and beyond the current dilemmas of race relations fear. They must examine that fear from spiritual, affective-symbolic, and phenomenological perspectives without reacting to, ignoring, or adopting that fear—or by doing so at a lesser intensity. To daily combat the Catch-33, a spiritual reality for inspiration, a cultural heritage for rootedness, and an appreciation of the extended self for companionship are needed to make sense of the nihilism and apathy inherent in Catch-33 politics.

Figure 2.3 examines the benefits of racial socialization if it is assumed that battling the psychological trauma of racism is essential to the development of healthy children of color. It is presumed that these same principles can apply to other "isms" involving gender, sexuality, age, and so on, in which reframing outer-world hostilities can promote self-development.

What can be done about the potential for Catch-33 apathy or hopelostness? Despite the fact that natural villages and support for combating racism occurs and that Catch-33 is not destined to happen to all oppressed persons, its likelihood is still of grave concern. That is, all of our suggestions will be based on a belief that rugged individualism does not work for building healthy relationships. It's not that it does not work at all, just that it is less productive for building healthy relationships.

We propose that it takes a village to raise a child, a teenager, an adult, an elder, a family and anyone else in between—from the cradle to the grave. Ultimately, cultural socialization, as we propose, can serve the larger goal of developing metaconsciousness skills in interpreting the systemic nature of racism (see Figure 2.3). Metaprocessing is not just thinking, it is thinking about the way to feel and to consider one's own thinking. It's like the difference between being given fish to eat and learning how to fish for oneself. It's like that moment or sets of moments when people realize that they are living within a tragedy and figure out the matrix and then, how the matrix works. Meta-analytic feeling and thinking stand to promote the appreciation of resistance toward either-or reality dynamics that contribute to the dehumanization and self-dehumanization of African Americans.

Figure 2.3
The Meta-Art of Racial Cultural Socialization

The initial step in challenging the self-dehumanization is to refuse to accept Westernized "either-or" ways of knowing as the only ways to know (Asante, 1987). These either-or methods are necessary under certain circumstances, but they have the potential to be destructive to the extended definition of self. What makes them self-destructive is the inherent refusal to self-critique the hidden hegemony, the hidden "matrix." People must begin by critiquing what they think they know and apply a both-and framework to it. So, cultural socialization must influence meta-analytic consciousness in three arenas: divine, affective-symbolic, and phenomenological (Figure 2.3). These three areas of self-consciousness relate specifically to more specific areas of self-knowledge (spiritual or divine, worldview, affect, other, and personal style) as is seen in the following list.

AREAS OF SELF-KNOWLEDGE

- Spirit—how people make sense of existence and purpose
  - Spirituality, religion, ancestor, and divinity acknowledgement
- Worldview—how a people make sense of their experiences
  - Humanism, both-and, social time, direct experience, realism, Catch-33

- Affect—how people relate to emotions of self
  - Empathy, deep feelings, vitality, happiness, anger, stress
- Other—how people relate to worldview, affect, styles of others
  - Rhythm, interrelatedness, sharing, communalism, resilience
  - Ebonic confluence, gift, connect, racial socialization, distrust, oppression awareness
- Style—how people apply spirituality, worldview, affect
  - Movement, orality, verve, improvisation, expressive individualism, poetic vernacular

These categories can each be expressed either verbally or nonverbally.

ARENAS OF META-ANALYTIC CONSCIOUSNESS

The divine arena involves the development of self-knowledge that acknowledges Creator and community wisdom—spiritual entities larger than our individual selves. Cultural socialization in this arena can teach a person how to metaprocess about the nature of reality—past, present, and future. Reality questions relate to teleology—where we come from, how the world orients itself, and what is the purpose and meaning of life. A major benefit of learning spiritual metaprocessing is that it can teach a person how futile it is to control or expend harmful anxiety about matters that cannot be controlled. This relief allows a person to focus on more productive activities. Another benefit is the worth of acknowledging the Creator's power (however Creator is defined) to manage material reality and its emptiness to satisfy the self. Understanding a spiritual reality and not just a religious reality, can explain how a person's fate is ordered by more than what is seen and experienced. And finally, it can give people hope, something higher than their talents and trauma to believe in (Mattis, Fontenot, & Hatcher-Kay, 2003).

Affective-symbolic meta-processing skills helps in identifying the way people think and feel about themselves in the context of others, from their own cultural history and vantage point. Ultimately, the meta-processing skill of asserting one's heritage, culture and self in the context of others, however "others" are defined, is key to not succumbing to the numbing of dehumanization that occurs in "nice" race relations where racial tension is avoided at all costs. Sometimes, "others" can mean other African Americans or family. Essentially, there are four benefits to affective-symbolic metaprocessing: (1) helps people connect with cultural roots that define their past, present, and future, (2) integrates feeling and thinking rather than separates them arbitrarily, (3) helps people to be open to different problem-solving strategies, (4) helps people assert their affective and cognitive understandings.

The third type of metaconsciousness that can develop from both-and cultural socialization is that of phenomenological consciousness. The set of skills people are likely to develop here is the appreciation of their own self-striving and self-creating and all of the experiences that are a part of that process. It is the confidence in their own journey in such a way that it can be validated from within rather than from without. It's integrating the trauma and the triumphs of their lives and helps them to reframe rather than ignore situations of oppression as unreflective of internal abilities but external ambivalence. It helps them to identify culturally empowering situations and embrace them. Basically, there are several benefits of racially socializing toward developing a phenomenological metaconsciousness: (1) to appreciate one's meaning-making process; (2) to distinguish between one's meaning-making and the meaning-making of others; (3) to create and self-define rather than imitate and be enslaved to another's reality; and (4) to gain personal style self-knowledge and wisdom and apply it to one's life.

The five areas of self-knowledge associated with the three categories of meta-analytic consciousness can help researchers and interventionists more aptly apply racial and cultural socialization processes to the lives of children and families throughout the life span. That is, it is proposed that racial and cultural socialization must address these five areas if it is to be effective in helping youth manage a confused and race-conscious and -phobic society. This work mirrors the work of others who have posited the psychological health promotion that is derived from an Afrocultural social ethos that includes spirituality, affect and communalism realities. Jagers and colleagues have found inverse relationships between this ethos and individualistic, Machiavellian attitudes as well as aggression and delinquent behaviors (Jagers, 1996; Jagers & Mock, 1993; Jagers, Smith, Mock, & Dill, 1997).

PROTECTIVE, PROACTIVE AND ADAPTIVE ASPECTS OF RACIAL/CULTURAL SOCIALIZATION

Jones (1997) analyzed three views that explain why ethnic minority youth maintain positive self-esteem despite the level of group-based stigmatization they receive. The first two views are based upon social stigma and social identity theories by Crocker and Major (1988) and Tajfel and Turner (1979), respectively. Crocker and Major (1988) proposed that stigmatized individuals or groups are protected by (1) attributing negative appraisals by the majority culture to their own prejudices which allows African Americans to avoid internalized acceptance of those negative perceptions; (2) comparing their behaviors with other African Americans rather than with those of the majority culture which results in less negative standards of evaluation; and (3) devaluing the dimensions or domains that the majority culture group deems important (e.g., reliance solely on culturally irrelevant scientific knowledge) and esteeming those dimensions that a particular group African Americans uphold as important (e.g., interpersonal competence).

On the basis of social identity theory which suggests that a person's positive social identity happens as a function of the favorable comparisons between the in-group and the stigmatized group, Tajfel and Turner (1979) suggested three ways that positive self-evaluations can be developed in the face of social hostility. One, social mobility assumes that stigmatization can be decreased as long as the stigmatized group can move toward the in-group in some way. An example might be that of an African American individual or family that espouses basic White middle class values, living surroundings, behaviors, lifestyle, and language to the rejection of their distinct cultural expressions. This move may decrease some racial hostilities but it is not entirely clear how family members in this scenario rid themselves completely of their cultural distinctiveness. Often a person's color makes this a temporary reality until a racially shocking encounter episode occurs (Cross, Parham, & Helms, 1991). The second, social competition, assumes that an attack by African Americans or some subgroup, let's say, in the form of a riot or boycott, against an institution of the majority culture can enhance the social status of this group. The third way that positive self-evaluations can be developed, according to Tajfel and Turner, is social creativity, which suggests that the stigmatized group can change the dimensions of comparison, change the values assigned to the esteemed dimensions, or find a lower-status or more stigmatized group to make comparisons with. This is where racial socialization comes in.

In addition to social stigma and social identity theories, Jones (1992) proposed that the final view comes from self-affirmation theory (Steele, 1988; 1992). This theory proposes that it is natural for an individual to protect the self by affirming it rather than trying to resolve the conflict that comes from negative perceptions of the majority culture. Steele (1992) discussed this perspective when he analyzed disidentification and the rejection of academic definitions of self in academic settings in which the unwarranted but persistent devaluation of African American undergraduates is systemic. It is only natural for students to look for relationships, sometimes nonacademic ones that affirm their talents and their existence.

All of these viewpoints highlight the way individuals and groups may create or maintain protective processes in the face of overwhelming social adversity. Lacking in this work is a perspective that identifies interpersonal, interactional, or familial communication processes that mediate the development of positive self-esteem. Racial socialization may be most meaningful if it can be found to differentiate families and individuals with high and low levels of self-esteem, self-efficacy, and other self-perception variables. Some expressions of cultural uniqueness or cultural promotion may in fact be dangerous if perceived by some as threatening the existence of the majority culture in either minor or major ways. Jones (1992) reiterated this point:

There is good news and bad news from these analyses. The good news is that in spite of continued widespread racial bias in our society...victims of stigmatizing bias can and do maintain positive identities and self-esteem. The bad news is that the result of these social cognitive strategies may often be under-performance in important domains in which such bias takes place. If this is true, the pernicious effect of psychological adaptation to discriminatory circumstances is a self-fulfilling perpetuation of the attitudes and beliefs of the majority population that "justify" bias (for those who accept the bias) and automate biased reactions in those who seek more egalitarian personal beliefs.

Given the effects of racial intolerance, the larger task of socializing children to develop a protective and positive racial identity is not only important but necessary (Perry, Steele, & Hilliard, 2003).

Three types of racial socialization have been proposed by Stevenson (1997) as identified by adolescents and parents and these were briefly mentioned in chapter 1. Proactive race-related messages include telling children that they are special and ought to be proud of their cultural heritage ("You come from a proud and prestigious legacy of great and talented leaders"). The focus in these messages is on the talent of the individual, not the power of the oppressor. Protective racial socialization represents messages and interactions that give guidance on managing the oppression of a larger society and its members ("You have to work twice as hard and be twice as smart if you are Black just to be considered equal to Whites"). We believe that both Protective and Proactive interactions are necessary for African Americans, across the life span, to interpret accurately and cope with the racial confusion. This amalgamation of proactive and protective teaching we call *Adaptive Racial Socialization*. In sum, racial socialization represents the lifelong memories that make up "Who I Am" and the "Who We Are" stories. And yes, these stories form the foundation of African American children's identities. Previous research from an adolescent perspective on these racial socialization types have found that African American male youth who report having higher levels of adaptive and proactive racial socialization show higher scores on measures of psychological adjustment (Stevenson, 1997).

"LEMMINGS OR LEADERS": FROM META-ANALYTIC CONSCIOUSNESS TO APPLIED SELF-KNOWLEDGE

Simply put, meta-analytic racial consciousness is necessary for all African Americans of similarly positioned cultural groups to refrain from applying rational thinking to absurd realities. Rationality is irrelevant in an absurd universe in which a person's skin color is a marker for either unprecedented opportunity or undeserved hostility. To apply rational thinking to racism in America can lead only to self-blame and doubt, much like what happens to sexual abuse survivors who haven't fully healed through the experience to be angry at their molester. Self is an easier target to blame because rationally, a person thinks, "if I had only done...or if I only had not done..." Absurd realities can be challenged only with meta-analytic cognitive strategies, one of which is "This shit is crazy." A more developed meta-analytic strategy could sound like "What kinds of fears must someone be overwhelmed by to view me as an animal, and incapable of most human expressions, feelings, and behaviors?"

Our point is still simple, yet complex. We believe young boys with histories of aggression should learn about their absurd and surreal positioning in the American societal landscape. We believe that they should understand most assuredly how they are more followers (i.e., lemmings) rather than cowboys or leaders when they do not appreciate the absurdity of systemic racism. And we believe that teaching them about these realities is more difficult than experiencing Black History Month, BET channel, and Kwanzza combined. It takes relationships from a caring community of folks willing to appreciate who they are as humans, as boys, as somebody's child despite the violence within their context and mistakes in their histories or their families' histories. It takes "getting in the face" of boys who can appreciate that kind of attention without the element of hostility. Catch-33 is not just a catchy phrase but a warning that a person's image is an important commodity in the interpersonal exchange we call life. The very fact that American hostility toward difference after the September 11 tragedy led to the misidentification of Arab Americans as dangerous and assaults on them should be a sign that a person's sense of comfortableness can change overnight, like the weather. Invisibility can become conspicuous, in a moment's notice. But even this too is predictable, if it is assumed that the absurdity of racism is a constant in American life. Instead of wondering "why police disproportionately stop Black and Latino youth over and over again" folks should be asking, "Why are we unprepared when it happens over and over again—and unprepared for the next time it will happen?" As DuBois makes clear that behind the problem of the color line in American society, there lurks the ultimate Catch-33 question, "How does it feel to be a problem?" If that's the question we are asking ourselves, then we are lemmings for sure.

SUMMARY

The concepts of Catch-33, conspicuous invisibility, and triple psychological bind are meant to augment, not detract from the work of various scholars who have found that the invisibility helps to explain the mental health crises of many African American males. Franklin (1999), for example, has written a wonderful paper on the psychological dilemmas of being invisible in a racially hostile world that is intolerant, ambivalent, and downright violent toward African American men. He has opened a wonderful door for African American scholars to process their personal and intellectual strivings. We expect that it will have an impact not only on the way we conduct clinical interventions for African American boys and men but also on how we develop theory (Franklin & Boyd-Franklin, 2000). Our contribution to this work is to illuminate some of the "both-and" qualities of being invisible and to propose that the very covert and blatant messages and actions toward African American boys and men are inseparable from those elements that are invisible. These processes are conspicuous and blatant as well as invisible and silent or subtle and the interrelationship of this phenomenon must be explored simultaneously.

Catch-33 proposes a different reality paradigm that Black folks, but especially boys and men, must struggle through. It is one that presupposes that Black men must often face situations that offer "damned if you do," "damned if you don't," and "just damned" options. The final "just damned" option is one that comes only after realizing the tragic historical and contemporary castelike status opportunities that America is most comfortable in assigning to Black men. While America is the "home of the brave and the land of the free," for Black men, it is a hypocritical democracy. The images and stereotypes for Black men are uniquely different than for other racial/gender groups in our society. The intransigence of these images is systematic and structural and once that is realized, many Black boys may abdicate to the pressure and "psychologically give up." The invisibility syndrome is not just a phase or a passing fad—it is an American structural phenomenon. Solutions to the Catch-33 do not reside in waiting for America to resolve or work through its race relations dilemmas. On the contrary, those solutions must be meta-analytic, atypical, and deconstructive of the peculiar arrogance that serves as a backdrop to American fears of race tension, and foundational to the perpetuation of the syndrome of invisibility, with all of its conspicuous characteristics. This phenomenon makes necessary the imparting of cultural socialization strategies in multiple forms provided by many different caring people.

In the movie where Clint Eastwood makes the famous pronouncement, "Go ahead, make my day," it is not coincidental, we believe, that he is addressing two young Black men, men dressed in hoodlum gear, apparently stealing from a store. The question, "Do you feel lucky?" is the question all Black men must answer, since often, life and death are reduced to a game, a game of disproportionate chance and probability with the cards stacked against Black boys and men. Because not only is the Marlboro Man, cowboy, rogue cop image of White male racial identity so clear in the psyche of Black boys and men, it is most consistently juxtaposed to the centuries old image of Black manhood as confused, hostile, criminal, aggressive. Black boys and men are situationally if not always consciously stuck in the throes of answering White folks' questions rather than creating their own. A meta-analytic view of conspicuous invisibility has the potential for helping Black boys and men to rewrite the scripts of American identity and survival. So a debt of gratitude is owed to Anderson Franklin and other authors writing on the psychology of Black men for leading us toward that end. Still, we believe that Catch-33 dynamics are reflective of an absurd reality, the acceptance of which can only lead to self-destruction schemas for Black males (i.e., "I ain't going out like no punk!"). Cultural socialization is meant to represent a diverse compendium of strategies and conceptual frameworks that make this absurdity explicit and more visible for challenge.

Given the understanding of Black psychology and some of its African philosophical roots, the larger systemic craziness of racism, and the "Catch-33," we now turn to the way cultural socialization strategies are applied in a violence intervention and prevention project we call PLAAY. It is no coincidence that these strategies are concretized most in a PLAAY component we affectionately call "CPR." The obvious goal is to raise the boys' awareness to the need for life-giving worldviews to replace the worldviews where luck and dehumanized fate are the daily questions of this age.

REFERENCES

Akbar, N. (1985). Our destiny: Authors of a scientific revolution. In H. P. McAdoo & J. L. McAdoo (Eds.), *Black children: Social, educational, and parental environments*. Newbury Park: Sage.

Akbar, N. (1989). Nigrescence and identity: Some limitations. *The Counseling Psychologist, 17*, 258–263.

Asante, M. (1987). *The Afrocentric idea*. Philadelphia: Temple University Press.

Bell, D. (1992). *Faces at the bottom of the well: The permanence of racism*. Basic Books: New York.

Biafora, F. A., Warheit, G. J., Zimmerman, R. S., Gil, A. G., Apospori, E., & Taylor, D. (1993). Racial mistrust and deviant behaviors among ethnically diverse Black adolescent boys. *Journal of Applied Social Psychology, 23*, 891–910.

Brooks, G. (1968). We real cool. In Chapman, A. *Black voices: An anthology of Afro-American literature*. New York: Mentor Book.

Canada, G. (1998). *Reaching up for manhood: Transforming the lives of boys in America*. Boston: Beacon Press.

Clark, R., Anderson, N. B., Clark, V. R., & Williams, D. R. (1999). Racism as a stressor for African Americans: A biopsychosocial model. *American Psychologist, 54*, 805–816.

Crocker, J. & Major, B. (1988). Social stigma and self-esteem: The self-perspective properties of stigma. *Psychological Review, 96*, 608–630.

Cross, William E. Jr. (1998). Black psychological functioning and the legacy of slavery: Myths and realities. In Y. Danieli (Ed.), et al. *International handbook of multigenerational legacies of trauma. The Plenum series on stress and coping*. New York, NY.

Cross, W. E., Parham, T. A., & Helms, J. (1991). The stages of Black identity development: Nigrescence models. In R. L. Jones (Ed.), *Black psychology* Berkeley: Cobb and Henry.

Darity, W. A. (2003). Employment discrimination, segregation, and health. *American Journal of Public Health, 93(2)*, 226–231.

Davis, P. H. (1997). Melanie Klein, motherhood, and the "Heart of the Heart of Darkness." In J. L. Jacobs & D. Capps (Eds.), *Religion, society, and psychoanalysis: Readings in contemporary theory.* Boulder, CO: Westview Press.

DuBois, W. E. B. (1903). *The souls of Black folk.* Kraus International Publications.

Ellison, R. (1951). *Invisible Man.* New York: Random House.

Fanon, F. (1967). *Black skin, White masks.* New York: Grove Press.

Franklin, A. J. (1999). Invisibility syndrome and racial identity development in psychotherapy and counseling African American men. *Counseling Psychologist, 27*, 761–793.

Franklin, A. J & Boyd-Franklin, N. (2000). Invisibility syndrome: A clinical model of the effects of racism on African-American males. *American Journal of Orthopsychiatry, 70(1)*, 33–41. American Psychological Assn/Educational Publishing Foundation, US.

Harrell, Shelly P. (2000) A multidimensional conceptualization of racism-related stress: Implications for the well-being of people of color. *American Journal of Orthopsychiatry, 70(1)*, 42–57.

Jagers, R. J. (1996). Culture and problem behaviors among inner-city African American youth. *Journal of Adolescence, 19*, 371–381.

Jagers, R. J. & Mock, L. O. (1993). Culture and social outcomes among inner-city African American children: An Afrographic analysis. *Journal of Black Psychology, 19*, 391–405.

Jagers, R. J., Smith, P., Mock, L. O., & Dill, E. (1997). An afrocultural social ethos: Component orientations and some social implications. *Journal of Black Psychology, 23(4)*, 328–343.

Jones, J. M. (1992). Understanding the mental health consequences of race: Contributions of basic social psychological processes. In D. Ruble, P. Costanzo, and M. Oliveri (Eds.), *The social psychology of mental health: Basic mechanisms and applications.* New York: Guilford Press.

Jones, J. M. (1997). *Prejudice and racism* (2nd ed). New York: McGraw Hill.

Krieger, N. & Sydney, S. (1996, October). Racial discrimination and blood pressure: The CARDIA study of young Black and White adults. *American Journal of Public Health, 86(10)*, 1370–1378.

Kunjufu, J. (1985). *Countering the conspiracy to destroy Black boys, Volume I.* Chicago, IL: African American Images.

Landrine, H., & Klonoff, E. A. (1996). The schedule of racist events: A measure of racial discrimination and study of its negative physical and mental health consequences. *Journal of Black Psychology, 22*, 144–168.

Majors, R. & Gordon, J. U. (Eds.). (1994). *The American Black Male: His present status and his future.* Chicago: Nelson-Hall.

Mattis, J. S., Fontenot, D. L., & Hatcher-Kay, C. A. (2003). Religiosity, racism, and dispositional optimism among African-Americans. *Personality and Individual Differences, 34*, 1025–1038.

McKay, C. (1953). *The selected poems of Claude McKay.* New York: Bookman Associates.

Morowitz, J.G. (1997). White experimenters, White blood, and other White conditions: Locating the psychologist's race. In M. Fine, L. Weis, L.C. Powell, & L.M. Wong. *Off White: Readings on race, power, and society.* New York, NY: Routledge.

Myers, L.J. (1988). *Understanding an African-centered world view: Introduction to an optimal psychology.* Dubuque, IA: Kendall/Hunt.

Myers, L. J., Speight, S.L., Highlen, P.S., Cox, C.I., Reynolds, A.L., Adams, E.M., & Hanley, C.P. (1991). Identity development and worldview: Toward an optimal conceptualization. *Journal of Counseling and Development, 70,* 54–63.

Nobles, W. (1989). Psychological nigrescence: An Afrocentric view. *The Counseling Psychologist, 17,* 253–257.

Nobles, W. (1991). African philosophy: Foundations for Black psychology. In R.L. Jones (Ed.), *Black Psychology.* Hampton, VA: Cobb & Henry Publishers.

Nyborg, V.M. & Curry, J.F. (2003). The impact of perceived racism: Psychological symptoms among African American boys. *Journal of Clinical Child and Adolescent Psychology, 32(2),* 258–266.

Perry, T., Steele, C., & Hilliard III, A. (2003). *Young, gifted, and black: Promoting high achievement among African-American students.* Boston: Beacon Press.

Spencer, M. B., Cunningham, M., & Swanson, D.P. (1995). Identity as coping: Adolescent African-American males' adaptive responses to high-risk environment. In H.W. Harris, H.C. Blue, & E.E.H. Griffith (Eds.), *Racial and ethnic identity: Psychological development and creative expression.* New York, NY: Routledge.

Steele, C.M. (1988). The psychology of self-affirmation: Sustaining the integrity of the self. In L. Berkowitz (Ed.), *Advances in experimental social psychology.* San Diego, CA: Academic Press.

Steele, C.M. (1992). Minds wasted, minds saved: Crisis and hope in the schooling of Black Americans. *Atlantic Monthly, 269(4),* 68–78.

Steele, C.M. & Aronson, J. (1998). Stereotype threat and the test performance of academically successful African Americans. In C. Jencks & M. Phillips (Eds.), et al. *The Black-White test score gap.* Washington, DC: Brookings Institution.

Stevenson, H.C. (1992). Invisibility revisited: Challenging the negative images of black males. *AFTA Newsletter, American Family Therapy Association, 48,* 15–19.

Stevenson, H.C. (1997). Managing Anger: Protective, Proactive, or Adaptive Racial Socialization Identity Profiles and Manhood Development. Special Issue on Manhood Development. *Journal of Prevention and Intervention in the Community, 16,* 35–61.

Stevenson, H.C. (1998). Raising Safe Villages: Cultural-ecological factors that influence the emotional adjustment of adolescents. *Journal of Black Psychology, 24,* 44–59.

Stevenson, H.C. (2002). Wrestling with destiny: Cultural socialization of anger and healing for African American males. *Journal of Psychology and Christianity, 21,* 357–364.

Stevenson, H.C. & Davis, G.Y. (2003). Racial Socialization. In R. Jones (Ed.), *Black Psychology,* 4th Edition. Hampton, VA: Cobb & Henry.

Stevenson, H.C. & Renard, G. (1993). Trusting ole' wise owls: Therapeutic utilization of cultural strengths in African American families. *Professional Psychology: Research and Practice, 24(4),* 433–442.

Tajfel, H. & Turner, J.C. (1979). An integrative theory of intergroup conflict. In S. Worchel & W.G. Austin (Eds.), *The social psychology of intergroup relations.* Monterey, CA: Brooks-Cole.

Utsey, S.O. (1998). Assessing the stressful effects of racism: A review of instrumentation. *Journal of Black Psychology, 24,* 269–288.

West, C. (1993). *Race matters.* Boston, MA: Beacon Press.

Williams, D.R., & Williams-Morris, R. (2000). Racism and mental health: the African American Experience. *Ethnicity and Health, 5,* 243–268.

PART II

"If We Must Die":
Examples of PLAAY
Project Interventions

CHAPTER 3

"If We Must Die": CPR for Managing Catch-33, Alienation, and Hypervulnerability

*Elaine F. Cassidy, Gwendolyn Y. Davis,
and Howard C. Stevenson Jr.*

If we must die, let it not be like hogs
Hunted and penned in an inglorious spot,
While round us bark the mad and hungry dogs,
Making their mock at our accursed lot.
If we must die, O let us nobly die,
So that our precious blood may not be shed
In vain; then even the monsters we defy
Shall be constrained to honor us though dead!
O kinsmen! We must meet the common foe!
Though far outnumbered let us show us brave,
And for their thousand blows deal one deathblow!
What though before us lies the open grave?
Like men we'll face the murderous, cowardly pack,
Pressed to the wall, dying, but fighting back!
       —Claude McKay, "If We Must Die"

Claude McKay (1922) believed in informing political minds and in no other poem is that more evident than in "If We Must Die." Born in Jamaica in 1889, McKay wrote and published the poem in 1919 in the *Liberator*. Written after World War I, this poem is decidedly revolutionary in tone and emphasis and meant to remasculinize Blacks who decided to fight back against the White violence and race rioting that took place in Black neighborhoods. The fire and spirit of "If We Must Die" were not lost on the world; Winston Churchill used it to rally British troops in their fight against the Nazis, even though it was originally written for African Americans struggling against racial violence and hatred. McKay eventually became the official poet laureate of Jamaica, but many African Americans will remember him for his words that ignited beaten spirits and helped African Americans acknowledge their strengths and contributions to the world and themselves.

In essence, the PLAAY program is also meant to help boys reframe their perceptions of themselves and the meaning-making energy they apply to daily activities. We believe that no component of PLAAY is more useful in helping Black boys do this than CPR, or cultural pride reinforcement.

"LET IT NOT BE LIKE HOGS HUNTED AND PENNED IN AN INGLORIOUS SPOT, WHILE ROUND US BARK THE MAD AND HUNGRY DOGS": MANAGING SOCIETY'S EXAGGERATED FEARS

Few dispute the fact that Black boys are harassed by society's exaggerated fears (Ferguson, 2000; May & Dunaway, 2000; Meeks, 2000). With that in mind, there should be little mystery about the kinds of therapeutic topics and conversations that should be developed to help Black males manage this harassment. We cannot say it any more bluntly. To create interventions for and conduct research with African American males and fail to consider the larger systemic problem of racism is to engage in what Frederick Douglass accused America of doing more than a century ago— that is, engaging in a comfortable hypocrisy by wanting "crops without plowing up the ground." How can any intervention effort with Black males be fruitful if it fails to address, or "plow up," the systemic racism that challenges their daily existence?

Perhaps it is useless to entertain programs that downplay or minimize the reality of systemic racism. The facts and consequences of racism do not have to be disputed as we have tried to suggest in chapter 2. Even so, disputes will occur over whether racism should be addressed in intervention and research, but those who wish to dispute its reality and impact waste the time of others who seek to address why Black youth are struggling in today's world. Rather than ask whether exploitation of Black youth is occurring, it is more important to discuss why the world is bent on exploiting our young Black males.

Such is the critical consciousness backdrop for CPR, which is the psycho-educational and group therapy intervention component of PLAAY. This component attempts to provide cultural socialization to Black youth by integrating discussions of the how's and why's of racism, including strategies for managing racial politics in America, and promoting understanding of why anger management is so crucial in a culturally stylistic and relevant atmosphere.

It's hard to be angry without consequences in America if you are Black and male. It's doubly hard explaining this concept and reality to Black boys. A difficult but serious truth we have learned throughout the PLAAY project, especially during the CPR component, is this: *To be Black and male does not mean that one understands the danger of such a status or the societal perceptions that accompany it. Moreover, even if one understands the unique challenges of being Black and male in America, this does not mean one knows how to combat it.* Most African American boys learn, without being taught directly, to internalize the values of Western American society (especially its dimensions of inferiority-superiority strivings); to desire and accumulate materialistic "trinkets" and trophies of their superiority; and to rest their manhood, identity, and self-worth on two major pillars—being "the Man" and being "the Man with Things." The key problem we see among many of the boys we work with is not just that they want these things and their social benefits, but that they also want the manhood clarity that these things bring. The confusion of manhood prominence is far too often clarified by the accumulation of material trinkets. To help the boys understand the Catch-33 that exists for young Black males is really the underlying thrust of CPR. And while it is not often that boys understand their Catch-33 dilemma, we believe we are dropping seeds each week in CPR that may help them begin to take notice of it. In essence, in re-addressing Frederick Douglass's wise words, we hope to plow up the ground and reap a bountiful crop from a fertile, but well-tilled soil.

"IF WE MUST DIE, O LET US NOBLY DIE": BASIC ASSUMPTIONS BEHIND CPR

Perhaps it makes sense to share our assumptions in the PLAAY project about the way traditional psychological and educational services misunderstand Black boys. These ideas are not new and have been written about extensively by scholars such as Amos Wilson, Linda Myers, Jawanza Kunjufu, Margaret Beale Spencer, and countless other African American social scientists. Although inaccurate and disturbing, we consider the following assumptions to be the most common ones directed at Black boys today:

1. Black males are aggressive and they are troublemakers.
2. Black males are overly sexual and not to be trusted.
3. Black males must be kept at a distance.
4. Black males can hurt you if you get too close.
5. Black males must be controlled first and talked to second and affectionately care for them last.

When CPR was originally created, the goal was to provide group therapy for African American boys or individuals and make it relevant to their lives. It was meant to be a place for Black males to learn and accept life-saving information about the way the rest of the world sees them and pathologizes them, and to present this knowledge to them in a way that it can be used for self-protection. Emotional self-defense is necessary to deal with the daily challenge of racism, but it must be initiated and maintained by an individual if it is to serve that person well. The relevance of using emotional self-defense is that without it, the boys are more likely to use physical self-defense in social situations where it is inappropriate. As Bob Marley declared, "None but ourselves can free our minds." It is impossible for students to learn emotional self-defense skills unless they are in an atmosphere in which they feel safe enough to disclose their basest fears and daily vulnerabilities. The death rate of American Black young boys and men is outrageous and unacceptable to every caring human on the face of the earth, and we take this assertion as a premise: No boy should be subjected to the horrors and deadly consequences of being misdiagnosed, misrepresented, and misunderstood, without having someone there to intercede for them or to fight for them.

The essential ideas of PLAAY are based on the works of several noteworthy scholars, including Arthur Whaley (1992), Amos Wilson (1990; 1991), Carl Bell (1997), Rodney Hammond and Betty Yung (1991), and Roderick Watts and Jaleel Abdul-Adil (1997). In addition to offering boys opportunities to discuss their fears and strengths, CPR is useful because it provides the boys with opportunities for receiving additional reinforcement about their behavior in the movement interventions of TEAM and MAAR. The primary goal of CPR is to discuss the meanings, realities, and consequences of being young, Black, and male today. Because violence has claimed so many lives and dreams of young Black boys, CPR lessons often focus on topics related to violence prevention. Other topics, which are indirectly related to violence, include understanding how to cope with fear and anger, developing and implementing anger management strategies, understanding one's cultural heritage and the importance of gender and racial identity socialization and protection, and visualizing future success and aspiration. In addition, to make the sessions more relevant, most workshops include discussion of current events from the popular media that involve real life experiences of African Americans (e.g., "Driving while Black"). Our hope is to reach these kids and make these discussions meaningful to them, so we use videotapes, guest speakers, role-play activities, writing assignments, and small-group interaction as teaching tools.

The theoretical model of PLAAY is filtered throughout the curriculum. In addition, care is taken to include metacognitive strategies throughout each session to help students think and feel about *how* they think about certain topics and *why* they think what they do. Each hour-long session may include two or all of the following three components: teaching, which lasts for 20 minutes; acting, which can include role playing and often lasts 15 minutes; and discussion/talking about the major topic, which lasts for 10 to 20 minutes. African psychological values and racial socialization processes are applied, and there is a concerted effort to teach students to deconstruct the world around them using gender, race, and culture as particular themes, and then to act out their thoughts or recollections through role-play activities. Examples of aggression (as well as solutions to prevent aggression) that take place in life as well as those that are observed in professional sports (including basketball) are highlighted throughout the CPR education, mostly in the teaching component, to demonstrate precipitating factors, or "triggers," related to aggression. A few sessions address situations that occur during the basketball (TEAM) or martial arts (MAAR) components in order to reinforce teachings about self-knowledge and self-management. The CPR curriculum is divided into two main groups related to African American psychology. The first group of sessions target self-knowledge or -awareness and the second set focuses on community-knowledge or other-knowledge.

Teaching self-knowledge involves helping students gain awareness of what precipitates violence among young people (i.e., their triggers), what hinders it, and what helps people avoid it. But CPR discussions are also realistic, so they also focus on what the boys can do when they feel that they cannot avoid violence, keeping in mind strategies that may be age-appropriate and culturally and gender-relevant for them to use. We try to have the boys discuss how they might avoid violence without invoking the image of being "sweet" or a punk. A second goal of CPR is to help youth become more aware and appreciative of others as an extension of themselves, especially those in their families and communities.

A major part of the CPR intervention is to promote an appreciation for communalism and community responsibility by having young adolescents share stories about their lives, their neighborhoods, and their fears and triumphs regarding potentially violent situations. Some of this communalism can be reinforced in the TEAM basketball component. In addition, it is important to help these boys maintain skills that can be reinforced at home if their parents are involved in the COPE component (described in chapter 6). Learning how to discuss these issues with family members is a vital skill to learn, and we gather data on the teens' abilities to actually engage in this type of family communication. A final goal of CPR is related to helping teens gain a historical and contemporary perspective on issues of race, culture, gender, and violence. Keeping in mind the way the past is linked to the present, we initiate discussions with the boys that focus on how historical events have affected their lives, hoping that it will raise their level of consciousness about racial and gender politics in America.

"SO THAT OUR PRECIOUS BLOOD MAY NOT BE SHED IN VAIN": INCREASING YOUTH INVESTMENT THROUGH CULTURAL RELEVANCE

This line of Claude McKay's poem helps us realize how important it is to create and implement a program that is culturally relevant and meaningful to the boys so that they feel safe to share their worries and fears. But what exactly is "cultural relevance" as it applies to the PLAAY program? In our opinion, cultural relevance must involve an experience and include an atmosphere that reflects the basic cultural expressions implicit in the language, mannerisms, looks, and style that the participants identify with. The boys identify with this atmosphere because it might resemble that found in the homes and neighborhoods in which they live. Asa Hilliard (1983) is quite right when he asserts that psychology cannot be separated from the language style of a people, and so the appreciation of Ebonics or hip-hop language is really the appreciation of a way of being. With that in mind, from the start of the PLAAY program it was important for us to ask ourselves these questions: Can the boys talk in the group the way they would talk if they were home, comfortably at home, with family and friends? And can they talk as if they were on the streets, comfortably on the street (if that is possible)?

To us, cultural relevance is more complex than language. It's about connection. It's about taking a thing and massaging and adjusting it so that it comes alive for the person or people that a teacher is communicating with. This thing, a lesson for example, should connect on a number of levels (e.g., language, mannerism, rhythm, and way of expression). As the audience, the culture of urban Black males requires a fluidity of style and expression in the learning and appreciation of the thing (lesson). In African American communication contexts, Asante (1987) says that cultural relevance in speaking transmits more than words. Styling becomes an example of cultural relevant communication and "a key element of style is rhythm created by tone, accent, and meaning. Thus to *style* is an action, and when one styles one is engaged in creating a relationship" (p. 39). Cultural relevance is a combination of spontaneous stylistic communication that fits with the communication patterns, and meaning-making values of the audience.

So where is this kind of culturally relevant atmosphere? Anywhere in most poor and not-so-poor Black neighborhoods, of course! But, for many Black men, one place that provides the most openness and freedom and opportunity for intense debate is the barbershop. More politics, religion, sports, and scandal of all kinds have been debated, deciphered, and dissected by Black men in barbershops than this world will ever know. The vibrancy, passion, and unbridled freedom for people to say what they want regardless of how ridiculous it may sound is the hallmark of barbershop

talk. People don't even have to have a point or good argument to participate in that freedom. They just have to assert their theory and assert it
strongly. This is a different type of group therapy, but similar to most therapeutic encounters in which clients can feel open and free to be and to
express themselves. The only difference is that the barbershop is missing a
therapist or a maestro (like the one Ernie Barnes, the Black artist portrays in
his artwork, of the same name, "Maestro" who leads a radio) to orchestrate
the multiple cultural strands of expression. That's where CPR comes in.

In observing the way other psychologists and researchers over the years
have constructed group work or interventions that do not consider the
specific realities of young Black males, it appears that many do not know
what this culturally relevant mandate means. Most are used to saying the
words "culturally relevant," and some truly want to integrate this concept
into their work, but few are able to pull it off because it seems to require
making real a concept that most would rather keep abstract. It is difficult
to make any intervention truly culturally relevant, but, even so, it is necessary to make it more meaningful to students and increase their investment in it.

"THEN EVEN THE MONSTERS WE DEFY SHALL BE CONSTRAINED TO HONOR US THOUGH DEAD!": WHEN FEAR FUELS BOYS TO LIVE EACH DAY AS THEIR LAST

As therapists, we are obligated to focus on the most essential matters
and dangers that affect youth and their families. As researchers, we have
an equal obligation to study the most salient aspects that affect children's
lives, and waste less time on esoteric, hypothetical psychological realities
that are distal from the challenge of preventing needless injury and death
to Black children. As human beings, we are compelled to feel the pain of
Black boys who every day find a way to hide their tragedy, incredible
losses, stigma, and fears of imminent nonexistence. So while it may not be
visible that these boys contemplate death, and while they may not initially
admit that they fear for their lives, we believe as village parents and fellow
human beings that overexposure to poverty, violence, and family discon-
nection can eventually create an unhealthy, self-destructive paranoia. This
is true for children all over the world, not just in urban America, but still
our focus here is on Black youth, who disproportionately face dangers to
their lives and limbs. These dangers make it necessary for us to teach
about death and its meaning in the youths' lives. Yet, because we can't
assume that Black youth will reveal a fear of death (as if they are not
human enough, while being and pretending to be the toughest mother-
fuckers in the neighborhood), we must ask the difficult questions: Do you
think about death? Are you scared to die? And what would you die for?

To assume that boys who live in violent contexts do not contemplate death is to assume that, by closing their eyes, the thing that they fear has disappeared. But there is a psychological death as well that people must consider in addition to their physical expiration. The young men in CPR are constantly asked to consider the meaning of living healthy and whole as well as dying young. The fear of living is not much different from the fatalism of death and without deconstruction or examination fatalism wins over life choosing. Contemplation is a funny thing for adolescents, and often Black boys ponder death or nonexistence by acting out their thoughts and fears through certain behaviors.

We take issue with a general view of Black boys exposed to violence or living within violent contexts as people indifferent to pain and suffering. This view suggests boys so disposed contract a chronic deadening of the senses towards human tragedy and can lead to a justified inhumane harassment of them by authorities who will not extend themselves intellectually, emotionally, or morally on behalf of the boys.

Furthermore, we reject the notion that Black males *cannot* ponder existentialism. CPR is often about bringing to the discussion some of the scariest things these youth face, so that they might ponder those things ever so differently than before (in contrast to when their "homies" are the advisors and the audience). To have caring, therapeutic adults, family, and peers around them who understand the larger racial, cultural, and health consequences of being Black and male is absolutely necessary when these boys have these discussions—and it brings meat to the notion of village.

We know that it is difficult for children of all ages and ethnic backgrounds to wrap their minds around racial intolerance and violence. Hate crimes seem absurd by their very nature, so the human reaction to deny, disbelieve, or pause before contemplating their reality is normal. We should not shudder when we see such reactions. Yet, without teaching, how should students come to grips with the sad reality that some Americans are negatively targeted, simply because of their skin color, gender, sexual orientation, physical size, or other quality, as menaces to society?

"THOUGH FAR OUTNUMBERED LET US SHOW US BRAVE": THE IMPORTANCE OF VILLAGE IN CULTURALLY RELEVANT INTERVENTION

In its purest form, CPR is a Black psychology class on race, class, and gender. In its most practical form, it's culturally relevant group therapy. The therapeutic skills used by group leaders in CPR cover a wide range of methods, such as using confrontation; hugging; rapping; uncovering family dynamics; deconstructing the meaning of rap and hip-hop music and lyrics; engaging in role plays about relationship troubles; and having leaders confess their own challenging life issues. In addition to providing nur-

Table 3.1
CPR Curriculum and Themes

Topic	Target Areas of Change	Activities, Discussion Questions, Tools
Introduction to CPR	Introduction to the program; Cultural Pride – What is it?; The need for support and encouragement	What is CPR? Why is it necessary for survival? What is Culture, Pride, and Reinforcement?
Mind Control: Who's zooming who?	Who's zooming who?; Reactive vs. Proactive decisions; Who makes your decisions?	Video segment: BOYZ 'N THE HOOD Responses to "Boyz 'N the Hood" segment What happens when others make choices for us? Are some of us "puppets on a string"? Video segment: TALES FROM THE HOOD
Violence: options to fighting	Self-defense; Aggression; Strategies for de-escalating conflict	Why do people fight? Is fighting worth it? What do we accomplish by fighting? Do people really want to fight? What can we do to avoid fighting? What are some alternatives to fighting? Video segment: TALES FROM THE HOOD
Manhood	Fatherhood; Manhood apart from physical and sexual prowess; Black man issues	What is a (black) man? **How do you learn to be a man?** Who in your life would you identify as "men"? Video segment: SOUTH CENTRAL

(continued)

turance to young and old boys in efforts to develop their critical consciousness and engage them in cultural socialization training, the goal of CPR is to help these boys develop their divine, phenomenological, and affective symbolic consciousness. We are not always successful in stimulating divine appreciation, but often the topic of religion, faith, God, and "higher powers" is brought up and discussed in conversations about the death and dying that so often accompanies urban life for these boys. In effect, we use CPR to trigger the lofty goal of future healing of the boys' emotional challenges, but it is also meant to offer them opportunities to

Table 3.1
Continued

Fathers/ Fatherhood	Experiences with fathers & father figures; Learning to be a man; role playing "If Dad Should Come Back"	What is the role of a father? What happens when fathers are absent? How can you learn to be a good father if your father was absent? Video segments: BOYZ 'N THE HOOD, HE GOT GAME, or SOUTH CENTRAL; Song: JAY ZEE (DYNASTY)
Image/Perception of Black men	Stereotypes of black man; Self-fulfilling prophecy;	How are black men perceived by others? What's it like to be thought of in this way? Song: MOS DEF (MR. NIGGA)
Getting Stopped by the police	Self-protective skills; Survival; Understanding law enforcement and the criminal justice system;	Have you ever been stopped or picked up by the police? How did this make you feel? How did you respond? How do you think you should respond? What happens when you challenge police? What's your goal in this situation? Song: KRS (ONE) Video segment: MALCOLM X OPENING
Racism/Prejudice	Oppression; Diminished opportunity; Maintaining positive sense of self despite racism	What is racism, prejudice, do they exist? Give examples of racist experiences Discuss examples in media and press How does racism compromise your life chances? Song: MOS DEF (MR. NIGGA)
Fear is not an option	Fear is a natural and adaptive response;	What are you afraid of? Are we all afraid of something?

Table 3.1
Continued

	Does fear or emotional distress compromise decision-making?	How we react when we're afraid Are you a punk if you're afraid?
Cool pose: Avoiding victimization in peer groups	Our public face (the self we show to others) vs. our true self; Why image is so important	Are you who you show us? Is it necessary for guys to project an image of toughness? What happens when others see you as soft or sweet?
Respect	Respect/Disrespect; Fear vs. respect	What is respect/disrespect? How do you show it? Who do you respect/disrespect, and why? Are you respected? Why or why not? What can a person do to get respect?
Trust; Ask staff about who they are	Depending on others; Trusting ourselves/Trusting others	What is trust? Who do you trust, why or why not? How do we know when someone is trustworthy? What happens when we aren't able to trust the people that we care about the most? Do others trust you? Why or why not?
Faith: Believing in something larger than ourselves	Belief; Hope	What is faith? Do you believe in things that you cannot see or touch? Does hoping, believing and praying make a difference?
What would you work for? What would sacrifice for?	Investing in things that are important to us; Disappointments; Getting what we want out of life; Working to potential;	Is there anything that you do or would work for? Why did or would you work for this? What do you think would happen if you sincerely worked for something? Do people really work for what they want or
	Maximizing talents	is it luck?

(continued)

Table 3.1
Continued

"If we must die": What would you die for?	What's important to you; Things/people worth dying for; Values	What does Claude McKay mean in the poem? Is there anything you would die for? Do you know anyone who has died for a good reason? And one who has died for no reason at all?
Drugs and the Black Community	Drug involvement (use & sales); Street economy	What are some of the reasons that people use and deal drugs? What are the short and long-term consequences of drug involvement? TIPS FOR TEENS
Relationships: Part I	Interactions and communication patterns between males and females	Do young men and women talk to one another respectfully or disrespectfully? Why and how does this relate to mind control? How are women vulnerable (likely to be hurt) in relationships with men? In what ways are men vulnerable in relationships with women?
Relationships: Part II	Relationships with parents; Productive vs. destructive relationships	Do we inherit our lives (the quality) from our parents? How do family patterns or cycles disrupt our lives? What happens when people disappoint us?
Anger	"Triggers"; Anger management strategies	What makes you angry? What makes you calm? When was the last time you got angry? When was the last time you got into a fight because you were angry?

receive support from elders and see it modeled for them, so that, ideally, they can learn how to band together and support each other. Indeed, it may take a village to raise young Black males today, so it seems useful to teach these boys the skills necessary to support each other early on so that they can build a village together to help them heal emotionally.

Table 3.2
Therapeutic Skills Used by Facilitators in CPR Intervention

	Skill to Be Observed	1	2	3	4	5	6	7	8	9
Affection	Greets students as they enter or during CPR session									
	Create atmosphere that encourages students to speak or disclose personal life issues ("passionate barbershop"); structures group									
	Provides emotional support and encouragement to students									
	Shows respect/respectfully handles disrespect from students									
	Connect issues that arise in CPR to the child's emotional, family, neighborhood, school, or male life									
Correction	Challenging distorted, underprocessed or mistaken beliefs or knowledge about self, others, or society									
	Therapeutically Explores potential emotional conflict; posing reflective questions; asking for clarification									
	Uses cultural style and expression to intervene									
	Illuminate students personal/familial trigger or vulnerable situations									
	Uses warning, step-outside, and removal system, if necessary									
	Explains/shows ways to manage emotions w/o losing status;									
	Physically mediates conflicts between students, if necessary									
Protection	Follows daily topic/uses multiple methods (role-play; video; rap)									
	Culturally socializes boys to ponder cultural identities/realities/histories									
	Flexibly shifts strategies based on student's strengths and limitations									

An example of the CPR curriculum over the course of 15 or so sessions can be found in Tables 3.1. Table 3.2 describes the affection, correction, and protection therapeutic skills that the PLAAY staff uses to conduct CPR effectively.

"PRESSED TO THE WALL, DYING, BUT FIGHTING BACK!": WHAT WOULD YOU DIE FOR?

Using a culturally relevant perspective, the second half of this chapter provides an example of a CPR session with our psychological interpretation of the interactions among the boys who participated in that session. At the start of this session, a staff member recites McKay's poem, "If We Must Die," which provides a challenge to its listeners regarding senseless violence and death (the uselessness of dying for an unjust cause). The poem encourages people to fight for freedom and just causes. We ask the boys to

dissect the meaning of the poem and apply it to their lives, while we interject how this plea to devote one's life to a noble cause is not applied very
well among today's youth—many of whom are risking death and dying
over the way somebody looks at them or disrespects them in public.

This CPR group session reveals how the boys describe and manage
their feelings of hypervulnerability within violent neighborhoods and
contexts. The group even reveals several strategies to the PLAAY project
staff. The boys discuss their experiences of being victimized and having to
fight for their personal belongings which represent their hypermasculine
identities. This leads to a discussion of what the boys could envision
themselves dying for. For this reason, we have titled this session, "What
Would You Die For?"

During each CPR session, boys sit in chairs arranged in a circle. To this
particular session, seven boys, ranging in age from 14 to 19 years of age,
are in attendance. Three African American male staff members sit inter-
spersed in the circle along with the boys in the group. One of those three,
Coach, is designated the group leader that day. The other two staff members, who are women, sit along the periphery of the circle, listening and
joining the conversation at different points.

The session begins with Coach, the group leader, reading McKay's
poem. Before he begins reading the poem, the boys are in conversation,
looking at each other, at the floor, or around the room. Once Coach starts
reading the poem, they sit quietly and give him their attention. The poem
is read.

Coach: Anybody tell me what the poem is about? Anything you remember about
the poem—just tell me what you think it's about.

Dandridge: About having pride.

Coach: OK. Having pride. Anybody else?

Dandridge: Standing up for what you believe in? (The rest of the boys in the circle
are quiet and do not show much expression.)

Coach: Standing for what you believe in. Definitely. Anything else? (long silent
pause) What about this part? What about "If we must die, let it not be like
hogs." What does that mean?

Mitchell: Go out fighting. (Mitchell answers Coach immediately in a loud, clear voice
with no apparent hesitation. He looks at Coach, then looks over his shoulder.)

Coach: OK. That's almost it, but that's not exactly it. (Mitchell looks at Coach
again.)

Mitchell: For a purpose and a moral (again, Mitchell's voice is clear and loud).

When we first observe Mitchell's behavior during this part of the session we think that he appears confident. His behavior seems, in many
ways, hypermasculine. He answers without hesitation and speaks in a

voice that is noticeably louder and clearer than that of the other boys. He seems fearless and brave, but we soon realize that this façade has a hyper-vulnerable dimension hidden beneath it as we observe and listen to Mitchell some more.

Coach: OK. That's it. What kind of purpose? (Mitchell is looking down at his hands as Coach is talking.)

Mitchell: (still looking down at his hands) Any purpose that suits you, so that you don't die like a coward.

(Mitchell's voice is higher than before. He places emphasis on the word "coward.")

Coach: Oh, that's good. (Coach looks around the room at other students.)

This interaction reflects the hypervulnerability that might underlie Mitchell's manly outward "toughness." He diverts his attention away from Coach when he is pushed to describe the kind of purpose that is worth dying for. His response is vague; he does not provide details of a purpose that is truly worth dying for. He does, however, reinforce his "manly" point: It is a purpose worth dying for as long as the person dies as a man, not a coward or punk.

In the next sequence it becomes clear that Mitchell and other students continue to focus on the way they might die rather than the reason for their death. They seem focused on superficialities (how did the man seem when he died? Did he seem scared?), but they are not prepared to look beneath the surface and figure out whether some steps leading up to fights or death are truly worth the battle.

Staff3: You said a type of purpose. (She looks at Coach) What type of purpose would he say? In the poem they named a purpose.

Mitchell: I don't know. What is it?

Staff3: They said noble. Do you know that word "noble"? A noble purpose? What would be a noble purpose to die for? (Pause)

Dandridge: Die with heart.

Staff3: Die with heart. OK.

As Dandridge's response shows, these boys seem to ask themselves, "Does the person seem fearless when he dies?" If so, then he died for a good reason. What seems to matter to them is the end, whether the person died as a true man, not the means. They understand the meaning of the poem which is if they die for something that is brave, the death is not senseless. However, maintaining manhood is a noble thing and dying or living like a punk is the most senseless thing to the boys. The conversation continues, and we soon learn that Mitchell has thought about noble purposes for which to die.

Coach: What would any of you die for that has a noble purpose? (Mitchell responds immediately)

Mitchell: My family.

Coach: Family. Who else? But first, would any of you die for a noble purpose?

Mitchell: It depends on what it was. (Mitchell is looking around the room)

Coach: OK. What is a noble purpose for you? What is your name?

Mitchell: Mitchell.

Coach: Mitchell, what is a noble purpose for you?

Mitchell: Depends on what it was! (His voice is higher when he says the word "was.") My mother. (His voice is lower once again when he says this)

Coach: OK. You would die for her.

Mitchell: Yeah. Um, (pause) probably do me my family. I don't have nothing else, really, except for that.

Mitchell shows a softer side in this moment. He admits that he would die for his family, especially his mom, and that he values them. He may even feel calmed by the realization that he has something precious enough to sacrifice himself for, as was indicated by his voice returning to normal when he talked about his mom. As we see in the following interaction, however, he seems animated and upset when he discusses other "noble" things for which he would die.

Coach: Uh hum. How 'bout a stranger? (Would you die for a stranger?)

Mitchell: My sneaks.

Coach: You'd die for your sneaks?

Mitchell: Yeah. (He responds in a voice that is higher, louder than before)

Coach: What's so special about your sneaks?

Mitchell: I'm not gonna let nobody take nothing from me.

Coach: What about your shirt?

Mitchell: That too! Anything that I paid for. Ain't nobody take nothing.

Coach: What kind of sneaks you got?

Mitchell: It's not what I got! I could have Bobo's. They're not taking them either. (A few others laugh. However, throughout this conversation about sneaks and clothing, the other boys do not give Mitchell eye contact. They look at Coach, at the floor, or at their feet while the two of them talk.)

Coach: So, it's just the stuff that belongs to you.

Mitchell: Yeah. It's the point that somebody disrespecting me and trying to take your stuff.

Coach: OK, that's good. So being disrespected is a noble purpose.

Mitchell: Yeah. (The other boys in the room are quiet. They do not respond.)

Coach: To die for. All right.

Again, Mitchell's high voice, his strong inflection on certain words, and his loud speech indicate that this is an emotional topic for him to talk about. When we see these kinds of behaviors in people, we often assume that they are scared, angry, or reflecting an experience of having been disrespected. Mitchell may very well be feeling both of these emotions, but he might also be feeling something that so rarely is attributed to young Black males: sadness and depression. This may be a difficult reality for Mitchell to admit to himself. He answered the question in a socially acceptable way by saying that he would die for his family. Most people would agree that it is a noble cause to die for one's family. Now, however, he is venturing into territory that few can understand——except for the other boys in the room, who seem to share Mitchell's sentiment by acting in similarly distressed ways as he talks. Mitchell seems to be the spokesperson for the group when he dramatically declares that he, like the other boys in the room, feels compelled to stand up for his manhood when his masculinity is at stake. Who cares what the reason is for the fight? The fight is not about the Bobo's or the shirt. It is about someone threatening his very manhood and demanding that he answer them, in the moment: Are you "sweet" or are you "the man"? In the next dialogue transaction, we can see an example of hypervulnerability in the immature view of being disrespected. Disrespect to hypervulnerable youth means to be rendered inconsequential, meaningless, and inferior. A less fragile identity would not so easily believe that an insult could change who an adolescent is.

The discussion continues. Now Montrose joins the conversation and begins to challenge Mitchell's opinion. For the first time during the session, an opinion is introduced that stresses that all fights may not be necessary to show one's manhood.

Coach: Somebody else. What else would you…What noble purpose would you die for? Somebody said family….

Coach: OK. What did you say, Montrose?

Montrose: (He is reclining, as if stretching) I'd get shot for my family, but I ain't takin' a hit. I ain't tryin' to die for 'em. If I'm there—If I'm there while they shooting, then I get shot. (Montrose is smiling). You know what I'm sayin', but, man, look! I ain't jumpin' in front of nothin'. I'll come to your funeral, you know what I'm sayin', and cry. (Nervous laughter comes from the crowd)

Staff3: Let me ask you this. If a situation was going down that involves your family and people was coming in there, and there was some shooting going on….

Montrose: That don't matter—my man….I wouldn't get shot at if I ain't got nothing to do with it. I ain't got nothing to do with it.

Staff3: If you thought you could step in and pull it out. Would you try to step in and help?

Montrose: Yeah, that's one thing if I could talk someone out, without somebody getting hurt, but if somebody come up on you and start shooting, man, I'm gonna be across the street.

(Montroses' voice is higher as he says this last sentence. Nervous laughter comes from the crowd. Somebody says, "That son of a bitch!" Montrose continues.) Look, I ain't taking no bullet for *no*body! (Laughter continues. One boy pretends to shoot someone as he's laughing. He says, "Someone come right up to you and go 'Pop!'" Mitchell is looking at this boy across the circle and says, "Get shot there right after the fight!" (Montrose continues) I'd never do that. I'd never do that.

Coach: What about your family? Somebody said family. Is everybody your family? (The group responds: No.)

Coach: Cousins?

Daniel: It depends. If I think, if I think they'd do it for me, I'd do it for them. Not everybody in my family.

Mitchell: To me, it depends on if they're older or younger though. My mom...though if it was somebody younger than me, I'd die for 'em because they gonna live longer than me.

Montrose: (jumps in) Ain't nobody here talking about no moms on the corner getting shot. For *real* (higher voice), man, be serious. If it was my mom, yeah....

Mitchell: I'm talking about family.

Montrose: But if me and my cousin standing there, somebody run up on you shooting...What's the first thing you wanna do if you ain't got no gun? You want to run. Am I right or am I wrong? Ain't gonna try to stand him, man, you ain't gonna just do it!

Coach: Let's just say that people who we might care for who might get shot or die is a rare thing. It doesn't happen every day. We hope dying doesn't happen—it only happens to us once in our lives, right? So the question really is, if you had to be in that place in that choice, what would you do it for? So maybe it's a rare thing that your mom might get shot, but if the situation came up, that's the issue.

Montrose: Well, if me and my mom was walking and someone started shooting, I'm sayin', yeah, I'd lie and go for cover, you know what I'm saying? (Montrose reads disagreement on the face of another group member) Come on, but, man, that's not....If you're standing on the corner with your man and someone run up and go, Pop, Pop, Pop!, and you ain't got no gun, whatcha gonna do? (His voice gets louder and higher so as to defend his remarks to the rest of the group which he may feel is questioning his comments. At this moment, Montrose is demonstrating the absurdity of confronting an armed person. His arms are outstretched in a culturally embattling fashion or in a manner to imitate someone who is unarmed and foolishly confronting an armed person.) You ain't gonna stand there and go, "Ah, Shit What? What? What?" (The boys begin laughing and have side conversations. Montrose continues.) You'd turn around and run!

Montrose is a realist. He is aware that there are circumstances during which a person is more at risk to being hurt or killed. He is the wise one in the crowd, the one willing to step up and present a voice of dissent. He brings the conversation back to a point where the real danger in their lives is discussed. His argument is well taken: Though it is not particularly common for their mothers to be shot at, shootings among young Black males on street corners is common. As the wise man in the group, Montrose offers a unique position. Maybe the real "man" should choose to run instead of fight, especially if he is not prepared to go against others who are better equipped for the challenge. Soon, others start to respond to Montrose's point, including Mitchell.

Mitchell: (His voice is high and he is talking above the crowd) I would run too if you and your boy were caught with no gun!

Brandon: We're talking about your mom....If you were on the corner with your mom. Would you go running from your mom?

Staff1: I think you guys need to listen to what Coach said. He said, "What noble cause would you die for?" OK, what you guys are talking about are isolated circumstances. He's asking for what noble cause. What is it in your life....hold up....

But all members of the group are showing that they are distressed during the conversation. As was the case before, they speak in high voices, stress certain words to get their points across, and talk in loud voices. Most, at this moment, are talking in side conversations.

The conversation now takes a more somber turn. While before the boys talked about how they would die for their mothers, they made no mention of fathers. At this point, Coach talks about his son and how he would die for him, especially to protect him from harm. Most of the boys have their arms folded and are sitting quietly. This is the first time during the session that fathers and fatherhood are discussed. The conversation continues, and now some of the boys, especially Mitchell, focus on talking about their dads.

Coach: There might be something you might do differently if the person you loved for and cared for was around you. Now some of you said there is somebody I wouldn't die for.

Mitchell: If I was closer to my dad, I would die for him too. Since you're not close to somebody, it's just like being strangers. (Someone from the crowd says, "Yeah.")

Coach: All right, so you would die for him.

Mitchell: So just like you see someone on the street—they getting shot, I don't know a fuck about 'em. Like that—excuse my language. (Kalenga laughs)

This is a sad moment because Mitchell is putting a caveat on the issue of family. He makes a strong point that there are some people in your family that you would die for and some you may not want to do anything for.

Mitchell is talking about the loneliness attached to father loss and absence. He is longing to be closer to his dad—in some ways, he seems to *want* to die for his father—but, in reality, the opportunity is not there for him to do that.

Coach: OK, what were you saying before? (Coach looks at Brandon)

Brandon: If it ain't my mom, my grandmom, or my grandfather, I'm ain't dying for them.

Coach: OK.

Brandon: All right, people who live in my house, let's put it that way and my grandmom. But anybody else, I ain't jumping in front of no bullets, no trains, no cars, nothing. I ain't jumpin' in front of nothing.

In the following sequence, Montrose once again forces the boys to be realistic, not hypothetical, and think about who would die for them. Again, the conversation turns to focus on fathers.

Montrose: Man, we sittin' here talking about people we'd die for. Gotta start thinkin' about the people who'd die for you, man. Know what I mean? (His voice is higher at the end)

Coach: Who would die for you? Do you know somebody?

Daniel: There's a lot of people who'd die for you. You just don't know. (The boys are all talking, having side conversations. Someone says, "That's what I'm saying!" Another says, "There's a couple of people.")

(Daniel continues): There's a lot of people who'd die for you, you just don't know. OK, you might say that all right, it's like, you might like, you said, you said, you ain't close to your pop, but you never know your pop...

The boys seem to be wishing for father involvement and caring despite all evidence to the contrary. It's possible that the boys could have been taken to the philosophical and psychological place of processing who would die for them through many of the group role-play strategies. These kids may seem to have faith that their fathers will protect them and that there is a loneliness that comes from the fact that they haven't experienced this protection yet.

Mitchell: (He interrupts Daniel) My pop might take a bullet for me, but I wouldn't take one for him! (Montrose laughs, arms crossed)

Staff1: But the point is, who would die for you?

Mitchell: Well, it's probably fewer people who'd die for me than I'd die for them being as though I would fight for anybody that I know—I would fight with anybody I know. But if it's like 15 and I'm running 2, I ain't gonna lie...(laughter from the crowd)

(Mitchell continues): If it's like 10, I'm gonna fight. If it's like 15 or 20 and I'm not ready. I'll catch up with them later!

(There's a suggestion that retaliation would be possible when the odds are against you. Someone from the crowd says, "Yeah.")

Coach: Do you know somebody who will die for you? The invisible man or super-person that will show up that you don't know. Let's just put them on the back-burner. Do you know somebody who will die for you?

Again, the boys talk about hypothetical situations instead of discussing realistic situations in which others might die for them. Dandridge talks about a hypothetical situation of pushing an old lady away at the train station if someone tries to shoot her. The boys join in and talk about other hypothetical situations in helping strangers. It seems much safer for them to discuss the "what if" rather than the "what really is."

The conversation soon turns again to issues of manhood and respect. Perhaps they return to their discussion of these topics to feel powerful again after they exposed their hypervulnerable sides in their discussions of father loss and absence.

Coach: What if, um, do we have brothers, do we have brothers, who die like hogs?

(They continue talking about hypothetical situations and stories in the news—the Jasper, TX lynching, a bullfight).

(After some diversion in the discussion, Coach continues): A lot of brothers—Latino and African American—like what Brother Hassan was talking about last time—sometimes we might die over a pair of sneakers. The sneakers might mean something like respect—like you (Mitchell) were saying....

Mitchell: It's not the fact that it's materialistic. I can go buy another pair today or tomorrow. It's but the point that somebody's just looking at you like "Damn, this thing is sweet. Let me get him right there." Looking at you like that—I've never been robbed.

(Someone from the crowd says, "Me neither.")

Coach: But would that be a cause to die for...

Mitchell: In a way.... (He is trying to talk over the crowd. His voice gets higher and louder.) Yeah. Look, look. In a way, yeah, in a way, no. Because of the simple fact, because of the simple fact—when somebody took something from me when I was older—when I was younger—I said it would never happen again. And ever since then, like when I was little, growing up like that, nobody never really tried to take nothing from me. So why should I let this person take something from me and have me feeling like now I'm a bitch now cuz somebody took something from me. I feel like that's disrespect.

Staff1: ARE you a bitch?

Mitchell: NO!

Staff1: Like Coach said, that's dying like a hog....

Mitchell: I didn't say I would die for it....I said nobody gonna take nothing....

Staff1: You said that earlier....

Mitchell: Yeah, cuz somebody gonna take it from me, ain't nobody gonna take anything off my back.

Staff1: So it's worth dying? Like Montrose was saying....He was saying on the side somebody put a gun up in my face and say, "Listen, give me your sneaks...."

Mitchell: (He leans forward and points at the boy across the circle) Half the time they ready to kill you any old way!

(Then he leans back. Conversations develop among the boys in the crowd)

Mitchell: So what's the point (voice raised higher than before)? I'd rather die with my sneaks on than die with them off!

(He is leaning forward)

Mitchell stands firm that it is worth dying for his respect and manhood. Montrose, however, once again interjects with a voice of reason. Montrose points out that, even when you fight back, you may not be in control and may have things taken from you. Fighting for what's yours does not prevent others from taking things from you. Dandridge eventually agrees with Montrose.

Montrose: (Montrose's arms are crossed) There's a good chance they're gonna take your shoes off after you die! (He laughs)

Dandridge: If you hesitate to take them off and then you take them off, they might bust you off then too!

Mitchell: Look. Look. Look. (People are talking. Mitchell is pointing to those across the circle from him) If they gonna shoot you, they gonna shoot you, regardless. If they gonna kill you, they gonna kill you, regardless, cuz it's your time to go. You don't know when it's your time to go. If you've given up or...or....some people....I seen somebody they didn't give them nothing. They didn't take it from them. They just went about their business. They weren't trying to kill nobody. They just had a gun and just wanted to see if they could stick someone up. If it's your time to go, it's gonna be your time to go. Don't nobody in here know when they're going to die.

Dandridge: I disagree.

Sadly, Mitchell's comments reflect the fact that he seems to feel powerless over his fate. These comments reflect an ironic disparity between his outward behavior and his true feelings. Perhaps he acts in hypermasculine ways in efforts to gain control of situations around him, while, on the inside, he feels a hypervulnerable hopelessness that stems from feelings of resignation and lack of control over his own fate. To the boys, avoidng being a bitch means to prevent dying like a hog. The irony is that boys risk dying like a hog, honorless and humiliated (at least in the eyes of the group facilitators), as they protect themselves from public ridicule. Is it possible that underneath the hypermasculinity is the hypervulnerable fear that their fate includes "dying like a hog?"

The group concludes with Coach talking about how they, as young men of color, are in the highest risk group to be killed or injured from acts of violence. The boys express an awareness of the fact that their safety and lives are at risk each day. On another sad note, Kalenga concludes with a final thought about respect. Throughout the session, a few of the boys talked about how it was necessary to engage in violence to earn respect from others. As a final thought, Kalenga notes how violence among and against young Black males actually reflects how they, as a group, receive less respect, not more, as a result of the violence they experience.

Coach: You guys are at the highest risk to be murdered and shot than any other group in America....You are a target....The statistics bear this out....And some days, we are also at risk, Brother Staff1 and I are also at risk.....

Mitchell: You at risk every day!

Kalenga: But we're at higher risk though. People don't do things wrong to old heads like that, man. You ever thought to do something wrong to old heads? You gonna do something wrong?

Daniel: They would mess our heads up!

Kalenga: EXACTLY! It's just like that! People respect old heads more than they respect you.

We end the session by first appreciating the sharing, then summarizing the thoughts and wisdom generated, and finally by trying to explain how the sharing is connected to growth, development, and psychological safety. The CPR group is the backbone of the PLAAY project. It's the place we are able to interact with the boys on the most intimate basis. It is especially important that the staff be on the alert to challenge any disrespect by other students as the boys reveal their most personal selves. While many of these sessions may end on a note of caution, over time the boys not only come to expect the sharing but long for it. When a staff member misses a session because of unforeseen circumstances, the boys want to know where they are and why they were not in the CPR group. The elements we expect in most therapeutic encounters, such as attachment, transference, and demand for equanimity of self-disclosure, are all visible in this experience.

As we try to explain to Black boys more about the complexity of being Black and male in this society, there is a certain sadness we share with them. This sadness comes from the experience of wondering why we even have to culturally socialize them in the first place. If we don't tell them about the complexity of Black manhood in America, we are allowing them to remain vulnerable. If we tell them about this Catch-33, we extend their vulnerability to some degree. Damned if we do, damned if we don't. The benefit, however, is that by doing so, we have the opportunity to challenge the last and final "damned." This is possible not only because boys have a choice to accept or reject some or all of society's negative conception of them as they explore these deeper dynamics. It is possible also because the Catch-22 is no longer invisible. Sometimes, it is only when people are at the bottom of the well that they are most ready to look up and see the light calling them. Our boys are not damned if we don't accept that premise. They don't have to accept it either. And they are our boys because we or someone we know must interact with them sooner or later. The late Robin Harris, a very well-known Black comedian, used to have a comedy sketch called "Bay-Bay's kids." These were children who would terrorize babysitters, family, friends, and the entire neighborhood with their negative behavior. In our view, even Bay-Bay's kids need love and support and the opportunity to know and reject the mantle of Catch-33. Even Bay-Bay's kids are our kids.

CPR is named so for a reason. If Black males do not get in touch with the sadness that underlies the insecure masculinity, they are taking risks with their lives, which our current society is all too ready to snuff out. Developing critical consciousness skills can be life saving for Black boys who live under our current circumstances in a "patrol and control" nation. Knowing the Catch-33; understanding how Black male anger triggers fears in our majority culture; and how this fear has historically been violently exercised on Black males; and embracing choices to sidestep, challenge, and jump over these fears can save a brother's life. And we hope it saves more than just one brother's life.

The next chapter explores one strategy to shake up the internal self-control challenges that Black boys experience. Martial arts represents one way we try to teach boys to know themselves and the internal frustrations that arise at the most unpredictable moments. Defending yourself is important. CPR represents a psychological self-defense. Knowing themselves before they battle a dangerous world is essential to survival on the streets. Let's discuss how psychological and physical self-defense work together.

REFERENCES

Asante, M. (1987). *The afrocentric idea.* Philadelphia: Temple University Press.
Bell, C. C. (1997). Promotion of mental health through coaching competitive sports. *Journal of the National Medical Association, 89(8),* 517–520.
Ferguson, A. A. (2000). *Bad boys: Public schools in the making of black masculinity.* Ann Arbor: University of Michigan Press.
Hammond, W. R., & Yung, B. R. (1991). Preventing violence in at-risk African-American youth. *Journal of Health Care for the Poor and Underserved, 2(3),* 359–373.

Hilliard, A. (1983). psychological factors associated with language in the education of the African-American child. *Journal of Negro Education, 52(1)*, 24–34.

Kunjufu, J. (1983). *Countering the conspiracy to destroy Black boys*. Chicago: African American Images.

Marley, Bob. (1983, 1989, 1991, 1992, 1994, 1996). Redemption Song. In T. White (Ed.), *Catch a Fire: The Life of Bob Marley*, rev. ed. by Timothy White © by Timothy White. Used by arrangement with Henry Holt and Co., New York and the author.

Maxwell, W. (1937). *A Long Way Home*. New York: *New York Times*, 1969.

May, D. C. & Dunaway, G. R. (2000). Predictors of fear of victimization at school among adolescents. *Sociological Spectrum, 20*.

McKay, C., & Sherman, J. R. (1999). *Selected poems by Claude McKay*. Mineola, NY: Dover Publications.

Meeks, K. (2000). *Driving while black: What to do if you are a victim of racial profiling*. New York: Broadway Books.

Watts, R. J. & Abdul-Adil, J. K. (1997). Promoting critical consciousness in young, African American men. In R. Watts & R. Jagers (Eds.), *Manhood Development in Urban African-American Communities*. New York: Haworth Press.

Whaley, A. L. (1992). A culturally sensitive approach to the prevention of interpersonal violence among urban Black youth. *Journal of the National Medical Association, 84*, 585–588.

Wilson, A. N. (1990). *Black-on-Black Violence*. Bronx, NY.: African World InfoSystems.

Wilson, A. N. (1991). *Understanding Black male adolescent violence: Its remediation and prevention*. Bronx, NY.: African World InfoSystems.

CHAPTER 4

PLAAY Fighting in Martial Arts

*Nimr Hassan, Elaine F. Cassidy, Diane M. Hall,
Gale Seiler, and Howard C. Stevenson Jr.*

Understanding the psychological meaning behind movement and style
has long been the focus of theoretical interest within the field of Black psychology (Boykin, 1977; 1978; Gallaher, 1992). For this reason, it is one of the
foundational principles of the theoretical background of the PLAAY program. Movement as a psychological intervention for African American
youth is not a new concept, but an understudied one. The ways in which
African American movement is exoticized and diagnosed is remarkable.
Neal, McCray, Webb-Johnson, and Bridgest (2003) found that teachers
rated African American youth with culturally stylistic movement as lower
in achievement, higher in aggression, and more likely to need special education services than students with traditional movement styles. Previous
studies by Wade Boykin and colleagues were concerned with style,
rhythm, movement and music as important contextual influences on the
performance of academic tasks by African American youth (Allen &
Boykin, 1991; Boykin, 1977, 1991; Boykin & Allen, 1988; Boykin, Allen,
Davis, & Senior, 1997; Dill & Boykin, 2000). These researchers have repeatedly shown that African American children often perform cognitive functions better when they are allowed a considerable amount of movement,
rather than low or no movement. In fact, in studies in which African American children were compared to White children, African American children
consistently performed better in high-movement expressive contexts.

In our program, we use martial arts as a forum for psychological intervention. We chose this athletic medium because it is movement-focused,
developmentally appropriate, multisystemic, and culturally relevant to
young Black males. The form of martial arts we use is not like the karate,

kung fu, Bruce Lee styles most people think of when they hear the phrase "martial arts." Rather, the kind used in the PLAAY project, known as Koga Ha Kosho Shorei Ryu Kempo, or "Koga Ha," combines breathing, movement, balance, focus and coordination to help boys learn to stay in control and avoid danger—by hopping away, employing misdirection (physical, verbal, and psychological), and using the appropriate defense as a last resort, if attacked. Our martial arts component is known as martial arts anger reduction or MAAR, because its purpose is to use movement, both individual and between boys, to reduce the anger and panic that may emerge when the boys are faced with daily conflict, and to help them avoid behavior that may have placed them in danger in past incidents.

PSYCHOLOGY OF MOVEMENT

Movement is commonly used to treat as well as prevent physical injuries. For example, patients are often told by their family physicians to exercise regularly to maintain a level of good health. Rarely, if ever, are people told to use movement as treatment for psychological issues. We believe that, just as you learn about a knee injury by observing the fluidity and challenges in a person's movement, you can also learn about that person's psychological distress by observing that person in action.

It makes sense that some people place great value on being able to "move right," given that movement is considered by some to be a form of intelligence. For example, Howard Gardner (1993) refers to physical movement as "bodily-kinesthetic intelligence," one of six forms of intelligence common to all individuals. When we watched Michael Jordan glide through the air with all of his scoring weapons, every bit of his peripheral vision, and every element of his mental acuity intact, we watched a genius in action. And when we watch someone like the smaller Dennis Rodman frustrate larger men like Alonzo Mourning because of the way he can out-rebound larger opponents and fit into spaces with wiry, Gumby-like body movements, we are seeing bodily intelligence at its best.

Indeed, it takes some kind of intelligence and skill to move, and even more know-how and skill to master movements. Actors and athletes rely heavily on movement in their respective venues and are often considered incredibly skilled in kinesthetic ability. But all of us rely on movement to make statements in the social world. How we walk and talk reflects what is going on with us beneath the surface. In this way, our movements reflect our personality strengths and limitations. This is no less true for staff members or adults working with boys. In so many ways, we communicate with our bodies how we feel about the young people we work with.

One example occurred during the first year of working with the boys at the discipline school. One of our undergraduate staff members went through our training and participated in some staff meetings and was eager to work with African American males. During some of the MAAR sessions, it became clear that the boys were watching her as she was standing far away from them. She expressed eagerness to participate when not in the presence of the boys, but during the session, she often gave off messages that she was tense, robotic, and slightly fearful. This behavior persisted for several sessions and it became obvious, although unspoken, that the boys were wary of this behavior. It was our belief that it was somewhat frightening to the boys as well, and their response to it was to test her distance by coming physically close to her to see what she would do. It was their way of trying to decrease the emotional distance as well as check out their assumptions, like "playing with her emotions." They were simply being adolescents in our opinion, trying to connect with her, but she wasn't responsive. Connection cannot be made if staff members are unwilling to critique their own fears—even those fears that are revealed in body language and movement. This is true for race relations in general, but when staff members are working with Black boys, their lack of racial and personal identity introspection is a deadly combination—for the boys.

MANAGING EMOTION AND TOLERATING FRUSTRATION

We believe there is enormous room to improve the psychological difficulties associated with frustrated mobility. But what exactly is "limited" or "frustrated mobility"? It is the experience of humiliation due to involuntary movements that are not in a person's immediate control. As Howard Gardner notes, voluntary motor activity often involves an interaction between a person's perceptual and motor systems. Some involuntary activities, however, proceed so quickly that feedback from perceptual or kinesthetic systems is impossible. It is during these involuntary activities that some people may feel a total lack of control and, consequently, feelings of utter frustration at being unable to control their bodily movements (Gardner, 1993; Gardner, Kornhaber, & Wake, 1996).

We think frustration can be used to help young people deal with the psychological challenges that may emerge from movement-related difficulties. "Frustration tolerance," or the ability to manage and move beyond one's frustration threshold, can help them overcome movement challenges by helping them recognize their weaknesses and choose strategies to deal with them. Perhaps it is no surprise to hear that frustration can often lead to feelings of anger, and vice versa, among youth. With this in mind, it makes sense for us to appreciate the link between frustration and anger and strategize ways to help young people deal with their frustrated/angry feelings during movement activities.

Limited mobility, however, is often influenced by factors outside the individual. That is, ecological and cultural contexts can determine the level of kinesthetic prowess that is necessary for acceptance in certain arenas. Among Black youth, we are especially interested in these contextual dynamics because they simultaneously determine the language and movements that accompany social interaction. Keeping this in mind, understanding limited mobility in a cultural ecological context becomes essential in not misidentifying and misdiagnosing Black youth as hyperactive, aggressive, or both. So movement can become a trigger for identifying a person's propensity for violence or acceptance, for engagement or avoidance, for rejection or appreciation. Since society has projected criminality, hostility, and animosity onto Black male movement, teachers and therapists have to rethink their own reactions to Black male movement. There should be an appreciation of the fact that just identifying the anger in students' movements can be very useful in understanding them and working with them.

Anger is a natural response to dangerous social situations and the more we know about how it is expressed verbally and nonverbally, the more helpful we can be when boys use movement to express it. Researchers have determined that anger is precipitated by two primary aspects: whether a person possesses enduring personal characteristics that lead to angry or frustrated feelings and whether a person experiences a momentary cognitive-emotional-physical state of anger or frustration. According to Lazarus (1991), people are likely to feel angry, and perhaps frustrated, if their ego identity is momentarily threatened in some way. But if the person is angry to begin with, that is, if the person has an "enduring personal characteristic" of anger, any type of frustration can increase the probability, intensity, and duration of the anger that person feels. Research by Zillman and Bryant (1974) has shown that this can happen even if the anger felt is completely unrelated to the current provocation. We still believe that there is usually a set of circumstances that can explain the anger of Black males. Moreover, we believe that the view of impulsive aggression is overused, especially given the tendency to "patrol and control" these young men. Attempts to find out the meaning of anger and aggression exacted by or experienced by these boys is rare and therefore a variety of strategies are necessary to appreciate the "both-and" problematic/healthy nature of anger expression. Movement is one arena in which we can observe how anger in boys is provoked. By adding the element of movement, we are attempting to increase the opportunities to observe this anger "in the moment" or "in the movement" and have some influence on it, once "understood."

The various components of PLAAY are designed to help the student identify, express, self-monitor, and reduce the frustration and anger that accompany the immediate awareness of failure. The martial arts component is developed particularly to frustrate the boys in little ways as they become aware of their lack of knowledge and skill in something that they feel confident they should know how to do. The goal of this is to stretch their ability to tolerate frustration, or increase their "frustration tolerance," as competent alternative strategies are developed and implemented to help them manage their frustration.

MOVEMENT AS INTERVENTION

Expressive movement psychotherapy has been successfully applied to ameliorate psychological adjustment challenges (Dosmantes-Alperson & Merrill, 1980). Other expressive movement researchers have also identified that independent judges can assess personality traits and emotional meaning from watching the movements of others (Boone & Cunningham, 2001; Frable, 1987; Katz et al., 1993). In discussing the skill required to move well, Sir Frederic Bartlett (1951) writes about the complexity of skilled performance functions. He notes that skilled performance is influenced by signals that performers pick up from their environment, in combination with other signals. What Bartlett is referring to here is the amazing psychological communication that occurs within the individual as he or she makes movements. This interaction of intra- and interpersonal emotional experiences is on display while people are making sense of their social context. This opens the door to an arena of psychological intervention and poses the question "What do individuals experience when they are engaged in skilled and unskilled movement that relates directly to their psychological and social adjustment?"

Many of us take for granted the amount of energy and the degree of complexity that goes into basic motor functions. It is only when we lose these basic abilities that we become cognizant of their importance and nuances. The moment we stub our toe, we realize its importance to the walking process. The same is true for a broken finger or a backache. Often, until these events happen to us, we overlook their relative importance to our daily movement tasks. Once we are aware of the limits of our mobility, we are immediately in touch with the frustration of immobility or limited mobility.

Understanding this frustration is similar to understanding the frustration of young people who have difficulty transacting with the world using their bodies or bodily intelligence. What if our social competence and the quality of our interpersonal relationships were influenced by how well we communicated through our movements? Among African American youth, cultural style and the integration of cool is essential to effectively move on in a healthy developmental fashion. With this in mind, it is our assertion that social competence for youth requires a mastery of movement communication. We believe that you can learn about an individual's personality, psychological strengths and limitations, and potential by understanding his or her movement expressions and bodily intelligence.

If that is so, then how do we help assess and develop bodily intelligence in the African American males with whom we work?

The frustration that people feel from not being able to influence their bodily expressions is a unique one that, in our opinion, can be reduced once its source is identified. We think we all can learn to observe our bodily and emotional expressions and change them, if we so desire. Many of us as adolescents used television, for example, to help us maneuver the latest styles, attitudes, and movements. *Soul Train* was a popular show during the 70s and 80s for many young people, not just because the latest music was being played, but because the latest dances were being performed and in an hour youth across the country could learn a move, practice it without the intrusion of "player-hatin'" classmates, and make better inroads into the world of "Black cool." Managing the tension of being Black and cool just wasn't possible by watching *American Bandstand.*

We can receive feedback about our strengths and weaknesses in movement, just as we receive feedback about our academic potential. During MAAR, students learn ways to think about their movement by using their metaconsciousness. This means that they learn to "think about what they are thinking" while they are engaged in movements that seem reflexive or second nature to them. These boys are aware that they have certain "reflexes," or movements that they use when they are simply, as they put it, "not thinking." We help them reflect on those reflexes so that they can break old patterns of movement and create new ones that are more informed, and perhaps more effective, than the reflexes they used to use.

There are multiple frustrations related to limited mobility. People may feel frustrated that their physical limitations might prevent them from completing a task well or completing it at all. Along with this frustration may be the awareness they have of their lack of accomplishment or their failure. For adolescents in particular, who already feel as if their vulnerabilities are constantly on display, it may be particularly challenging to experience and tolerate movement-related limitations in front of their peers.

Dealing with this frustration is a metacognitive social demand, is it not? Movement frustration brings about a type of egocentric "thinking about one's thinking." But that is not all. It also brings about a perception that "others are thinking about how I am unable to move effectively in this moment." It is intensely frustrating to fail to complete an expected movement and watch that "failure" take place. However, it is even more psychologically frustrating to think how others, especially one's peers, may be watching this failure. Certain thoughts may go through a person's head, such as "They are watching me and expecting me to be able to do this. Because I can't, they think I'm stupid," or "I believe I should be able to complete this task in front of everyone and if I don't, maybe I *am* stupid." These thoughts are directly related to adolescents' active expression of identity. As we've explained earlier in the introduction, some adolescents are so caught up in being the person their peers expect or contexts require them to be that they are "doing identity" instead of "being" whoever it is they need or want to be.

Searching for and choosing an identity is an important developmental task for adolescents. We therefore target these identity-related behavioral and cognitive frustrations in our interventions because we believe they contribute to acting-out behaviors of youth who are frustrated. This double-frustration ("What I think about my failure" and "What I perceive they are thinking of me") can cause young people to spiral into more intense physical interactions, ones that do not necessarily have to occur, such as aggression. Help can be provided, however, if we recognize the source of those frustrations and intervene with young people before explosions occur.

In designing any type of intervention, it is necessary to realize that all young people are not the same. This is especially true of those who engage in aggressive behavior. Intervention is not helpful or effective if it fails to appreciate the unique and varied ways in which young people spiral into anger and aggression. By observing the boys during movement-related activities, we can see the unique ways they handle frustration. These activities provide the boys with opportunities to express themselves, in their own ways. They also help them improve their bodily intelligence. In our opinions, bodily intelligence is not so static or genetically based that it cannot be improved. Rather, we believe this type of intelligence is mutable by virtue of maturation and feedback, even resilient to change, once it has been properly taught. We therefore believe that movement ability is teachable and we agree with Carl Bell's assertion that, like courage, it "can be cultivated and fortified" to have long-term benefits for youth (Bell, 1997).

MARTIAL ARTS MOVEMENT

We use martial arts as our vehicle for movement-related intervention because it has been applied to ameliorate the troubled lives of wayward youth and improve the self-control, concentration, and mental health functioning of children and adults (Ferrari, 1999; Riggio, Lippa, & Salinas, 1990; Theeboom, De Knop, & Weiss, 1995; Williams & Elliott, 1999). Numerous researchers have found that the movement of martial arts yields special opportunities to manage the emotional struggles of angry adolescents (Delva-Tauiliili, 1995; Twemlow & Sacco, 1998). It is our goal to observe the balance between stress and mastery in the young African American males we serve. Helping youth manage the stress of coordinating difficult movements and gain confidence by mastering those movements is key to helping teens with histories of impulsivity gain self-control. In the PLAAY project, we attempt to work through these frustrations and triumphs to reduce the anger and aggression of African American youth who have histories of school problems.

STAFF TRAINING

Several elements of the martial arts instruction helped to establish a very effective teaching atmosphere. First, all staff members teaching the boys had experience with the training from the sensei (martial arts instructor) and they felt many of the same frustrations and had to overcome many of the frustrations that the boys would experience. This was helpful in a "keeping it real" adolescent reality that required instructors to be able to "walk the walk and talk the talk" of self-defense movements and knowledge. The sensei had the final say on decisions related to martial arts technique and strategy. Second, there was a focus on making sure instructors used nonthreatening verbal and nonverbal language and soft voices when managing classroom behavior. These were strategies designed to balance out and undermine the potential extreme outbursts or emotional expressions of the boys when they felt unruly. Third, numbers replaced words when students were commanded to move in left and right directions (e.g., 2 and 3) in order to make it easier for students to grasp coordination of hand and body instructions from the sensei. This represented a new way for the boys to gain control of their body movements. Finally, instructors included both men and women across the age spectrum from college undergraduates to middle-aged psychologists. Having the boys see men and women from different walks of life was important; it helped break down the barriers of resistance often represented in the giving-up comment "I can't do that." Table 4.1 describes the affection, correction, and protection competency skills used by facilitators of the MAAR sessions.

MAAR is designed to teach boys how to manage their emotions internally through exercises that stimulate minor frustrations that are visible in movement struggles involving what we call discoordination. Discoordination involves miscommunication between people's desire to perform a physical task and their ability to actually perform the bodily movements necessary to complete that task. What is important about the process of discoordination is that it places the egos of young men on trial as they become forced to use age-old strategies of physical manhandling to resolve the conflicts or ridicule that may result from their discoordination.

We believe that a lot of self-reflection and status concerns are evident during the basic MAAR exercises, which require students to follow clear but frustrating commands to stand, walk, and sit in a narrow and specific set of parameters and to coordinate their foot and hand movements in self-defensive fashion. In the view of the sensei, these command-generated movements (walking, sitting, standing, and hopping) reflect personality strengths and limitations. One major benefit of the foot, hand, and hop-

Table 4.1
Competency Skills for Facilitators in MAAR Intervention

	Skill to Be Observed	1	2	3	4	5	6	7	8
Affection	Greets students, sign-in as they enter the MAAR session								
	Uses appropriate voice for situation (calm or directive)								
	Shows respect and respectfully handles disrespect from students								
	Connects child's emotional life to problem behaviors in MAAR								
Correction	Reframes self-doubt beliefs about accomplishing new tests								
	Anticipates potential hypervulnerability conflict early								
	Redirects/distracts student from trigger or aggressive situations								
	Uses warning, step-outside, and removal system, if necessary								
	Physically mediates conflicts between students, if necessary								
Protection Self-Defense Self-Control Teaching	Teach student how to manage failure in exercises								
	Maintains the attention and motivation of the students								
	Explains meaning of Sensei teaching and demonstrates moves; especially breathing and box patterns, rope skips								
	Follow curriculum and uses multiple methods to teach; cultural socialization								

ping movements in MAAR is that they help students to begin to identify the difference between habits and ideas. Often, the boys believe they know their bodies and can control them at will, but during these exercises they realize fairly quickly that this control is ephemeral. They realize that they have developed habits that do not easily conform to their self-commands or to reception of commands from the sensei, and that another form of cognitive-visual-motor discipline must begin so that thought and action become one. Watching this frustration turn to mastery is wonderful; some students developed an intuitive sense of self-confidence.

In the "skills and drills" exercises, students are asked to straddle a round rubber spot on the floor, that is 6 inches in diameter. There are a number of spots placed equally distant from each other so that students who are moving in relation to the spots must also be aware of others who are equally distant from them moving in relation to their spots. One rope skipping exercise involves seeing how many rope skips can be completed in 1 minute with the goal of seeing whether any student could do 300 skips in 3 minutes. Because the students were afraid their classmates might cheat, they asked the instructors to count for them. In one session, the scenario went like this.

Two boys (A and B) take their position on the floor while their friends are encouraging each to win the contest of who can jump more rope skips in a 3-minute time period. Student A is a high-status youth who has more friends to root for him; Student B is a low-status youth whose chance of winning is perceived by everyone to be low. While Student B's mannerisms show that he does not believe he can win, he reluctantly agrees to participate. He has only one friend encouraging him to win, but even his friend thinks his chance of winning is low.

The instructor says "Go" and both boys start jumping. At the end of 30 seconds both boys have jumped the same number of skips. Student A is being encouraged to jump faster by his friends so that he can beat this "weak punk." Student B hears only his single supporter encouraging him to continue. At 1 minute Student A stops to catch his breath. Student B continues to jump. The group hollers and yells at Student A to keep jumping. Using derogatory language about Student B, they start to tell Student A that he is going to be beaten by the lower-status boy, a result that would represent a sin before God and nature. At 2 minutes Student B has jumped almost 300 skips. The tide of encouragement has shifted. Student B now hears the audience encouraging him to beat the 3-minute time limit. Student A is now being teased and is swiftly being demoted in the group's pecking order. He has caused his group, friends, "doggs" to look bad. If he looks bad, they look bad. In the space of 3 minutes, Student B is now viewed as having strength and a competence that brings him respect from all of the students in the classroom. He is now able to talk and mingle with the group. He has even picked up some new friends.

Over the years, we noticed that the pecking order was as evident in the ways students approached the MAAR exercises as they were in the daily social relations during the free times in the school hallways and cafeteria. Some boys who were "top-dog" in the school would attempt to exact their power during the MAAR exercises by demonstrating they were better than everyone else, sometimes claiming to be better than the sensei. Those students who were lowest in the pecking order received the most derision from high- and moderate-status youth. What was amazing to watch was how the varied exercises of the MAAR sessions illuminated the weaknesses of some of the high-status boys. Some could not coordinate the rope jumps and would often give up, cursing the exercise as childish and stupid while some lower-status youth could master this exercise with visible ease. With this show of competence, the lower-status youth could raise their status in the MAAR group quite dramatically and, in our opinion sometimes this change in status generalized into their social relations outside the MAAR classroom. Friendships were developed by many of the lower-status peers because others saw their willingness to try to conquer MAAR exercises that the high-status youths would not try or demonstrated fear of by not completing.

MAAR is also helpful to these boys because it provides them with opportunities to trust themselves, as they deal with discoordination and limited mobility, and to trust elders, who teach skills and strategies to deal with their movement-related difficulties. In addition to teaching culturally relevant, street-wise, urban-based self-defense strategies, we are very interested in the emotional coping strategies that youths demonstrate as they are trying to manage the frustrations of the MAAR experience. These demonstrations of emotional coping become wonderful rich opportunities to teach life lessons, but most important, they are opportunities to build relationships with the boys. These spontaneous therapeutic moments of play occur when working with youths who often are dismissed as insignificant and in our opinion, they are the moments in which youths test our resolve to care for them. It's an opportunity for us to prove to them that we are in their lives for this small amount of time for their benefit, not just ours. The following are excerpts of a MAAR session in which movement was used to build trust and respect for authority when several students decided to challenge the sensei's authority after struggling to master the self-defense movements.

Example 1: Managing Frustration and Motivation During Martial Arts Movement

In this series of qualitative segments, older boys, ages 15 to 18, are trying to perform a basic Koga Ha exercise, known as the octagon. The name of this activity stems from the fact that the boys jump forward, backward, and side to side in a pattern that resembles the shape of an octagon. The octagon is an ancient martial arts exercise system in which students are required to master eight different defense movements, all of which involve hand-and-foot coordination. These defense movements are expected to help the students move out of the path of an oncoming attacker. The exercise starts with students standing with their feet parallel over a rubber circle, or spot, which helps them keep track of their starting point and stay within a limited area on the floor. After each movement in the octagon, they are expected to return to the original position (marked by the spot) by landing with their feet straddling the spot. As they learn and perform this exercise, they are guided by the class's teacher, the sensei.

We have found that some boys inevitably become frustrated during this exercise because they have difficulty managing the foot patterns and coordinating them with the proper hand movements. They struggle to place their hands and feet in the proper positions, making it seem as if they do not understand the sensei's directions of "right" and "left." A corresponding dynamic that occurs among these boys is their constant need to "be cool." They negotiate and deliver the art of cool in all their social interactions. These issues are linked with the intense hypermasculinity demands of American manhood. We will discuss later how the procurement of cool and hypermasculinity mediates aggressive conflicts.

Sensei: Left hand up, ready, hop forward

The boys respond to the commands of the sensei. To hop forward in the first move of the octagon, the students hop with their left foot forward and their left hand up. They start in the original position; their hands are in what is called the kigan position, a protective positioning of the hands in front of the center of the body to prevent attack from an opponent. Once they hop, they are expected to switch their hands so that the right hand and forearm are in front of them, protecting their bodies. They hop with awkward trepidation, unsure how to coordinate their hands and their feet. Most of the boys end up looking at their feet and the feet of others to get their bearings, in desperation, but to no avail. Most hop with the right foot first, but even those who hop with the correct, left foot first are not sure that this is the correct footing. This frustration is expected and is produced for a purpose.

Sensei: Left foot. Left. Other left, military left. Ready? Original. Back over the spot. When we tell you to hop back, we want you to hop back with the right hand up. Hop back. Right hand. Original. Right hand, right foot.

The boys have to return to the original position before going to the second position of the octagon, which involves hopping back with the right foot back first and the right hand up to protect themselves. Again, they are unsure and confused about what to do, but they still try to follow the instructions and look cool in the process. In their attempts to look cool, some boys perform Koga Ha movements with exaggerated stylistic expressions during small breaks in the exercise. Some do the movements as dance movements, while others do Bruce Lee, karate-like impersonations, saying things like "Hiya! Ho! Hi!" These unique expressions create connections between boys in the class and add to their meaning-making experiences.

Sensei: When we tell you to hop left, we want you to hop left, hop left. With the left
   hand, left foot. Hop left. Original (meaning, back over the original "spot"). Good.

Boys: Damn! Darn!

The boys seem to curse when they become frustrated with their inability to master the instructions and perform the movements at the same time. It's like playing Twister, but with much simpler movements (ones that you might expect to accomplish standing straight up). Some of the boys are standing, just looking around trying to see who has it right, and others are hopping in untoward positions, sort of like cats at a water park.

Sensei: Come back to kigan (the original "resting" position during which participants stand with feet slightly apart and hands guarding the center of the body).
   Get your hands up. You guys are not getting your hands up to protect yourself.
   Hop right. Turn completely right. Original—over the spot. Now, the reason we
   want you to do this is there is going to be a practicum afterwards. We are gonna
   have each of you come up and do it. Let's do it again. Ready, hop forward. Left
   hand, left hand, left foot. Hop back—over the original. Hop back.

This process of practicing the first four movements of the octagon continues until the boys improve slightly, but none of them become so proficient that they feel able to brag about their performance. At times, despite their frustration, the boys ask sensei if their feet are arranged correctly. In our opinion, this demonstrates that the boys are engaged with and motivated by the teaching, despite the frustration they feel. This phenomenon has been ruled out by most educational and psychological professionals who believe it is not possible with aggressive African American youths like these. Moments like these are often lost in the process of teaching and intervening because the cultural windows of opportunity they represent seem minor in the eyes of professionals who expect dynamics among African American males to be obvious and bold. But these small moments represent the fertile ground in which meaningful relationships between staff and students can grow and where small wins are possible.

At times during these Koga Ha exercises, boys inadvertently bump into each other and laugh about their clumsiness. Although the laughter and tension mount because of their frustration and obvious lack of talent in martial arts, the laughter is not accusatory, as it is in other social interactions, such as in athletics when a person's abilities are on display among teens who show a range of talent. If "misery loves company," we think "cluelessness enjoys company" as well. In this arena, everyone is in a "clueless" condition; no one can claim bragging rights.

In African psychology, both-and represents a worldview that expects opposite experiences to coexist. Although the boys are frustrated, they are also motivated to learn. The sensei is in a situation in which he can build relationships with the boys by challenging them and motivating them to learn and improve. During these exercises, the sensei is also asked to respond to their unique concerns for authenticity and trust. As the boys' frustration mounts, they often need outlets for the constant sense of incompetence they feel. This is often called testing the limits in most psychological behavioral circles. We prefer to frame this behavior according to Michael Cunningham and Margaret Spencer's term of "reactive coping," given its broader cultural-ecological applications (Spencer, Cunningham, & Swanson, 1995).

Example 2: "PLAAY Fighting," Authority Testing, and Trust Building during MAAR

The boys continue to be led through the octagon by sensei. Later in that session, in a low-toned but direct manner, one of the boys invites sensei to a fight. Sensei attends to this invite before fully realizing the seriousness of the request.

Boy #1: Let's fight. (He has a serious look on his face and momentarily raises his arms and fists in a boxing position.)

Sensei: Who? You and me?

Boy #1: You and me. (He nods his head in affirmation.)

Sensei: (Immediately announces the fight to the class) Excuse me! (The boy smiles.) I have a request for a fight. Everyone in the class sit down. (*Boy #1* immediately goes to sit down and so do most of the other boys, which leaves a clearing in the middle of the room.) Except for you. (*Sensei* is speaking to *Boy #1*, but by this time he is almost in his chair. What is amazing at this point is that, even though each of the boys overheard the whisper-like request to fight from *Boy #1*, they eagerly sit down—perhaps from relief that the octagon drill is over and out of curiosity to watch the impending fight. One of the boys, whom we call *Boy #2*, is farthest away from *sensei* in the back of the room. *Boy #2* knows about the call to fight *sensei* and he remarks on *Boy #1*'s backing down from the fight.)

Boy #2: Yo, yo! Where you going?!

Boy #1: Hey, I ain't fightin' that dude.

Boy #2: C'mon, I'll fight you.

In our view, this is a group, not an individual, phenomenon. While one boy proposes to fight, the rest respond as if this has been on their minds all along. For adolescent boys, identity is developed in the process of doing and experimenting with danger. It is not just about "talking about fighting," it's about fighting that embodies "keepin' it real." A number of them have crossed the barrier that many adolescents or adults never cross (or forgot they crossed) and have tested the waters of indecision about physical engagement. Risk is visceral and makes people feel alive, especially if their existence in the world is questionable. They are more "courageous" in one sense, but their expectations are higher too. So the question on everyone's mind is whether sensei can truly fight or whether "he just talkin' shit."

Another interesting group phenomenon occurs once Boy #2 proposes to fight. After Boy #2 steps up to fight, they all want to fight sensei. Boy #2 is representative of the larger group's wonderment. He is the Marlboro Man, as it were, who steps into the breach of what many boys and men consider "real manhood or cowardice" and takes on the lesson that Boy #1 could not complete. It's time for the student to teach the teacher, and Boy #2 has initiated that lesson. Under the reality of male supremacy, the politics of manhood never consider danger entirely. Dying is often a foregone or irrelevant conclusion, but failing or succeeding to stand up to the fight is the statement of true manhood. So as the group makes room for Boy #2, the other boys follow his decree, saying, "C'mon, I'll fight you."

Boys: I'll fight you! I'll fight! Well, I would—(nervous laughter erupts sensing that something "real" is going to happen). He gonna' knock you the fuck out (more nervous laughter). He gonna body-punch you.

Sensei: Everyone sit down. (As *Boy #2* walks toward *sensei,* smiling, *sensei* immediately asks him—.) How do you want to do this? Full-speed, half-speed? (More nervous laughter from the group and physical demonstrations of martial arts moves. They are pre-empting the experience by imagining and acting it out. But the suspense, the unknown is thrilling, because everyone knows this isn't scripted.)

Boy #2: Full-speed, half-speed?

(Confused and put off by the question, *Boy #2* tries to figure out what comes next.)

Sensei: Yeh.

Boy #2: What you 'bout to do?

Sensei: Yeh, you said fight. How do you want to fight? Full-speed, half-speed?

Boy #2: What? We boxing?

Sensei: I don't box. You said fight. I don't know anything about boxing. Boxing is a sport.

Boy #2: I'll box. You mean half-speed, full-speed all this? (gestures martial arts hand and kick gestures as he asks)

Boys: He said, "Fight!" He said, "Fight! Half-speed, full-speed!"

Boy #2: (Seeing that the confusion of this fight situation is too quickly coming to clarity and realizing that all the "talk about fighting" is about to end, he responds,) "No, I'm cool," (and walks away. He walks to the other side of the room, still standing, however).

This is a seminal moment in sensei's relationship-building with the boys because he has responded to their call-out and has maintained his stature as a feared expert. But the challenge isn't over. As soon as Boy #2 leaves, Boy #3 appears, but with much more humility and appeal for injury-free contact. In fact, Boy #3 makes a special request for "no face hitting." Again, this is a group identity phenomenon that is cultural. It involves movement as the vehicle through which the boys are learning about the sensei and how martial arts relates to their emotional and physical lives. This is considered "PLAAY fighting" because we know that these "fights" are not ones of revenge or retaliation. Unlike these "PLAAY fights," there are no rules in street fighting and there is often a lot less discussion. Throughout these "PLAAY fights," the boys seek and establish rules so as to obtain their purpose without injury. Their purpose is simple. They want to find out: Is sensei the authority in this room or are we?

Boy #3: You want half-speed, full-speed? Okay, no face-hittin' (He touches his face. The group erupts in laughter).

Sensei: Now you got rules!

Boy #2: I ain't got no rules!

Boy #2 returns to the center of the room with outstretched arms, loudly revving himself up in both voice and physical boxing movements and gestures. He was using the time away to get himself prepared for the battle that he walked away from earlier. This is a strategy for preparing to take on difficult and scary tasks that one has to admire. The student understands that this is not easy, but he does not give up entirely either. He attempts to manage his fear by watching from a distance for a short time until he is ready to mount the effort.

Boy #2: I just don't want to mess around and then you'll kick me. (A reasonable explanation for not fighting the first time. There's more nervous group laughter which gets louder.)

Sensei: I *am* gonna kick you. I'm gonna' tell you seriously—(looking *Boy #2* directly in the eye.)

Boy #2: See, that's what I wanna know. Now if we gonna box, I'll *box* you! (He emphasizes the word "box" and talks more loudly now. His fists are in a boxing stance.) Whether I get knocked out or no!

Sensei immediately gets in a boxing stance and pursues Boy #2 who retreats as quickly as sensei pursues until he realizes that his backward-stepping is not fast enough to get away from sensei's advances. He then turns and runs to the door while the rest of the group and staff laugh loudly. Boy #2 concedes the point and the lesson and the challenge—game, set, and match—are essentially over.

Boy #3: (Still wanting to engage in some form of fighting asks very nicely) You wanna box or do anything? Anything?

Sensei: (Having the upper hand, *sensei* can now dismiss all challenges easily). I'm gonna give you a few hours. You only been in the class for an hour. If I knock you out in the first hour, then it would be bad. Have a seat.

Boy #3: Oh, scared of this, boy. (*Boy #3* seems glad and says this with soft acceptance and invisible gratitude and then he promptly sits down.)

In the octagon, the boys are finding that it is very hard to be frustrated and cool at the same time. While frustration can serve as a moderator to task performance, casting doubt in one's mind about one's ability, this frustration is internal and not likely to raise the same fears as external frustrations. Each boy is wrestling with himself, not others. Additionally, all of the boys are in similar situations of ignorance about self-defense. Ignorance loves company as much as does misery. Finally, the frustration is not so enormous that they will feel overwhelmed, just annoyed. We believe that the immediate and visceral learning of frustration and subsequent frustration tolerance (the ability to rise above the frustration felt) may eventually serve as a buffer to overcoming movement and social interaction challenges. At any rate, this example suggests that playing with the activity of fighting allows youths with histories of "having to fight" to take a break from the tension of it all and be boys who can't win all the time—and don't have to.

SUMMARY

The MAAR, or martial arts anger reduction, component of PLAAY provides one example of how movement is creatively constructed to challenge and influence developmental, cultural-ecological, and emotional issues of the African American male adolescent. The role of movement is to enhance the culturally relevant nature of the PLAAY intervention, but its primarily purpose is to deepen the level of knowledge we can gain about each boy. Self-knowledge is a key aspect of the PLAAY project for the leadership and for the male participants and as we integrate other components that emphasize racial and cultural socialization strategies, we expect that these strategies will enhance boys' self-knowledge in divine, affective-symbolic, and phenomenological ways. Movement, which is just one of many vehicles that can be used, opens the door for a variety of strategies previously minimized as inconsequential in the daily lives of Black youth. Here, we've understood movement but primarily as an intrapersonal reality. In the next chapter, we will explore the psychological implications of movement in an interpersonal reality—basketball.

REFERENCES

Allen, B. & Boykin, A. W. (1991). The influence of contextual factors on Afro-American and Euro-American children's performance: Effects of movement opportunity and music. *International Journal of Psychology, 26(3),* 373–387.

Bartlett, F. (1951). *The mind at work and play.* London: George Allen and Unwin Ltd.

Bell, C. C. (1997). Promotion of mental health through coaching competitive sports. *Journal of the National Medical Association, 89(8),* 517–520.

Bell, C. C. & Suggs, H. (1998). Using sports to strengthen resilience in children: Training heart. *Sport Psychiatry, 7(4),* 859–865.

Boone, R. T. & Cunningham, J. G. (2001). Children's expression of emotional meaning in music through expressive body movement. *Journal of Nonverbal Behavior, 25,* 21–41.

Boykin, A. W. (1977). Verbally expressed preference and problem-solving proficiency. *Journal of Experimental Psychology: Human Perception and Performance,* 3(1), 165–174.

Boykin, A. W. (1978). Psychological/behavioral verse in academnic/task performance: Pre-theoretical considerations. *Journal of Negro Eeducation, 47,* pp 343–354.

Boykin, A. W. (1991). Black psychology and experimental psychology: A functional confluence. In R. Jones (Ed.), *Black Psychology.* Hampton, VA: Cobb & Henry.

Boykin, A. W. & Allen, B. A. (1988). Rhythmic-movement facilitation of learning in working-class Afro-American children. *Journal of Genetic Psychology, 149(3),* 335–347.

Boykin, A. W., Allen, B., Davis, L. H., & Senior, A. M. (1997). Task performance of Black and White children across levels of presentation variability. *Journal of Psychology, 131(4),* 427–437.

Delva-Tauiliili, J. (1995). Does brief Aikido training reduce aggression of youth? *Perceptual & Motor Skills, 80(1),* 297–298.

Dill, E. M. & Boykin, A. W. (2000). The comparative influence of individual, peer tutoring, and communal learning contexts on the text recall of African American children. *Journal of Black Psychology, 26(1),* 65–78.

Dosmantes-Alperson, E. & Merrill, N. (1980). Growth effects of experiential movement psychotherapy. *Psychotherapy: Theory, Research, & Practice, 17,* 63–68.

Ferrari, M. (1999). Influence of expertise on the intentional transfer of motor skill. *Journal of Motor Behavior, 31(1),* 79–85.

Frable, D. E. (1987). Sex-typed execution and perception of expressive movement. *Journal of Personality and Social Psychology, 53,* 391–396.

Gallaher, P. E. (1992). Individual differences in nonverbal behavior: Dimensions of style. *Journal of Personality and Social Psychology, 63,* 133–145.

Gardner, H. (1993). *Multiple intelligences: The theory in practice.* New York: Basic Books, Inc.

Gardner, H., Kornhaber, M. L., & Wake, W. K. (1996). *Intelligence: Multiple perspectives.* Orlando, FL: Harcourt Brace College Publishers.

Katz, M. M., Wetzler, S., Cloitre, M., Swann, A., Secunda, S., Mendels, J., & Robins, E. (1993). Expressive characteristics of anxiety in depressed men and women. *Journal of Affective Disorders, 28,* 267–277.

Lazarus, R. S. (1991). *Emotion and adaptation.* New York: Oxford University Press.

Neal, L. I., McCray, A. D., Webb-Johnson, G., & Bridgest, S. T. (2003). The effects of African American movement styles on teachers' perceptions and reactions. *Journal of Special Education, 37,* 49–57.

Riggio, R. E., Lippa, R., & Salinas, C. (1990). The display of personality in expressive movement. *Journal of Research in Personality, 24(1),* 16–31.

Spencer, M. B., Cunningham, M., & Swanson, D. P. (1995). Identity as coping: Adolescent African-American males' adaptive responses to high-risk environment. In H. W. Harris, H. C. Blue, & E. E. H. Griffith (Eds.), *Racial and ethnic identity: Psychological development and creative expression.* New York: Routledge.

Theeboom, M., De Knop, P., & Weiss, M. R. (1995). Motivational climate, psychological responses, and motor skill development in children's sport: A field-based intervention study. *Journal of Sport & Exercise Psychology, 17(3),* 294–311.

Twemlow, S. W. & Sacco, F. C. (1998). The application of traditional martial arts practice and theory to the treatment of violent adolescents. *Adolescence, 33(131),* 505–518.

Williams, A. M. & Elliott, D. (1999). Anxiety, expertise, and visual search strategy in karate. *Journal of Sport & Exercise Psychology, 21(4),* 362–375.

Zillman, D. & Bryant, J. (1974). Retaliatory equity as a factor in humor appreciation. *Journal of Experimental Social Psychology, 10(5)* 480–488.

CHAPTER 5

Emotions in Motion: Teaching Emotional Empowerment through Basketball

Howard C. Stevenson Jr., Gwendolyn Y. Davis, Chad Lassiter, and Juana Gatson

Writing autobiography, looking back, trying to recall and represent yourself at some point in the past, you are playing many games simultaneously. There are many selves, many sets of rules jostling for position. None offers the clarifying, cleansing unity of playing hoop.
—John Wideman (2001), *Hoop Roots: Basketball, Race, and Love*

There is a life to doing; neither prolific descriptive writing, storytelling, nor praise are substitutes for it. To get the most out of life, to be able to freely dream or imagine, one must engage in the stream of life and resist spectating. This theme underlies the use of basketball as a vehicle for understanding the personality strengths and challenges of African American boys. Basketball has become more than an athletic activity in one sense, primarily because of the overwhelming American commercialism that surrounds it and transports it around the world. Ironically, the promotion of basketball is still spectating, but it usually centers on the theme of "basketball is fantastic," or translated—"Basketball is life." In another sense, basketball playing is a space in which people can be transported in so many ways, borrowing from fantasy, imagination, superstar idol images and yes, even their own talent. This is one of the thrusts of John Wideman's book, *Hoop Roots: Basketball, Race, and Love*. That is, there is nothing like playing the game. Talking basketball is just not the same as playing, mostly because a person's manhood is on trial every moment the game is on. But then again, manhood on trial is the game in every moment.

As has been mentioned in previous chapters, adolescence is concerned especially with demonstrating one's identity through action or "doing." Since doing is believing, what better place to understand the adolescent's way of doing than on a playground court. Emotions across the spectrum, even those of the most controlled male teens, are likely to reveal themselves when boys are engaged in a "friendly" game of hoops. We find this phenomenon to be true for boys with a history of aggression as well as adults and women or girls with no history of aggression, with youths in middle school and adults with multiple degrees and lots of education. While we wanted to study and use this arena to understand how conflicts and emotions for African American boys are "played out" for the purpose of helping them manage their emotions more efficiently, we do not believe that adults or the best athletes have better coping skills in anger management during basketball play.

TEAM stands for teaching emotional empowerment through athletic movement and is a program that primarily involves a set of culturally relevant in vivo intervention strategies for youth as they are actively engaged in basketball. Our goal is to teach boys about themselves using basketball play as the vehicle. Although we will teach basketball skills through challenging exercises and drills, supervised competition, and game-like situations, we are interested primarily in teaching them about life. We expect to learn how the boys manage conflicts (poorly or well) by observing how they negotiate their identities (cultural, group, and individual) during play and how they negotiate the movement demands of play. We believe that all youth (young and older) reveal psychological style, personality, and resources through their play and cannot hide these elements (Smith, Smoll, & Christensen, 1996).

But basketball play is like no other in American society. During the past two decades, basketball has surpassed major league baseball and professional football as the most publicly watched sport. In fact, internationally, it runs a close second to soccer. For urban African American males, it is even more mind consuming. Basketball has become popular in America and around the world primarily because the cultural style and movement creativity of African American athletes. The cultural style demands and opportunities in basketball are limitless. Because basketball represents a get-rich-quick avenue for urban Black males and it has become so popular and glamorized, it is a perfect arena for males to test out rugged individualistic masculine-challenging conflicts with other males.

This chapter describes the procedures we use to assess the experiences and expressions of anger exhibited by African American boys with a history of violence as they play basketball. The interventions we use are described as well.

WHY USE ATHLETICS TO HELP YOUTHS MANAGE THEIR EMOTIONS?

Research on Black young men has identified the protective importance of "cool pose" coping strategies (Goffman, 1959; Langley, 1994; Majors & Billson, 1992; Majors, Tyler, Peden, & Hall, 1994). Cool pose strategies include behaviors that prevent negative perceptions from devaluing the self-esteem of the individual. But they also apply to females. Community research demonstrates that violence and relationships for girls still follow values and rules resident in "survival of the fittest" male-dominated contexts. Cool pose dynamics can become destructive if they keep Black youths from expressing true feelings of anger and resolving them. The cool pose views are often integrated in athletics in which cultural and gender identity are expressed in style, creativity, and movement.

There is some research that solidifies the link between athletic participation and the academic aspirations and achievement of youth (Braddock, 1981, 1982; Dawkins, 1982; Dawkins & Braddock, 1982; Harris & Hunt, 1983; Otto, 1975; Picou, 1978; Riemeke, 1988). Athletic aggression is a relevant arena for observing the emotional difficulties of youth and taking steps to intervene (Braddock, Royster, Winfield, & Hawkins, 1991; Bredemeier & Shields, 1986; Elias & Soth, 1988; Harrell, 1980; Martin, 1976; Russell, 1983; Ryan, Williams, & Wimer, 1990; Segrave & Hastad, 1984; Thirer & Rampey, 1979; Varca, 1980; Wall & Gruber, 1986; Wandzilak, Carroll, & Ansorge, 1988). Athletic participation has been shown to decrease posttraumatic stress—related symptoms (McGrath, Keita, Strickland, & Russo, 1990; Smith, Smoll, & Barnett, 1995). It has also been linked to decreases in depression (North, McCullagh, & Tran, 1990), especially in female adolescents (Greenberg & Oglesby, 1997). Studies on exercise also indicate that sports participation is linked to significant decreases in smoking behavior among adolescents (Facts on Sport and Smoke-free Youth, 2001) and higher grade point averages (Griffin, 1998). In addition, athletic training in deep breathing and relaxation techniques has been shown to increase an individual's sense of personal control and empowerment (McCann & Pearlman, 1990).

On the playground or court, a variety of interpersonal angry and aggressive outbursts occur. This research has found that crowd behavior, hostile attribution bias, bolstered egocentricity, heightened interpersonal physical contact, and losing are factors that contribute to increased reactive and instrumental extrapunitive aggression. Bredemeir and Shields (1986) found that athletes often develop a "bracketed morality" and may become egocentric as a way to cope with the competition of the game. This suggests that egocentricity is more pronounced during athletics which can contribute to in-game aggression. Elias and Soth (1988) found that basketball helped aggressive youths feel less threatened when they received critical feedback, more cohesiveness as a group, and more comfortable in developing friendships with team members. While basketball focuses on interpersonal self-control skills, martial arts has the potential for reducing anxiety and aggression but with a focus on internal self-control skills (Bell, 1997; Bell & Suggs, 1998). All of this research points to athletics as a worthwhile arena for improving the pro-social behaviors of Black youth if intervention can be conducted live, "in the moment."

MORE EXPLANATION OF THE IMPORTANCE OF MOVEMENT

The African psychological perspective of Boykin and Toms (1985) is relevant here, particularly the characteristics of movement. Boykin and Toms (1985) outlined nine characteristics of African American culture and expression: verve, expressive individualism, rhythm, orality, social time perspective, spirituality, harmony, affect, and finally, movement. Movement is an area of psychological wealth that often goes untapped (see chapter 4 for a more in-depth review). Our goal is to use movement as one of the mechanisms by which students can manage their emotions while receiving mentored feedback from coaches, elders, and the PLAAY staff. Coaches have to be able to watch the boys during physical play and observe their movement, which reveals how the boys manage and appropriately express their affect.

The game of basketball is so important in popular culture that it has moved beyond sports to glamorized identity expression. Machoism and coolness are integrated in the movements of this sport, making basketball ripe for African American cultural expression in its multiple forms. We have witnessed on many occasions how the flashiness of certain basketball moves takes precedence over one of the most basic elements of the game—scoring. For many youth, embarrassing or dominating their opponents can be just as exciting as scoring the winning basket as the whistle signals the ending of the game. Crossover dribbles, made most famous by a Philadelphia basketball idol, Allen Iverson, can bring out the loudest praise as well as "ooohs" and "aaahs" from opponents and teammates alike.

Expressive individualism is so pronounced in the way boys and girls make their "moves" on the court that it is often hard to separate team and individual talents in the context of play. We do not want to separate the two, and we will be trying to help these boys, who are at differing levels of basketball skill, "get their games off." That is, the coaches and elders will help the boys to be as uniquely glamorous as possible by helping them maximize their basketball skill, and work on their weaknesses while helping them to avoid public humiliation as much as possible. As such, basketball play is a wonderful laboratory to study movement and assess with multiple emotions, including anger and aggression, and to intervene. Identifying the unique strengths and weaknesses of each boy in the basketball and social problem-solving arenas becomes key. It is our endeavor to help the boys generalize their abilities and new knowledge to other forms of social interaction, and relationship, in other contexts (school, neighborhood, and home).

RELATIONSHIP IS ALL WE HAVE

Once during a PLAAY session, the boys were still testing us and had colluded to steal the basketball. Near the end of this session, one of the undergraduate PLAAY staff members was operating the video camera when he witnessed a boy take the ball, hide it behind him, and walk slyly out of the back door of the gym. The staff member mentioned this to me (Stevenson) several minutes later and was dazed by the event yet hesitant about saying anything, fearing that it would bring some sort of conflict between the PLAAY team and the students. While some of the students were still milling around, I called out to the young man who we thought might have taken the ball or who might at least know something about the theft. He was shooting on the other side of the gym.

Jamal, what happened to our ball! Somebody took our ball!

He explained he knew nothing about it and continued to shoot shots intermittently. I pursued him even further.

Jamal, this is a problem. We need that ball. I can't trust you guys if you take my stuff. I need that ball, Jamal.

Jamal continued to claim ignorance and would not look at me. Now, it is essential to understand that adults cannot make youth do anything except by force, but that rarely brings about the kind of relationship we were trying to build. The issues of credibility, trust, and intimacy require there to be some common agreement on respecting each other. So I told Jamal that I believed he knew what happened and that it would be very hard for us to work with him or the other boys if we didn't get that ball back.

If I don't get that ball back, Jamal, I'm going to be very disappointed in you and whoever took it. I don't need to know who took it. I don't care about getting folks in trouble, but I do care about trusting folks I work with. I just want that ball back.

The pressure and tension were getting to him as he continued to ignore, deny, and fail to look at me directly. Slowly, he meandered out the door and I gave one last parting shot, "Jamal, I mean this! C'mon brother, you know what I'm talking about man. It's not just about the ball. It's about us, man!"

As he left, I felt quite helpless. But within five minutes, the ball came rolling in the back door. No questions asked. No one to blame. I still yelled, "Thanks Jamal!"

Most useful interventions are instances in which we apply the right response in the smallest of meaningful moments. Relationship, therefore, is a series of small but meaningful loosely interwoven moments in which we call the "other" to some level of commitment and loyalty. If the moment is "Will you know that I am testing your loyalty?" and we reply, "It doesn't matter because there's something wrong with you for testing me" then we are missing the moments and the meaning of relationship with these young boys. It could be a look, an attitude, or a gesture, but if it is a call to us, we have to respond in kind. Thus, call-and-response interactions are very useful psychological intervention moments—or at least they have the potential to be.

Relationship is still the most powerful influence we have on these young men. And if we have spent the time and shared the pains, that is money in the bank. There is some semblance of relationship that can be applied to hold students accountable. Protection and affection are not as meaningful without correction but discipline and confrontation do not have to imply loss of relationship. On the contrary, they should imply taking the relationship to another level.

TEAM—TEACHING EMPOWERMENT THROUGH ATHLETIC MOVEMENT INTERVENTIONS

There are three major types of interventions in the athletic portions of PLAAY. The first is called affection, and the goal is to connect to and within the emotional life of the students. The second is called correction; the focus here is on the multiple ways of intervening or confronting, and if necessary, reframing anger and aggression when they are revealed. The last is called protection; *the goal here is to teach* or coach by providing emotional choices through the play or emotional interactions students experience while in PLAAY.

Applying affection or connecting to the emotional life of the students is no easy task. There are many pitfalls but there are several steps to follow. One very significant step is physically affirming the existence of Black youths as they engage us on a daily basis. One rule we have tried to apply, not always successfully, is to greet the boys as they enter the room when we first see them in the mornings or in the beginning of any PLAAY session. Most of the time, this is a handshake, but sometimes, it involves hugs. For boys that appreciate that, we have found it sets the stage for managing tensions that might arise later. It's like putting money in the bank for a tense moment in the future. We can draw on this credit later when we emotionally challenge the students or when we intervene with them as they go through emotional challenges during the athletic movement conditions. During CPR sessions, the boys have told us how other people stand distant from them physically and emotionally. So they expect a generalized rejection response from the world.

As another step toward the goal of connection, it is essential for PLAAY staff members to be *active* both physically and verbally during the TEAM events. The more "present" the staff can be, the more likely the boys will see them as useful when they are intervening during frustrating moments. Connection involves an ability to observe and assess the personal strengths and weaknesses of each boy. This becomes data that can be used to build intimacy in the relationships with the boys. Still, inactivity, passivity, or invisibility on the part of the staff is not likely to be helpful.

In addition, individuals willing to work with young African American males in clinical contexts such as TEAM must be willing to receive feedback about their emotional challenges and to handle the same manhood frustrations. They must be able to be clear about their intentions for working with the boys because not only will the boys ask about those intentions in direct and not-so-direct ways, but they will also pick them up nonverbally. The potential for becoming an irritant to the boys and igniting frustration is there and that is why it is imperative that staff members be trained in both self-knowledge and creative psychological intervention skills. When it comes to power struggles with the students, staff members who do not know themselves, their frustrations, and their weaknesses are likely to just add emotional fuel to the fire when the boys are trying to work out their frustrations.

In the early sessions, when the staff challenged the boys to a game, beating the boys during the game was essential for establishing some credibility, not only in the game of basketball but in the manhood respect game. It is harder for students to respect a coach who is telling them about anger management during a game when the coach cannot play very well or has no track record. Conversely, it is important to teach the boys how to manage losing by letting them see that staff members can emotionally accept it when the boys are able to beat them—in basketball and verbal bantering or trash-talking. We have had moments in which staff have struggled with losing to the boys in basketball and has taken it personally, suggesting that the losing will undermine credibility or hierarchical respect. Ultimately, the principles of the project demand that we appreciate the need to gain respect by winning and losing gracefully in some of these rare staff-student basketball contests with the overarching goal to embrace the boys' emotional selves in both situations. To insist on total game dominance against the boys only perpetuates the same insecure masculinity dynamics that many boys learn in the streets and will only undermine relationship in the long run. And we are in this for as long as we can.

The second type of TEAM intervention, correction, involves confronting aggression where we see it. It is important to confront aggression without pathologizing the character of boys in natural social settings. This is possible by appreciating how aggression may be functional for some students as they negotiate the manhood demands of the streets (Anderson, 1990). These demands are just as visible in the school hallways, classrooms, and gyms. Appreciating that there is a "story" behind the aggression that youth experience can reduce the potential that counselors or confronters will fall into a "patrol and control" orientation and mentality.

Confronting aggression is accomplished by watching how boys are likely to explode and knowing the conditions under which hypervulnerability is possible. Trash-talking situations can be potential hypervulnerability-triggering moments. They can also be relationship-building moments. Again, "both-and" thinking is important when a particular behavior (i.e., trash-talking) can be bonding and when it is disruptive. Still, knowing that failure in the game can also trigger feelings of hypervulnerability helps.

Confronting aggression involves recognizing the social dynamics of tension before, during, and after physical conflicts occur. Sometimes, confronting aggression involves distracting two individuals as they begin to trash-talk in negative ways. Other times, it involves physically mediating the conflict by stepping in between two students who are squaring off with each other. When two students are intruding into each other's personal space, it is a signal that conflict could erupt. The game has many opportunities to distract or physically mediate conflict without being too obvious about it. Referees and coaches or any PLAAY staff member can call time-outs at any time to stop play or potential conflicts. Whispering is a strategy in which a PLAAY staff member might see a potential conflict and go directly to one of the participants and quietly but firmly give a message countering the disrespect or hypervulnerability the student is experiencing. "You don't have to believe that you are a punk like he said. Next time you go down the court, you can do all of your talking by taking that short jumper at the foul line."

Protection or coaching, the third type of intervention in TEAM, is about teaching the game of basketball solely for the purpose of developing the human spirit and encouraging character. PLAAY includes these elements, but the focus is more on helping students manage their emotional selves and to generalize these new skills to environments outside of basketball such as the classroom, the school hallways and cafeterias, and home and neighborhood contexts (Smith & Smoll, 1990). Learning to manage one's emotional self is not about "control" as much as it is about "understanding the self." As stated previously, in African American psychology, self-knowledge is the highest form of knowledge, and good coaching must be about encouraging, stimulating, and embracing the self-knowledge journey of Black boys.

A person's emotional style as a human being is one of those aspects of the self that requires understanding. In many ways knowing oneself is about developing character. So for us, playing basketball well is not necessary; it doesn't matter when we mix students of varying talents together. We expect students to be frustrated by the game, by the talent levels of teammates, and by their own challenging history of managing conflict. Given that we are not engaged in basketball competition in the traditional sense, the goal of basketball skills development is not primary. Skill development is useful, but not the most important aspect. The purpose of the coaching is to help students engage the social environment more ably.

Specific training for the coaches involves information on how to lead a group of students to play the game of basketball as a cohesive unit. Emphasis is placed on identifying potential conflict before it is expressed as well as reframing distorted and wrongful beliefs about the hostile intentions of others. Our coaches have to demonstrate competency in commanding and maintaining the attention of the teenage players, learning each player's strength and limitations, learning each player's catalyst for aggressive behavior, and coaching the players in ways that accomplish the goals of a particular game strategy while simultaneously confronting the precursor conditions in each player that are likely to stimulate aggressive behavior.

One common example of the way learning basketball skills can change social interactions is the situation in which some boys attempt to do more in the game than their basketball talent will sustain. Many of the boys will attempt maneuvers that are rarely successful. The way play of any sort can bring out this level of unabashed experimenting has to be appreciated. Still, the consequences of failure can be very devastating emotionally if the failure brings on social derision from teammates and opposing players.

Trash-talking is a skill on the basketball court; it not only can toughen the skin of sensitive boys but it can also show others, without fighting, that they can stand up for themselves. Unfortunately, when boys try basketball moves like a crossover, and the ball is stolen from them 95 percent of the time they attempt it, they may receive extreme criticism in the form of trash-talking or very direct hostility. These moments are hard to live down and can lead to aggressive conflicts. What is more frightening is that this hostility and trash-talking can move beyond the court to hallways, cafeterias and other public venues where the boys are trying to maintain dignity and manhood competence. Coaching students to protect the ball when they are dribbling or conducting a crossover dribble can save them from present and future social embarrassment. Coaching boys to take high-percentage shots and make high-percentage moves will not only increase their successes in the game of basketball but it will decrease the

Table 5.1
Competency Training for Coaches and Elders in TEAM Intervention

	Skill to Be Observed	1	2	3	4	5	6	7
Affection	Builds team cohesion and support among players							
	Responds appropriately to emotional experiences of student							
	Shows respect and respectfully handles disrespect from students							
	Supports and encourages the play of the students							
	Connects child's problem behaviors on court to emotional life							
Correction	Anticipates potential hypervulnerability conflict on court early							
	Tries to resolve conflicts during play							
Intervening	Redirects/distracts player from trigger or aggressive situations							
	Uses time-outs & substitutions to manage emotional outbursts							
	Physically mediates conflicts between students, if necessary							
Protection	Changes strategies based on player's strengths and limitations							
Teaching	Maintains and encourages attention, motivation and success							
Coaching	Teaches basketball skills (dribble, pass, shoot, block, defense)							
	Connects child's problem behaviors on court to emotional life							

amount of generalizable social critique that can pollute the emotional atmosphere of schooling.

Several strategies are used by the coaches or PLAAY staff. They include distraction, use of voice to curb aggressive intentions; encouragement of positive interactions, role playing of basketball moves that result in success on the court and represent alternatives to aggression that comes from experiencing frustrated play (e.g., blocked shot); whispering; reframing masculinity without aggression but inclusive of control, style, and competence; discouragement of peer disrespect; and encouragement to decrease aggressive behaviors. Table 5.1 describes the affection, correction, and protection skills that staff members are trained to provide. This training will be put to use on the court as well as during nonplaying experiences. Students are encouraged to settle disputes (e.g., anger at a team member for refusing to pass the ball) through verbal, not physical means. PLAAY staff members are encouraged to observe instances in which peers give positive or negative feedback (e.g., support or challenging comments), accept negative feedback, resist peer pressure, self-problem solve, negotiate conflicts, and follow instructions—and to then praise those efforts.

HOW AGGRESSION ERUPTS IN THE GAME

Since ego, identity, and gender dominance are often on trial for the boys when they are doing anything from walking in the hallways to playing basketball, we are interested in understanding how different boys are triggered to respond aggressively when challenged. Often, the challenge comes as a function of a boy's inability to demonstrate his talents and the competitive anxiety juices begin to flow (Smoll & Smith, 1996). These talents reflect his ability to be dominant during many moments in the game. For many boys, basketball is a relief from the pressures of the day, or at least the boys look forward to the relief. Unfortunately, since verbal and physical challenges to one's manhood can raise their ugly heads during the game, the respite is short-lived. We have captured many aggressive incidents on the court and have observed that they often begin with the failure of another teammate to engage the game at a high level of enthusiasm.

One example involves the student Charles, who was excited about the prospect of playing. The setting of the game was structured by the PLAAY staff. There was a referee, a timekeeper and scorekeeper, many PLAAY staff members and spectators to watch the game, many young women staff members who might be impressed, and worthy opponents to battle. You could see that Charles was ready for the game by his energy. Throughout the course of the game, you could hear the small but effervescent crowd of PLAAY staff members cheer out his nickname (name of a famous NBA player) over and over again. In the first half, Charles's play was fantastic. At one point, however, he made a nice pass under the basket to a teammate, Avery. Avery missed the layup, but got the rebound and passed to another teammate who made the shot and two points. Charles was upset, but he didn't show it too much. The same scenario occurred a few minutes later. Avery flubbed another of Charles's passes. The first half ended with Avery trying desperately to get the ball off for a last second shot, but couldn't really get a handle on the ball. As the team walked off the court, Charles's frustration was evident in his attitude as he began to mumble to himself.

During halftime, Charles and Avery were cooling off by walking back and forth. Charles continued to mumble but Avery had no idea why he was mumbling and proceeded to explain his first-half difficulties. One PLAAY staff member noticed that Charles was upset and encouraged him to explain his frustration. As the staff member was trying to connect with Charles, Charles and Avery continued to mill back and forth along the sideline until Charles's mumbling became louder, "You don't know what to do." And Avery started to catch on that the mumbling involved criticisms of his play. "You don't know what to do!" Attempts to distract Charles were not working, and when they walked past each other for a third time, you could feel the tension and hostility start to mount. "He don't know what to do." Charles screams louder, "You can't make a layup!" Avery responds "I'm not even talking to you!" as if Charles thought that Avery's explanations were directed at him. Avery and Charles are in the same physical space at this time. The staff member begins to feel the tension, see the physical proximity, and hear the loudness of the voices and moves toward the two boys. As Avery's voice gets louder he is also directing the shouting at Charles while standing toe-to-toe. Avery yells something to Charles, then says, "I'm not scared of you." Charles, the bigger of the two, then pushes Avery away from him while the staff member is getting between them. The staff member is able to touch Avery as he is being pushed back by Charles and continue to gently hold Avery and push him backward away from the encounter and away from Charles.

Charles starts toward Avery and the staff member slowly but rethinks and turns away, all the while saying, "You better stop coming up on me like that!" The staff member continues to talk to Avery face-to-face while simultaneously gently pushing him backward, saying "Let it go. Think about it. What do you want to do? It's no big deal. Just work it out on the court. Think about it" over and over again until Charles and Avery were at least 20 feet from each other. Other staff members joined in at this time to gently touch and come face-to-face with Charles. Now while the gentle push-backs are occurring, Avery and Charles are exchanging barbs and at one point, Charles decided to rush after Avery while he is across the gym, but PLAAY staff members intervene and reconnect physically with Charles by holding his hand and continuing the talk-downs.

This and other incidents are videotaped for the purpose of analyzing the triggers of aggression in boys with a history of aggression and of gaining an understanding about what natural strategies by staff members tend to work in these situations. The key elements of the intervention here are the gentle touching, the calm talk-downs, the use of built-up credibility and trust, the whispering before and after conflicts, the use of time-outs and stoppage of play to bring attention to the resulting or ensuing tension, and the use of multiple staff members with different personalities and intervention styles actively applying those styles throughout the session.

PROCEDURES AND PROCESS

The game is structured and involves two, three, or four quarters of six or eight minute limits. Whenever possible, a clock and scoring process is maintained and made public throughout the game because we are trying to re-create game-like conditions. This helps to put boys in a situation that intensifies the moments, team-building, and dependence on others to complete the task of winning. This concentration of game-like conditions also respects the boys' need to play basketball and have it attended to fully by the adults in their lives. One of the most overlooked aspects of organized sports is the way youth rely on the structure to receive praise from caring adults who take their participation seriously. The structure helps to ensure the attention. We think this is a very different emotional experience from free play in gym classes or situations in which students are allowed to do whatever they want with little adult supervision. The adult supervision and attention brings a degree of seriousness and respect to the play.

Initially, we meet at center court to remind the boys that the purpose of the game is to manage anger. We give them instructions on the rules of the game, who will be the referee of the day, how timeouts will be handled, and the consequences of not managing their anger. This takes about 5 minutes at most and is followed by stretching exercises or basketball drills such as lay-ups. The drills can take from 10 to 15 minutes. The goal here is to divide the boys into two equally matched groups who can then begin to build a sense of "teamness."

Following the game, we meet again at center court to identify moments in which anger management was not helpful, admit any mistakes on the part of the PLAAY staff, praise boys for their efforts (using specific examples in which students handled themselves admirably through restraint or working through some tension), and connect in any way possible before they leave the gym. TEAM always follows the CPR group, so on occasion we will give strong statements of praise to the students for their openness during the CPR group as well as their taking risks to share their life stories with us. We will end the TEAM session with hands held together in a final team yell.

In summary, we want to intervene during the moments of tension for boys as they engage in a sport that raises their level of imagination and motivation to points at which personality strengths and challenges are revealed (Smith & Smoll, 2002). These moments are pure in our minds in that they are unlike other therapeutic contexts in which the retelling of a person's social conflicts is days and sometimes weeks old. We are grateful whenever the boys tell us their stories, whether in movement or in words. And even if they are not aware of this storytelling, the preciousness of their identities deserve appreciation and should not be trampled on or worse—ignored. Basketball is more than a game; it's a place in which people's emotions are in constant motion. It's up to us to listen to those expressions without hesitation and to shun any noise of self-interest to distract us from the listening. The love of playing basketball for many youth is about the love of imagination and possibility and to be unable to play (skillfully or not) is perhaps to die, or worse to cease to exist. More than not, it is possible to witness these boys imagining themselves as Allen

Iverson or Michael Jordan, if just for a moment, only to realize that the biggest failure here is not that they won't reach the NBA. The biggest tragedy is to fail to imagine at all.

REFERENCES

Anderson, E. (1990). *Streetwise*. Chicago: University of Chicago Press.

Bell, C. C. (1997). Promotion of mental health through coaching competitive sports. *Journal of the National Medical Association, 89(8)*, 517–520.

Bell, C. C. & Suggs, H. (1998). Using sports to strengthen resilience in children: Training heart. *Sport Psychiatry, 7(4)*, 859–865.

Boykin, A. W. & Toms, F. D. (1985). Black child socialization: A conceptual framework. In H. P. McAdoo & J. L. McAdoo, (Eds.), *Black children: Social, Educational, and Parental Environments*. Newbury Park: Sage.

Braddock, J. (1981). Race, athletics, and educational attainment: Dispelling the myths. *Youth and Society, 12*, 335–350.

Braddock, J. (1982). Academics and athletics in American high schools: Some future considerations of the adolescent subculture hypothesis. *Journal of Social and Behavioral Sciences, 29*, 88–94.

Braddock, J. H., Royster, D. A., Winfield, L. F., & Hawkins, R. (1991). Bouncing back: Sports and academic resilience among African American males. *Education and Urban Society, 24*, 113–131.

Bredemeier, B. J. & Shields, D. L. (1986). Game reasoning and interactional morality. *Journal of Genetic Psychology, 147*, 257–275.

Dawkins, M. (1982). Sports and mobility aspirations among Black male college Students. *Journal of Social and Behavioral Sciences, 28*, 77–81.

Dawkins, M. & Braddock, J. (1982). Race, athletics and delinquency. *Journal of Social and Behavioral Sciences, 28*, 82–87.

Elias, P. & Soth, N. B. (1988). The inpatient basketball group as an alternative to group therapy: Helping the "bad boys" feel good about themselves. *Journal of Child Care, 3*, 45–54.

Facts on sports and smoke-free youth. (2001). Available at the World Wide Web on July 23, 2001 at http://www.cdc.gov/tobacco/research_data/youth/ythsprt1.htm. Atlanta, GA: Center for Disease Control (CDC).

Goffman, E. (1959). *The presentation of self in everyday life*. Garden City, NY: Doubleday.

Greenberg, D. & Oglesby, C. A. (1997). Mental health dimensions. In *Physical activity and sport in the lives of girls: Physical and mental health dimensions from an interdisciplinary approach*. Rockville, MD: SAMHSA.

Griffin, R. S. (1998). *Sports in the lives of children and adolescents: Success on the field and in life*. Westport, CT: Praeger.

Harrell, W. A. (1980). Aggression by high school basketball players: An observational study of the effects of opponents' aggression and frustration-inducing factors. *International Journal of Sport Psychology, 11*, 290–298.

Harris, O. & Hunt, L. (1983). Race and sports involvement: Some implications of athletics for Black and White youth. *Journal of Social and Behavioral Sciences, 28*, 95–103.

Langley, M. R. (1994). The cool pose: An Africentric analysis. In R. G. Majors & J. U. Gordon (Eds.), *The American Black Male: His present status and his future.* Chicago: Nelson-Hall Publishers.

Majors, R. & Billson, J. M. (1992). *Cool pose: The dilemmas of Black manhood in America.* New York: Lexington Books.

Majors, R., Tyler, R., Peden, B., & Hall, R. (1994). Cool pose: A symbolic mechanism for masculine role enactment and coping? In R. G. Majors & J. U. Gordon (Eds.), *The American Black male: His present status and his future.* Chicago: Nelson/Hall.

Martin, L. A. (1976). Effects of competition upon the aggressive responses of college basketball players and wrestlers. *Research Quarterly, 47,* 388–393.

McCann, I. L. & Pearlman, L. A. (1990). *Psychological trauma and the adult survivor: Theory, therapy, and transformation.* New York: Brunner/Mazel.

McGrath, E., Keita, G. P., Strickland, B. R., & Russo, N. F. (1990). *Women and depression.* Washington, DC: American Psychological Association.

North, T. C., McCullagh, P., & Tran, Z. V. (1990). Effect of exercise on depression. *Exercise and Sport Sciences Reviews, 18,* 379–415.

Otto, L. B. (1975). Extracurricular activities in the educational attainment proess. *Rural Sociology, 40,* 162–176.

Picou, J. S. (1978). Race, athletic achievement, and educational aspiration. *Sociological Quarterly, 19,* 429–438.

Riemeke, C. (1988). All must play: The only way for middle school athletics. *Middle School Journal, 19,* 8–9.

Russell, G. W. (1983). Crowd size and density in relation to athletic aggression and performance. *Social Behavior and Personality, 11,* 9–15.

Ryan, M. K., Williams, J. M., & Wimer, B. (1990). Athletic aggression: Perceived legitimacy and behavioral intentions in girls' high school basketball. *Journal of Sport and Exercise Psychology, 12,* 48–55.

Segrave, J. & Hastad, D. (1984). Interscholastic athletic participation and delinquent behavior: An empirical assessment of relevant variables. *Sociology of Sport Journal, 1,* 117–137.

Smith, R. E. & Smoll, F. L. (1990). Self-esteem and children's reactions to youth sport coaching behaviors: A field study of self-enhancement processes. *Developmental Psychology, 26,* 987–993.

Smith, R. E., Smoll, F. L., & Barnett, N. P. (1995) Reduction of children's sport performance anxiety through social support and stress-reduction training for coaches. *Journal of Applied Developmental Psychology, 16,* 125–142.

Smith, R. E., Smoll, F. L., & Christensen, D. S. (1996). Behavioral assessment and intervention in youth sports. *Behavior Modification, 20,* 3–44.

Smoll, F. L. & Smith, R. E. (1996). Competitive anxiety: Sources, consequences, and intervention strategies. In F. L. Smoll & R. E. Smith (Eds.), *Children and youth in sport: A biopsychosocial perspective.* Dubuque, IA: McGraw-Hill.

Smith, R. E. & Smoll, F. L. (2002). Youth sports as a behavior setting for psychosocial interventions. In J. L. Van Raalte & B. W. Brewer (Eds.), *Exploring sport and exercise psychology* (2nd ed.). Washington, DC: American Psychological Association.

Thirer, J. & Rampey, M. S. (1979). Effects of abusive spectators' behavior on performance of home and visiting intercollegiate basketball teams. *Perceptual and Motor Skills, 48,* 1047–1053.

Varca, P. E. (1980). An analysis of home and away game performance of male college basketball team. *Journal of Sport Psychology, 2,* 245–257.

Wall, B. R. & Gruber, J. J. (1986). Relevancy of athletic aggression inventory for use in women's intercollegiate basketball: A pilot investigation. *International Journal of Sport Psychology, 17,* 23–33.

Wandzilak, T., Carroll, T., & Ansorge, C. J. (1988). Values development through physical activity: Promoting sportsmanlike behaviors, perceptions and moral reasoning. *Journal of Teaching in Physical Education, 8,* 13–22.

Wideman, J. (2001). *Hoop roots: Basketball, race, and love.* New York: Penguin Books.

Youth99: Results of the Youth Risk Behavior Survey. (2000). Atlanta, GA: Centers for Disease Control.

CHAPTER 6

COPE: Community Outreach through Parent Empowerment

Saburah Abdul-Kabir, Teresa Herrero-Taylor,
Howard C. Stevenson Jr. and Pamela C. Zamel

Despite the attempts of intervention programs to address the individual needs of Black male youth, success in ameliorating the emotional stressors and coping challenges of insecure masculinity will not occur without serious attention paid to family dynamics. Individuals always operate in an interactional context, and although we have focused primarily on the societal, neighborhood, and gender interactions of Black males, the family interactional context is absolutely important. The PLAAY project has not intentionally focused on individuals, and we have always kept in mind the importance of systems theory and social interaction of the family. In the CPR groups, the boys openly testify and confess about family dynamics that are at the top of the list of both unprompted and prompted discussions. This chapter will describe our attempts to include the family in the PLAAY intervention experience. We were not as successful as we had hoped in attaining that goal, but when the experiences occurred, they were amazing.

THE BEGINNINGS OF OUTREACH TO PARENTS

For almost a decade, we have been involved with outreach to families in the West Philadelphia community. While it is well known in the research community that healthy parents produce healthy children, we were very concerned about the ways African American families were perceived by society at-large. Dr. Stevenson enlisted Saburah Abdul-Kabir to help develop a parent focus group with cultural flavor and style; thus, the birth of COPE, Community Outreach through Parent Empowerment. After

Table 6.1
Example of Brief COPE Curriculum and Themes

Principle	Sub-themes	Topics	Target Areas of Change
Stage 1: Empowerment for Self	You got dreams, child. What are they?	Session 1: *My First Name Is Not Mommy!: Taking Care of Self*	Isolation; Parenting Knowledge; Parental Self-Comp; Trust in Unique Strengths; Identifying Your Strengths and Stressors;
	Your inner child needs love, too, remember?	Session 2: *Fighting For My Baby, My Child? Re-membering Childhood Experiences and Building Positive Relationships with Your Child.*	Connecting Parents to the pain of parenting when they were children; Ineffective parenting strategies that leave them helpless; Intergenerational Considerations
Stage 2: Empowerment for the Parent	Your behavior is worth 1000 words	Session 3 - *What Do My Kids See in Me? What Do I See in Them? Culturally Relevant Adolescent Development*	
	You are the first teacher, so talk to the boy!	Session 4- *How Do I Control My Child So That He Controls Himself? Correction, Affection, And Protection for Black Males with Aggression Problems (Bay-Bay's Kids Need Love Too);*	Parental Monitoring
	Racism is real and boys need Cultural Socialization	Session 5- *Teaching Black Boys What It Means To Be Black: Cultural Pride Reinforcement.*	Cultural Socialization; Coping with Antagonism, Alertness to Discrimination, CPR, Cultural Legacy Appreciation, Explaining the Mainstream
Stage 3: Empowerment for Advocacy	Know the system or it will eat Your Young!	Session 6 – *How The System Sees You and Your Child (e.g., Teacher, Judge, or Probation Officer);*	Fear of Teacher & Classroom; Negotiating Skills
	Don't ever stop fighting!	Session 7 – *The Greatest Teacher: Fighting For My Baby, My Child, Part II.*	

much fine-tuning and piloting in Head Start centers, they introduced COPE to Philadelphia neighborhoods through the community-based settlement agencies. With a strong cultural component throughout and attention to a parent's history, COPE structure was designed to move parents toward a healthy place of empowerment. We constructed COPE so that it could be facilitated by a professional and a trained parent who had previously participated in the group process. The cultural components of COPE reach deep into the roots of African American psychology developed in the introduction and chapters 1 and 2 (see Table 6.1).

WHY COPE?

The challenging reality of being Black and male is not lost on the parents of Black boys. Sometimes the fear of losing their male child is so great, it overwhelms the parents' senses and disturbs their sleep; this is true for mothers especially. We have had parents say to us in parenting education groups, "As long as I get him to 18...." For so many, the very real potential of a Black male child not making it to his 18th birthday is a recurring nightmare. The question, "It's 10:00 P.M., do you know where your children are?" raises unique emotions for these parents. In some inner-city neighborhoods, it becomes critical to ask the question, "It's 4:00 P.M. do you know where your children are?" Most understand that Black males journey through dangerous jungles and some unnecessary but seemingly unstoppable pain. They realize that the manhood demands on boys start from the day they are born, with nicknames like "Little Man" to "My Little Man" to "Man of the House," and most parents are frightened of the future.

These parents are also caught in the conundrum of being Black, sometimes being poor, and living under the stressors of painful memories from their own childhoods. Having a teenage male in trouble with the legal, school, and neighborhood systems is just one more burden on their already overloaded backs. The ability of families to protect their children and themselves may be hindered by the crime, violence, limited resources, and racial segregation characteristics of many urban neighborhoods (McLoyd, 1998).

Nevertheless, families play a pivotal role in that they also can serve as buffers between children and environmental factors. The relationship between neighborhood violence and externalizing behavior has been found to be mediated by the quality of parent-child interactions (i.e., parent involvement in school activities) (Richters & Martinez, 1993). We have found that if the parents are struggling themselves with life stressors (ranging from relationship violence to substance abuse to mere isolation), in CPR, the boys will disclose that information as part of their story. If the parents are unable or less able to see the emotional life of their teenage boys (many longing to recoup childhood) because of being overwhelmed with personal life tragedy (which doesn't mean substance abuse and could mean simply new relationships, broken relationships, and family of origin pain), the boys will often tell that story too.

Our goal in COPE is to realize that young people are not the only ones who need a place to share what life is like for them. Many parents of the boys we work with are "missed, dissed, and pissed" too. They have issues that ought to be heard by someone who does not have an agenda, and who has time to listen. So COPE is meant to first bring a CPR-like group therapy/support/church/family experience to parents who are so overwhelmed with life, most of the times, that managing the storms of Black male adolescence has to take a backseat. The curriculum for COPE has been tried and tested in Head Start, In-Home Abuse Prevention, Youth Diversion, Family Reunification, and Young Adult reintegration programs, and in each setting the curriculum frame has been the same. We start with taking care of the parents first as human beings, not parents. They are human beings first. They have existential fears, forgotten aspirations, and broken promises and dreams that affect their parenting, work, and personal lives, and these must be heard. We aim to hear them. If the parents come to COPE, we aim to hear them.

SOCIAL AND STRESSFUL CONTEXT OF COPING

The Langston Hughes poem "Life Ain't No Crystal Stair" typifies the cry of many mothers who struggle with poverty while raising their children. Facing that reality daily is hard to imagine without having had some personal experience with it. The term "underclass" is popularized by many books and political debates, carrying with it both pejorative and realistic images (Katz, 1992). Yet and still, very little literature or governmental oversight has appreciated or integrated the phenomenological awareness of living through struggle, poverty, and the tyranny of the "isms." Often, because that voice is so sadly missing from debates about the conditions of poverty and the people living through it, the very desire to help is demonized and the poor are dehumanized in the process. American culture wants to assume that poor people who are on or who have been on welfare do not want to work. It is assumed that there are jobs available for people on welfare that will cover childcare, housing, and nutrition expenses. It is assumed that these men and women look and act a certain way (Geiger, 1995; Spakes, 1991; West, 1981).

When Black males get in trouble, agents of the social welfare and juvenile justice institutions often become pseudopolice by default—sometimes in opposition to the personal goodwill of conscientious social workers. Social policies and programs become mired in a maze of imagined "all hope is lost" theorizing. In a curious twist of ironic, "hopelost" and interdependent relationships, the helper through the fear of media castration participates in pathologizing and degrading the images of parents of Black males in trouble. We believe that the cause of "stopping crime" has too easily aligned with the negative images of Black males as societal culprits of crime. Fueled by these images, the negative attitudes toward parents of these young men-to-be contribute to parental and family resistance when "helpers" come calling and visiting.

DIGNITY MANAGEMENT AS A COPING STRATEGY

Amidst the struggle between "keeping society safe" and providing justice or human services to youths, one basic human commodity is often overlooked and too often stepped on. That commodity is dignity, and the process to obtain it is self-preservation. Dignity reigns supreme in a world in which everything else is literally out of a person's control. Meaning is defined mostly out of a sense that "I still have my dignity above all else"; and it becomes first on a small list titled "What the world cannot take from me." We believe this applies to parents who find themselves caught in the system as a result of their sons' actions. It is our endeavor to remind social service professionals that the precious resource of dignity and somebody-ness must not be forgotten.

It is our opinion that without a culturally relevant epistemology, all psychotherapeutic or social reform efforts that forget "somebodyness" will end in tragedy or, at the very least will have a decreased emotional effect on the parents. Why? Because the deeper-level meaning behind the cultural values and interactions of Black parents must be integrated in the intervention for them to feel safe using the service (Stevenson, Davis, & Abdul-Kabir, 2001). COPE is an attempt to bring this somebodyness back to the parent education/support/intervention process. We must understand what is strong in families who struggle with children in trouble, and we must acknowledge, honor, ask permission for, borrow, return, and integrate that strength into our psychotherapeutic techniques and social policies. It is our experience that once appreciated and respected for their wisdom, parents under stress will disclose their greatest fears, their horrible experiences, their personal remorse, and the behaviors that lead others to see them as unfit to raise their teenage boys. This mission is not one to deny that serious parenting issues may exist but that in a "both-and" world, parenting challenges and strengths coexist.

COMMUNITY-BASED PARENT EMPOWERMENT EDUCATION

While the literature on culturally relevant parent training programs is limited (Coard, Wallace, Stevenson, & Brotma, in press), we have proposed and applied a community-based parent empowerment model called COPE (Community Outreach through Parent Empowerment Education). The model relies on five core principles designed to develop effective researcher-citizen partnerships among low-income African American parents. The principles include a focus on trust, empowerment, cultural relevance, ecological fit, and gender sensitivity. Previous pilot research indicates that attention to these essential features will provide the context for successful parent education. Project COPE is designed to consider social and cultural adjustment factors that are central to survival and central to the kinds of stress low-income African American parents are likely to face (e.g., trauma related to racism and socioeconomic distress).

Central to the COPE model is the "village concept," that is, the identification and use of resilient community peer mentors who are successfully handling the kinds of issues faced by parents who are isolated and who may be engaged in social system conflicts (e.g., schools, protective services, and justice). It is important that the atmosphere of the group feel like a "village" by the time the parent leaves the first session—because this may be the only session they attend. This model acknowledges the importance of cultural relevance by recognizing the significance of cultural expression among participants (regardless of ethnic background) and the fact that these cultural expressions can be a source of strength in both the teaching style and group participation in a parent education format. The model also encourages parents to practice their new knowledge in play with their sons. It strives toward ecological fit by using resilient community members from neighborhoods similar to those of the target parents, in all phases of the project. Currently, COPE is being applied to home-based case management programs in community settlement agencies. Training is conducted to help create the capacity in the community-based agencies to facilitate COPE groups with the families they consistently work with. Their knowledge of the local neighborhood customs, history, and cultural expressions is essential to the success of the model and meeting the ecological fit assumption. Finally, the model includes gender concerns by actively evaluating methods for recruiting African American men (who are often neglected) and women and involving their unique gender development concerns in the creation and implementation of the parent education outreach activities.

Initially, shame and isolation often inhibit parents from attending a COPE group meeting. Another barrier is the very reason a parent typically really needs COPE to begin with—the emotional and economic burden of supporting a family and dealing with an adolescent with behavioral difficulties, often alone as a single parent. Approximately 70 percent of parents involved with COPE are single parents, and there is only limited involvement in their children's lives on the part of the other parent. Our curriculum tries to take those circumstances into consideration.

COPE CURRICULUM

The COPE curriculum has been developed based on the authors' previous experiences in providing parent education. Differences from traditional parent training include the use of parents as cofacilitators, operationalization of peer resilience strategies, use of culturally expressive presentation styles (e.g., role playing), use of empowerment activities, inclusion of specific cultural issues (e.g., discussion of the trauma and pressure of racism as a stressor that impedes effective parenting), and the building of peer support relationships. The curriculum is divided into three basic modules.

The first module is called *Parent as a Change Agent for Self.* Three of the sessions in this module focus on building trust and addressing mistrust between parents and facilitators, and on helping the parent identify strengths and weaknesses, stressors and coping strategies, wishes and hopes, and barriers to realizing those aspirations. All of this is expected to begin in the first phase but to continue throughout the rest of the sessions. The group style and support are expected to contribute to open disclosure of difficult life struggles. Strategies and ideas are provided by the group membership and the facilitators. Partnership here is defined as helping the individual (in collaboration with others) to identify personal life issues that contribute to stress and to identify personal assets that can be mobilized to combat the bustle of daily life. The focus is on relationships with men or women, race, socioeconomic and gender worries, family-of-origin relationships, effect of isolation on psychological status, stress management, health concerns, and taking care of one's health. A particular focus is on the rationale for and skills in developing friendships and community with other isolated parents. *Parent-Parent* collaborations are encouraged. Caring for self and others is a major theme throughout Phase 1 of this curriculum. There are four sessions in this module. **Session 1**—My First Name Is Not Mommy!: Taking Care of Self, **Session 2**—Managing Anger and Stress that Cramps Your Style, **Session 3**—Building Positive Relationships With Men and Women, and **Session 4**—Remembering Childhood Experiences.

The following segment between the facilitator and parents reveals the challenges of helping some parents consider their identities outside of their parenting. For some it is easy, for others, it may take an entire session.

Facilitator: Tonight is for you. We were going to start with a topic that we do like the second or third session but since you all are first timers the topic for the first timers is "My name is not Mommy." The reason why we say that is...or grandmommy in this case or grand-whatever, aunt, cousin...the reason why we say that is because a lot of times you spend a lot of your lives spent with your kids, taking care of your kids, and you might have a life of your own that you have thought about wanting. Or even thought about what would I do if I could just imagine for a second that my name was not mommy? That my name was whatever my first name is and I had a dream. What would my dream be for me? The kids got PLAAY during the day and I have COPE for night. What is it that I would want to do without worrying about my child...What is it that I would like to do just for me?

Mother: I would like to take that cruise to the islands.

At these points in COPE, invariably disclosure happens and some "testifyin" occurs that explains why imagining one's identity outside of mommy is hard.

Facilitator: Any particular island?

Mother: Cancun, Mexico.

Mother's son: Why do you want to go to Mexico? (The group laughs out of wonderment that this kind of discussion can ever occur.)

Majak's grandmother: Something other than Momma or Grandmother (in a pensive voice).

Facilitator: What does Majak call you?

Majak's Grandmother: Grandma.

Facilitator: Okay. We can't use that tonight. Use something else.

Majak's Grandmother: Majak can call me his grandma.

Facilitator: Well, what would you like to be?

Majak's Grandmother: To really be honest, because I have raised all of mine, I
would not like to be a grandmother, but I don't have any other choice. Well see,
I tell the honest truth about it. And I usually tell Joseph and Majak, "you know
you're very lucky because you have a grandmother that really cares." You
know what I'm saying? There are times...and I got three grandchildren, one
ten, Majak, and one fourteen, and you can imagine and I am a senior citizen,
what I go through. Listen, I could just...(laughs). But I mean, where would I
want to go? What would I do? (The group echoes these questions)

Group: Yeah, what would you do?

Majak's Grandmother: I would like to go to the Holy Land. That's what my dream is.

Facilitator: I understand that. Which part?

Majak's Grandmother: The part where Jesus was. The part where the Pope was.

Once parents disclose their fantasies, we try to find ways to make the
ideas practical and to devise doable experiences that support the goal of
enjoying oneself.

The second module is titled *Parent as a Change Agent in the Child's Presence,* and consists of focusing more directly on the role of parenting, the
relationship with the child, parental competence, and intimacy. In this second phase, the parents' partnership is with their children. Empowerment
is identified as understanding one's own responses to stress when children are present or the contribution of one's responses to the exacerbation
of that stress; understanding that parent-child relationships contribute to
educational failure or low motivation in young children; learning basic
stress-reducing child management strategies, and knowing when they
will work and when they won't; and understanding what one has and
does not have control over. *Parent-child* collaborations are encouraged.
The following four sessions make up this module. **Session 5**—Development Makes a Difference, **Session 6**—What A Parent Looks Like from the
Child's Perspective, **Session 7**—Discipline and Child Rearing, and **Session 8**—Teaching Children About Their Heritage.

The third module is titled *Parent as a Change Agent in School/Community
Contexts,* consists of teaching parents about the way school systems and
politics work and how best to work in the school and community context
to secure resources for themselves and their families. The purpose of this
module is to increase parents' involvement in the academic lives of their
children. Empowerment is defined as the parent being actively engaged

in the contexts of school and community as expressed by the parent's assertiveness in conversation with teachers and local leaders in key community institutions. Examples of topics include the politics of advocacy for a child's educational promise; understanding the world and stressors of teachers; and learning negotiation and conflict management skills. In the two teacher-parent sessions, the focus will be on the parents sharing with the teachers their views about schools and teachers. Issues of trust and mistrust will be addressed. *Teacher-Parent* collaborations are encouraged and developed during this phase. The sessions include **Session 9**—From A Teacher's Point of View and **Session 10**—School Politics and How You Can Advocate for Your Child. Because of the challenge of getting parents to the COPE sessions, we shortened this curriculum to seven sessions and Table 6.1 describes this integration of ten sessions into seven. The rest of this chapter will highlight some of the typical group dynamics experienced during the process of conducting COPE groups.

WHAT ARE SUCCESSFUL MOMENTS AND PROCESSES IN COPE?

Although success is often difficult to define, several instances were identified as successful moments during the course of our group work. These moments, which are stimulated by culturally relevant group processes, are observed when one or more individuals have been effectively supported. These successful moments are the reason and purpose for which COPE was developed. They are instances in which individuals felt any or all of the following: a sense of acceptance, relief, connection, support, nurturance, understanding, compassion, guidance, or resurgence of strength or will. Successful moments for us are stimulated, mediated, and interpreted through one major process—cultural style.

Cultural style can be exhibited during the course of speaking or listening (i.e., arm waving, hand gestures/movements, voice intonations, use of humor, etc.). When group members cultural styles are demonstrated, it is an indication that they feel comfortable in the group, and comfortable enough to be themselves. For the parents, especially in the context of their previous negative experiences working with professionals, being themselves and sharing themselves freely involve a certain level of comfort and trust. By focusing in the first two sessions on the parent as a person, we remove some of the blame attached to parenting difficult youth. Both the "breaking of bread" together and the nonjudgmental tone of the group meeting contribute to the parents' perception that the group is a safe place for them to relax and unwind. Cultural style can be observed in three behaviors: testifyin', emotional flow, and interaction with the facilitators.

Testifyin'

Testifyin' occurs when participants share personal and private information and pain in a brief period of time with people that they do not know
at all. Most parents seemed to have no idea of what to expect from the
group process. But it is essential to have a familiarity with the "call-and-
response" cultural style, which appreciates that people can and should
talk about their issues as they would around their own dinner table. "Be
yourself" or "tell your story" are familiar cries among the participants
who may see each other only once. The process is very reminiscent of
Black church congregations held every Sunday morning in which testi-
monials are solicited by congregants. It is a very powerful cultural experience; the burdens a person is carrying can be made lighter if they are
shared with trustworthy comrades who have gone through similar struggles and who also appreciate the cultural style and medium.

The following vignette contains some brief dialogue from a COPE
group in which parents are discussing their overwhelmed lives. One parent testifies that she is very stressed and that she has to do all of the work
around the house by herself. As she described what stresses her, she tells a
story of being the only one in her family of six to clean the house or cook
or take care of household duties. The session is very light and intense at
the same time as the mother describes her cooking talents and a typical
Sunday dinner, which seems like a feast for ungrateful people. The other
parents are impressed with the mother's skills and work effort, and in culturally stylistic and humorous fashion, want her to cook for them, too.

Parent #1: I made three sweet potato pies and made it for Sunday dinner. And I
put them in the freezer. So I made fresh collard greens, baked macaroni and
cheese, roast beef, mushroom gravy—

Parent #2: Uh-uh. (This is a small example of cultural style in the negative. This
parent disagrees with a grunt, but it's not a disagreement but an affirmation as
if she can't believe that this woman cooks all this stuff. As if to say, "No she didn't
make all this food?" As Parent #1 is describing the dish, she is making everybody hungry as they seem to be able to smell the food she describes.)

Parent #3: Are you going to give me your address?

Parent #4: I'm going right with you? (laughter from all the parents after realizing
how big a dinner this woman has cooked and how nice it would be to have
someone to cook this much for them.)

Parent #1: Mushroom gravy, potato salad.

Facilitator: You have any more sweet potato pie?

Parent #3: Oh, man, she gonna give me her address. (Again insisting while being
funny. The group laughs continuously.)

Parent #1: They all gone; I came home yesterday, the last pie dish was sitting on
the table.

Facilitator: Whaaat?

Parent #1: I mean they done ate all three. But I don't do it no—far as—more; if—when I cook a big dinner it would be like every other weekend. That's when I'm off.

Facilitator: What can I do for you? (Facilitator is trying to get the focus of the group on parent's overresponsibility in the family and how it may contribute to her stress despite the fact that she is an excellent cook and gets praise for it. The strategy for doing this is to ask the mother a question as if he is one of the family members that benefits from this scrumptious meal. Parent #1 immediately responds to this strategy and talks back to the family member by confessing her particular style—a style that reveals that she doesn't trust her family to care for her.)

Parent #1: You know what? I think really I'm set in a way, that, I just. I'm just used to doing for myself. I don't have the patience to wait for you.

The parent excites the group with her culinary talents but she is also telling us her coping style, that she doesn't trust other people to do things her way. She is overwhelmed by this workload but her personality style takes precedence and it appears to be too hard for her to rely on others to relieve her of the load. The session goes on until others begin to challenge her competence to allow her to see, ever so briefly, that perhaps her "rigid perfection" keeps family members from helping, enabling them to be underresponsible, and her to be overresponsible. Inadvertently, this dynamic leaves her lonely and alone in a house full of people and empty pie dishes.

The suggestion from the group was to let go of her competence, let others help her even if imperfectly, admit that she needs something from them that only they can provide, and allow them to care for her. By having the whole group affirm her competence in a culturally stylistic way following the first part of her testimony and then having the group support yet challenge the limits of her cooking competence in the latter part of the group process, the parent was able to acknowledge that her emotional needs may not get met under the current set of dynamics—no matter how many scrumptious Sunday dinners she makes.

Emotional Flow or Release

When participants are testifyin', it is not uncommon for there to be raucous laughter, tears, or both that physically demonstrate that they are engaged in this process. Testifyin' and emotional release are two indicators that the atmosphere in COPE is safe enough that parents who are coming for the first time may feel comfortable disclosing personal information to strangers.

Parents become frustrated dealing with a multitude of difficulties. Often, many parents are dealing with other issues such as death of family members, health issues, social and emotional difficulties, relationship problems, limited supports in place, poverty, single parenthood, and work stresses. Often times, parents and children both need therapy but have difficulty accessing services because of the circumstances that exist in their personal lives. Time, childcare, health, work schedules, and economics can all serve to impede the process of reaching out for help. In fact, the personal and family problems that require therapeutic intervention are usually the same problems that hinder the ability of many families to seek the therapeutic intervention they so desperately need. This places many parents in a psychological bind, feeling as if they need to put out fires on a daily basis but unable to truly address the source of the flame. It puts them in a position of needing to choose their battles based on urgency, which typically means that they deal with the symptoms of the problem instead of the problem itself.

The aggregate of their various difficulties has a profound emotional effect on parents, which can render them unable to properly address their emotional pain or the original source of their difficulties. The group process provides them with an outlet for their emotions so that they may continue to fight the good fight and face their challenges. The aforementioned example in which the mother attended only one session touches on the need many overwhelmed parents have for emotional release. In that case, the mother of a young man used the group in the moment to handle the pain of dealing with the juvenile justice system and the courts. She shared with the group her anger and frustration that her son's father was not more involved and her need to give her ex-husband custody of her son to force involvement. Sensing that she was heavily burdened, the group listened and consoled her during her time of need.

It is important to keep in mind that the emotional needs of parents vary. For some, repeat attendance is necessary to achieve maximal benefit from the group. For others, just knowing the group exists as an outlet for self-expression and support is sufficient reassurance. It is important to consider individual variation in the context of the group process. Some parents need only one session, while others may be able to attend only one session. Using the analogy of their situation as a boxing match, a COPE session is the training camp that can prepare a parent to reenter the ring. The COPE session is the 60-second reprieve between rounds that allows a person to live to fight another day. There was one mother, who after weeks of phone contacts and missed sessions, finally made it to a COPE session, willing and ready to share her story. As soon as introductions were completed, this mother began to lift the pressure valve and let the steam flow. This degree of intense release of emotional pressure would have typically taken weeks to address through COPE. However, for this overwhelmed mother the cathartic benefit of sharing her story once in the group context permitted her to reenter the ring and keep fighting. Just as quickly as she entered the group, she never returned.

Interaction with Facilitators

Connection to the group facilitator or other group member(s) may be reflected through eye contact or head nods, sharing of personal information ("testifyin'"), reaffirming or repeating what others have said, asking questions of others, offering suggestions or guidance to other group members, or giving the facilitators instruction and permission to intervene with their children. The following segment shows how we explain PLAAY to parents for the first time. Initially, the group facilitator describes the cultural pride reinforcement component of the program and then moves on to detail the basketball component of the program.

Saburah: ...They learn how to express their feelings verbally instead of physically. And how to express them verbally in a manner that someone can understand them without (makes punching gestures with her hands)...in a way that you can be heard and the person is going to respond to you in the same way. So that's...And the cultural part is to let them know who they are as Black young males and what it means to be a minority male in this society. That's on Tuesdays and Thursdays. After that we do the basketball component. Through basketball, they learn the game, they learn control. Again, if you are thinking and using...yeah, the team working together...it's also using your body and your mind. It also brings up their emotions and we can deal with it in the moment. If he goes on saying to him (makes hand gesture) instead of wanting to fight right there on the court, we have a counselor right there who can take you out. Where is that anger coming from? Why did you have to respond like that? Because that's not something he has to wait until next week to go to his therapist to talk about it. And it's in the moment and it's right there. And it's a game that all the boys love and they get emotional about it, and we want them to get emotional about it. And it works well. And those are the components. It takes place four days a week, four mornings per week. Every morning that they come to school, we are there. I don't know if there is anything I didn't cover. I think I covered everything in COPE, PLAAY, and MAAR. Are there any questions you might have about COPE?

Majak's mother: Well, like, if you have a problem with them, do you call my grandmother or do you just call the counselors at school?

Saburah: We are their counselors. I've known Majak all this time (chuckling).

Majak's mother: Oh, really! You see I have an answering machine and grandmom doesn't so I'll make sure that you have my number.

Saburah: See, we don't deal with them like we are their teachers. We don't deal with any academics. We are just some folks who came there and want to be a part of their lives and want to make a difference in their lives and hope that they remember us and hope that we do make a difference in their lives. But uh, no, Majak and I have spent many times out into the hall if (chuckling, group laughs). But no I am not a member of Miller staff.

Facilitator: We don't physically grab them. We might give him the best look that we have ever had. We will talk back to him.

Saburah: I will take him off to the side, but I don't physically do anything.

Majak's mother: Well, that would be good if you do. (group laughs)

Another mother: Me, too. Snatch him right on up (shaking her head in approval).

Saburah: Each of us staff has our own way of dealing with the boys. You know, I'm a mother of six and so I'll do something with these boys... I will talk to Majak in a way maybe Pam would talk to them in a different way. Each of us deal with them on the spot. We don't go to nobody. We don't report them to anybody. The worse they may get from us is to be put out and they hate that. They have to go back to class and be put out of the program for that day. And I mean they have to really, really do something bad for us to put them out. They don't want that. They don't want to get sent out of the program for that day. So...

The parents here didn't mind if we applied physical discipline with their sons if they get out of hand, which is something we would not do. But they are giving us their permission to use a variety of discipline strategies that reflect an appreciation for a certain cultural style of parenting. This cultural style includes many strategies with different variations but may be reflected in the behaviors of "snatch him up" or giving him "the look." This is one example of how parents' interactions with us in humorous cultural stylistic fashion affirm not only that it is okay to "be Black" during the COPE sessions but also that it is okay to apply culturally stylistic parenting strategies with their children. We have been given permission to become surrogate parents or "aunts and uncles" for their children.

There are opportunities for in-the-moment intervention to be implemented throughout the COPE process. Connected to this is a common dynamic among some parents who wait until they come to COPE before they reach their breaking point, where it is socially and emotionally safe to bottom out. In one case, facilitators had made numerous unsuccessful attempts to involve one particular mother in COPE. She did not attend until the school threatened to forbid her son to return to school if she did not come to COPE. Out of necessity, the program director became involved at that time. This school situation provided a unique opportunity for in-the-moment therapy with this mother and her son. When she was in crisis, she decided to turn to the program for support. Our intervention sometimes includes hugs and affection, which may be all we can provide if a situation is desperate, but more intensively, it allows for brief family systems therapeutic intervention.

At times, phone contacts provided some parents with a much-needed opportunity for in-the-moment intervention with COPE support staff. As such, although the original purpose of phone contacts was to serve as an attendance reminder, it ultimately also afforded parents in a state of crisis the chance to speak to someone who knew their sons and was safe and trustworthy.

The COPE staff has provided various levels and types of support to parents. There have been instances in which court hearings have been attended, hospital visits have been made to children or youth who have been shot or experienced loss. We have offered support to their parents or guardians and written reports to juvenile court proceedings to attest to a youth's and parent's involvement and progress in our program.

Connection with Each Other

When COPE is going well, we expect this type of support group to be very healing for the participants as they bond together over how to manage parenting African American male teens in a racially hostile society. Taking the time to participate in the group allows them to take a step back and reflect on their situation. Many parents often lead chaotic lives and have difficulty finding the opportunity for sufficient reflection. Over time, the process facilitates a deeper understanding of themselves and their challenges.

An additional benefit is that provided through listening to the difficulties and experiences of other parents. This can provide a different perspective of their own problems, especially since many parents do not realize that there are other parents who share similar difficulties with their teenage boys. It is not just them, other parents struggle with how best to raise their children. The group process serves to normalize their problems and make parents feel less alone or isolated. Parents can learn to understand themselves better as they understand others better as well. The group experience affords emotionally isolated parents the opportunity to connect with others similar to themselves. They all struggle with the responsibility of parenting and fear that their children are a reflection on them. Being the parents of boys in trouble make their involvement in parenting intervention groups difficult because they expect to be blamed for their sons' misbehaviors.

The COPE groups provide a safe haven for sharing the challenging aspects of their lives and for safely disclosing their personal shame. After all, are they not the mothers and fathers of these "delinquents"? Isn't it all their fault? In COPE, we try to help parents work on altering their perceptions of themselves as just "mom" or "dad." Many struggle vehemently at times but begin to see themselves as individuals, not as defective parents. Often, before their participation in the groups, they lost themselves in their problems and their problems became a key aspect of their presented identity.

To resolve the problem of a loss of dignity and emotional overload, it can be beneficial to talk to others with similar life and family situations. A sense of relief is often felt when parents share their story and hear similar stories from other parents. For example, there were two fathers who connected with one another by sharing their stories about their sons' academic and emotional difficulties. Perhaps for the first time, there was no shame regarding their family situation since the other person understood both their situation and their pain. Ultimately, they served as a source of support for one another. They exchanged phone numbers and began to take the same route home together. A great weight lifted off his shoulders, one father was able to find a supportive social worker to help his son receive wraparound social services and also he received a letter from the PLAAY project director to present to the courts on his son's behalf. When the father first came he wanted to send his son to a residential group home for incorrigible youth. He was frustrated, angry, and overwhelmed. He was not to be talked out of it by the COPE facilitators in the beginning. But by the end of the seven sessions, he had changed his mind and picked up a friend in the process.

FIGHTING THE POWERS THAT BE: PARENTS AS CHANGE AGENTS IN THEIR CHILDREN'S LIVES

The development of adaptive parental coping mechanisms that involve the effective engagement with the social, justice, and educational systems that interact with African American boys is critical.

Over time parents begin to develop alternative coping methods, ways of being, and perceptions of their situation. Although many were aware of some of these strategies before attending the groups, their participation in the groups served as the impetus for: recognizing the importance of using alternate coping and parenting strategies; using the strategies when faced with challenging situations; and later realizing that they can be very effective and beneficial to them. A unique sense of vulnerability is often felt by parents. They are concerned about the safety of their sons as African American males and the fact that their sons' lives and their futures may be in jeopardy. The possibility of losing them to the criminal justice system looms large as they witness the demise of other adolescents in their neighborhoods and families.

Perhaps for the first time in their lives, problems are being focused on in the context of a positive, supportive environment. Typically, government agencies and institutions (i.e., schools, courts, etc.) involve parents of problem youth in a manner that is punitive, hostile, and derogatory. Whether this is intentional or not is less important than the fact that folks often feel punished, angry, and put down. Especially with children who have recurrent behavioral difficulties, there is an assumption that their parents are defective and do not have the ability to properly parent. This message is often sent in subtle ways to parents who over time begin to internalize the negative perceptions others have projected onto them. But parents who know this and can sidestep its emotional stress will be way ahead of the dehumanizing politics. Anger management is crucial here so that their children will receive the best services from a reticent human service system. COPE strives, sometimes unsuccessfully, to provide an outlet that serves to reaffirm a positive identity in parents who themselves have been victimized by a system that has demoralized them as individuals—and to turn that negative energy into advocacy for their boys.

Feelings of helplessness and being overwhelmed often dissipate as group members begin to feel empowered to make positive changes in their approach to their difficulties. Constructively, they can begin to more fully explore options available to them since they are taking the time to think about their situation with the support and guidance of others. Designed to empower parents to become advocates for their children, COPE can increase knowledge of the politics of the juvenile justice system and reduce the fear parents feel as a result of having little control over their situation. COPE can help them understand what they have control over and what options they may have.

In summary, we hope to help parents tap the strengths that exist in them and in their lives. COPE enables them to discover their own strengths so that they are better able to tap into existing resources and support in their families and communities. Despite the rhyming and playful significance of the names of PLAAY components, each is named so for a reason that relates directly to the work of the component. Our next chapter is about ROPE, the combination of rites of passage ceremony and an ongoing support group to acknowledge and provide support for the PLAAY youths as they continue their journey from boyhood into manhood.

REFERENCES

Coard, S.I., Wallace, S.A., Stevenson, H.C., & Brotma, L.M. (in press). Towards culturally relevant preventive interventions: The consideration of racial socialization in parent training with African American families. *Journal of Child and Family Studies.*

Geiger, S.M. (1995). African-American single mothers: Public perceptions and public policies. In K. Vaz (Ed.), *Black Women in America*. Newbury Park: Sage Press.

Katz, M.B. (1992). *The underclass debate: Views from history*. Princeton, NJ: Princeton University Press.

McLoyd, V.C. (1998). Changing demographics in the American population: Implications for research on minority children and adolescents. In V.C. McLoyd & L. Steinberg (Eds.), *Studying minority adolescents: Conceptual, methodological, and theoretical issues*. Mahwah, NJ: Lawrence Erlbaum Associates, Inc.

Richters, J.E. & Martinez, P. (1993). The NIMH community violence project: I. Children as victims of and witnesses to violence. *Psychiatry, 56,* 7–21.

Spakes, P. (1991). A feminist approach to national family policy. In Elaine A. Anderson & Richard C. Hula (Eds.), *The reconstruction of family policy*. Westport, CT: Greenwood Press.

Stevenson, H.C., Davis, G.Y., & Abdul-Kabir, S. (2001). *Stickin' To, Watchin' Over, and Gettin' With: African American Parent's Guide to Discipline.* San Francisco: Jossey-Bass.

West, G. (1981). *The national welfare rights movement: The social protest of poor women.* New York: Praeger.

CHAPTER 7

Life After PLAAY: Alumni Group and Rites of Passage Empowerment (ROPE)

Gwendolyn Y. Davis, Pamela C. Zamel, Diane M. Hall,
Erick Espin, and Vernita R. Williams

The social and emotional development of African American boys are essential to the future of Black family and societal relationships. The ripple effect of the disproportionate imprisonment of young Black men is underestimated and avoided by civil rights advocates and politicians alike. It is our opinion that the reduction of future negative life outcomes for everyone these boys come in contact with is dependent on how well they learn the skills of self-knowledge, cultural empowerment, oppression management, interpersonal competence, and emotional expression. In all the components of PLAAY there is a concerted effort to develop intense relationships with the boys, to stretch their tolerance of frustration, and show them the compassion of other caring adults. Applying these varied strategies for two to three periods a day for four days in a five-day school week over an average of 20 weeks is important, but not sufficient, in our estimation. As we began this project, we knew that a rites of passage program was essential to commemorate the accomplishments of the boys. What we did not know was that one or two ceremonies would not be enough. Staff members decided that meeting with the boys after they left the school-based portion of PLAAY would be a way to help maintain relationships with many of the boys and to continue gathering follow-up data.

The rites of passage program (ROPE) was intended for graduates of the first four components. Another name for this component is the alumni group. A ROPE ceremony occurs at the end of each intervention sequence as a review of the teenagers' growth, their accountability to the larger community to which they belong and the community's accountability to them, their strengths and limitations during the previous year, and their future mission to avoid the use of violence in handling interpersonal conflicts.

This chapter reports on the challenges and processes involved in following the boys in the PLAAY project after they completed the school-based intervention (Stevenson et al., 2001). But first we must explain that PLAAY is an intervention research project. The intervention research itself yielded many quantifiable outcomes, the specifics of which cannot be fully examined here. Up to this point, we have tried to tell the story of these experiences rather than communicate the results through reductionistic summaries which are best represented in journal review articles. Nevertheless, we will summarize some of the major findings regarding the impact PLAAY had on many of these students before their involvement with the ROPE portion of the project.

EVIDENCE OF PLAAY IMPACT

Previous implementation of the PLAAY project in a behavior academy setting yielded information on approximately 164 youths. A smaller subgroup of about 90 were randomly assigned to a PLAAY group and a control group. We targeted youth with a history of aggression to see whether we could assess the diversity of students classified as angry and aggressive. We found relationships between some of the mental health measures and anger expression and fighting behaviors that are worth reporting.

In a preliminary investigation of the pretest measures, we found that *anger suppression* is related to aspects of depression, including cognitive difficulty, sad mood, and low self-esteem whereas *anger acted outward* toward others is strongly correlated with pessimism, irritability, and instrumental helplessness. At high levels, both anger suppression and anger acted outward are associated with youth health risks and a history of aggression (Deffenbacher, Lynch, Oetting, & Kemper, 1996; Johnson & Greene, 1991; Johnson, Spielberger, Worden, & Jacobs, 1987; Renouf & Harter, 1990; Siegel, 1984), but rarely are aggressive youths of color thought of as depressed or depressed in particular areas of cognitive and emotional functioning, despite evidence to the contrary (Roberts & Sobhan, 1992). Moreover, we have found that racial socialization experiences from family members may be protective and risky since they are differentially associated with anger expression styles and aggression (Stevenson, Reed, Bodison & Bishop, 1997; Stevenson, Cameron, Herrero-Taylor, & Davis, 2002).

Mainstream racial socialization experiences for teenagers and young adults are significantly correlated with anger control, anger suppression, anger acted out, and low self-esteem (Constantine & Blackmon, 2002). We interpret this to mean that the "both-and" nature of learning how to fit into mainstream American society has advantages and disadvantages with respect to anger. As adolescents are receiving messages of assimilation and fitting in, they are also aware of the deference and race denial stances that such assimilation may require. Cultural pride reinforcement socialization is positively associated with anger control, which we believe is a beneficial outcome (Stevenson, Reed, Bodison, & Bishop, 1997). Anger control is often associated with positive outcomes in school adjustment and interpersonal and social relationships and is inversely related to aggression and fighting behavior (Stevenson et al., 2002). Furthermore, anger suppression and acting out are often highly associated with behavioral and physiological health illnesses.

We believe that CPR along with the other components of PLAAY (which stress various types of racial socialization experiences here presented) promote the ways in which families socialize their children to feel proud of their culture, their heritage, and themselves. These can be particularly useful for aggressive youth for whom some aspects of depression are prominent or interacting with anger and aggression. The CPR component is designed to address some of these issues through a group therapy focus with strong culturally relevant strategies and materials to promote cultural critical consciousness, or a frame for which the boys can make better sense of their experiences and feelings.

The PLAAY project was identified as a major reason the absenteeism rate of the behavior academy decreased during the time between the program's initiation in January of 1999 and June of 2001. The behavior academy's student attendance rates increased from 62 percent to 69 percent and average unexcused absences decreased from 38 percent to 26 percent during that time. Moreover, the number of total suspensions dropped from 328 to 117 (Family Resource Trend Report, 2000). Although there were other programs in the school, the principal and the district truancy statistician identified the PLAAY project as one of the primary reasons for those improvements.

RESULTS OF RANDOM-ASSIGNMENT EXPERIMENT

In a preliminary review of the prepost treatment effects of a subgroup of the behavior academy youths who were randomly assigned to either PLAAY or control conditions, it was found that PLAAY students responded differently from control students in several post administrations of rejection sensitivity, feelings of rejection, and anxious expectation measures (Stevenson, Davis, Cassidy, Zamel, & Williams, 2003). Using pretest scores as covariates in a MANCOVA (Wilks's $\Lambda = .534$, $F = 7.48$, $p < .0001$, $eta^2 = .10$) with rejection sensitivity variables as dependent variables, there were significant effects for angry psychological reactions ($F = 7.63$, $p < .01$; $eta^2 = .10$), rejection feelings ($F = 10.10$, $p < .002$; $eta^2 = .13$), anxious expectation ($F = 19.43$, $p < .0001$; $eta^2 = .23$), angry expectation ($F = 24.21$, $p < .0001$; $eta^2 = .27$), and angry feelings ($F = 3.73$, $p < .05$; $eta^2 = .05$).

Results provided mixed support for hypotheses of better rejection sensitivity health outcomes for PLAAY students. When confronted with situations of interpersonal conflict in school classroom, playground, and neighborhood contexts, PLAAY students reported significantly lower levels of angry psychological reactions to rejection and rejection feelings compared with control group students. In contrast, PLAAY students reported significantly higher levels of anxiety and anger feelings before an interpersonal conflict, while feeling more angry after an interpersonal conflict compared to control group students. Mostly, they were feeling more.

We feel that students involved in PLAAY intervention components are sensitized more directly toward identifying and experiencing their feelings in greater ways than are students who do not receive the treatment. Being able to express anger is a key component of the project. In addition, there is concern about the concept of rejection sensitivity for students who frequently receive real, not just perceived, rejection messages and experiences. The ability to identify rejection where it exists is viewed by our team as a strength, not a weakness, most especially in contexts in which dangers of various emotional and physical sorts are prevalent. Rejection sensitivity can be a weakness in contexts in which "watching one's back" interferes with learning and social interaction. The energy it takes to be hypervigilant is wasted in contexts in which processing new information is essential. In CPR groups and by teacher and parent report, we learn how often these boys face significant health and injury dangers. Prolonged exposure to danger is of course problematic for emotional competence; however, rejection sensitivity can be a necessary skill in dangerous contexts. Being able to express the feelings attached to rejection is a positive step in the direction of emotional maturity and coping.

There were no significant differences between PLAAY and control students on measures of depression and anger expression at posttest. These results help to point us to the potential benefit of more refined development of the individual components of the PLAAY project. In particular, a major goal is to help students reduce their reactivity to rejection by being aware of it when it is actually occurring as opposed to attributing hostility where none exists. This is necessary for racially charged neighborhood contexts in which there are significant institutional authority-neighborhood distrust and conflicts as well as in nonracially charged contexts. As students move beyond the confines of the behavior academy, oddly enough they move into more dangerous contexts. As they reenter the regular school system they are fearful. They are very fearful that they will be tossed into a large pressure-cooker in which territory and turf combined with intense manhood politics are the order of the day. Many of the boys talk of the behavior academy as a reputation nightmare at times, but all in all they consider it a relatively safe environment because of the extra scrutiny and predictable structure. In regular school settings, the ringing of the bell to change classes brings hundreds of students into hallways along with overstimulating emotional conflicts that can flood our boys and make them forget their best interpersonal skills.

For these and other reasons, which the boys report as a "tough life," our staff decided to construct a program for boys after they leave the behavior academy. We had many hopes of maintaining the connections we had developed so adeptly at the school and seeing how long they could last. In addition, we hoped that the benefits of "feeling more" could be found to persist in those boys who would continue in the ROPE. The idea of "ROPE" is that we may need to continue to throw out a "lifeline," as the boys try to swim in the deeper part of the ocean. Everybody needs a lifeline now and then, but we feel being Black and male requires the Coast Guard to be on call with many ropes, long and strong.

EARLY CONCEPTIONS OF ROPE AND THE ALUMNI GROUP

Initially, we thought of the rites of passage empowerment program as a ceremony process. That is, it was meant to bring together the family, teachers, and friends of the PLAAY students for a ceremony that would commemorate their successful participation in the many components of the PLAAY program. This ceremony would be at the end of the program and would acknowledge the students' individual strengths and weaknesses, telling stories about funny and challenging moments throughout the year, include teaching around the importance of cultural pride, seeing the community as important, and helping the students move to the next stage of their lives as young men. Following the first year of the project, it became clear that one ceremony would not capture the dynamics of the time spent with these boys nor would it address the serious issues they all faced when they left the program. Gwendolyn Davis conceived of the idea we call alumni group, which was meant to involve all the boys who wished to be involved. It became a monthly meeting to track how they were doing in their new schools and to provide more CPR training and experience. So although ROPE started as a ceremony with several connecting events (for example, including COPE parents in the ROPE ceremony), it turned into a monthly CPR lifeline group experience. Students who became friends at Miller were able to see each other again at the alumni group. For our purposes, ROPE represents the end-of-the-year ceremony as well as the alumni group experience at the school.

ROPE CEREMONY

A Rites of Passage ceremony is conducted at the end of each intervention sequence to mark the students' successful completion of the three major components as well as their initiation into the fourth and final component, the ROPE program. The purpose of the ceremony is to review each student's growth during the previous year, acknowledge his strengths and limitations, and provide an opportunity to affirm his mission to avoid the use of violence to handle future conflicts. The ceremony also serves as a ritualized expression of the student's transition from PLAAY member to PLAAY alumnus. During the course of the program, the boys engage in thoughtful discussions about society, racism, manhood, fatherhood, brotherhood, and employment. During the past four years, we have observed that they seem to gain a better understanding of their past mistakes; their relationships; and their emotions, including anger and fear.

It is our intention to celebrate the path these boys traveled with us as well as illuminate the path that lies ahead of them. It is our hope that our ceremony conveys not only our pride in their accomplishments and our feelings of connectedness with them but also our expectations and definitions for them as future alumni and young adult members of society. One biblical passage illuminates our spiritual hope for these young men who traverse treacherous territories and are in great need of divine intervention;

Your word is a lamp
to my feet
And a light to my path.
    —Psalm 119:105

Still, prayer and trust in spiritual resources are reasonable strategies for managing the overwhelming hope for the survival of young Black males. We have relied on this reality on more occasions than one. PLAAY staff members have different religious and spiritual traditions that appreciate the role of prayer in working with these young men. The benefit of prayer in difficult unpredictable life circumstances is that it allows the participants to stop wasting energy in trying to control the uncontrollable. The ceremony reflects the reliance on these resources in subtle ways.

Typically, our ceremony has been performed in an auditorium with an audience of parents, teachers and fellow students. While this ceremony may be conducted in a smaller, more intimate setting such as a library or gym, we have found that our students actually prefer a larger, more formal setting for the ceremony. In traditional rites of passage ceremonies, the audience represents the larger community to which the young man belongs and will be held accountable to, and it is the community that will be accountable to him. Members of the audience are witnesses to the young man's testimony to take on additional responsibilities in the community and to fulfill his personal and social obligations. As a result, these witnesses are expected to help the youth uphold his promises by adjusting their own expectations for him in the future and by providing gentle reminders when necessary of his testimony at this ceremony.

Parents and teachers are invited to our ROPE ceremony to act as both supporters and witnesses. We recognize that they will play a critical role in helping students stay true to their mission in the future; at the same time they are helpful to us in being there to shower our students with the attention and recognition they deserve for their present accomplishments.

The ceremony commences with a brief summary of the boys' involvement in each component, and mention of notable signs of growth. Parents, school administrators, and teachers are thanked and blessed in the opening prayer for their cooperation and contributions. Members of the audience are encouraged to express their own thanks and blessings as well. The opening prayer holds significance for its emphasis on spirituality and its appreciation for a higher power. Spirituality is one of the key principles of CPR, and thus throughout the intervention, the boys are encouraged to consider a nonmechanistic interpretation of events so that they may gain a richer understanding and stronger connection to their own spiritual reality.

Following the opening prayer, the program director reads the poem "If We Must Die" to remind the boys and members of the audience of our common purpose. This poem underscores the historical and political importance of our program's mission of preventing long-term anger and aggression in African American youth. As well, it challenges us all to bring meaning to our lives and to never waste our God-given talents.

The reading is followed by a musical piece performed by one or more of our PLAAY students. In the past, we have had beautiful and uplifting piano and steel drum performances. This is an opportunity for the students to express their creativity and individuality while the community expresses delight and gratitude for their unique gifts and talents. The message we hope to convey here is one that we repeat time and time again in our CPR sessions: individuality, not individualism, is the key to a healthy and safe community.

Next, we have a short demonstration of the kata performed by a select group of PLAAY members. The kata is a floor exercise that is taught in our martial arts component (MAAR); it combines a series of complex hand-and-foot combinations requiring students to use balance, coordination, movement, and agility. The purpose of this performance is to provide the students with an opportunity to demonstrate their competencies related to this challenging exercise. It is in the accolades of the audience that we hope our boys come to recognize and appreciate their own mastery. Likewise, we hope that the boys reflect on how their past difficulties with this exercise, including their experiences of frustration, discoordination, breathlessness, and defeat, have each contributed to their ultimate success.

Following this performance, the students are requested to return to their seats and all members of PLAAY are asked to stand for the rite. The eldest

member of our team proceeds to read the following passage. She makes
sure to pause after each verse so that the students may repeat after her.

I will make every effort:
>   to be my brother's keeper,
which means looking out for others as well as myself.
>   to honor my parents,
and others who have sacrificed and cared about me.
>   to respect others,
even when I don't think they deserve respect.
>   to believe in myself and not give up,
even when the world is unfair to me.
>   to be an example for my family, friends and community and abide by
>   society's laws,
even if I feel they are unfair to me.
>   to apply myself,
and not waste my God given talents.
>   to be true to myself,
and make decisions that are in my best interest and fair to others.
>   to not bring harm to others,
with my words or my fists.
>   to be humble to a Higher Power than myself
and remember that God created me and has a reason for my being here.

It is in the rite that we make our expectations explicit and ask the students
to make a commitment to accept the roles and responsibilities associated
with being a young adult in our community. Themes of self-development,
cultural awareness, and accountability are all brought together in the rite.
By repeating these statements, the young men are publicly affirming who
they are, who they are not and who they will be. In addition, this aspect of
the ceremony is conducted in a way that appreciates orality, an important
aspect of African American culture, and specifically uses the "call and
response" tradition that comes directly from traditional African culture.

Next, the "passage" is read aloud to formally present the young men
before us to the community at large with our prayers and blessings. Following a long round of applause, each student is called to the podium and
presented with a certificate and a small gift. In addition to the child's own
name, each certificate is inscribed with a nickname or motto. These nicknames are chosen by the staff to affirm something special or unique about
the young men and read aloud to the audience. The students are also presented with a PLAAY T-shirt as a token of our appreciation for their participation and hard work. In closing, roses are presented to the parents of our
students in the audience. We express our gratitude to these parents for their
own commitment, wisdom, competence, and community accountability.
Sometimes these ceremonies have gone smoothly and sometimes they
have been interrupted with raucous ridicule by classmates but we persist

through any distractions to stay committed to the ceremony's completion for the boys. At times, talking through with the boys about the emotional pressure to receive positive feedback from others while experiencing ridicule has been the focus of the discussion following the ROPE ceremony.

Following the ceremony, a small reception is held with food and beverages. We have found that this smaller, more intimate setting is more conducive to the sharing of stories and memories. It also provides additional opportunities for the staff to give constructive feedback to students about their individual strengths and weaknesses. Words of encouragement are exchanged as well as parting words. During this time, students are provided with the details of the ROPE program, including the date and time of the next monthly meeting.

PREPARING FOR WORK

A more recent and newer subcomponent of ROPE is called EMPLOY (education, mentoring, and job placement of youth). Students participating in the alumni job skills training group meet weekly and work in both group and individual activities. There are three areas of focus in the jobs curriculum: (1) obtaining, completing, and returning a completed job application; (2) practicing interviewing skills; and (3) learning about work environment expectations. Students will be assessed on their reading and mathematics achievement. For students with academic difficulties, work with educational specialists will be provided. Throughout the process, students also are assessed on their job skills (e.g., putting lists in alphanumeric order, filing, etc.).

Throughout the curriculum, whether working in a group or one-on-one, staff members act as coaches. This involves giving students very specific feedback about positive areas, as well as areas in need of improvement. In addition, many of these students have self-esteem issues. Interacting as coaches with these students provides a context in which the students feel that they have an advocate and someone who will provide assistance in a nonjudgmental manner. As staff members get to know the students and their particular potential weaknesses, role plays are individually designed to gently challenge and push the students to think differently about particular issues.

For the first objective of the curriculum, students role play asking a potential employer for a job application. Staff members discuss with students the importance of dress, language, and first impressions. Students are given job application prototypes to complete, with the assistance of the staff. Students are encouraged to think creatively about job skills they may have and to work toward finding all information needed to present a complete application (e.g., former supervisor's name and phone number). Students may practice this several times before an application is considered ready. In addition, students with previous employment will work on creating a resume. Finally, students make an information card, with all of their application contact information on it. It is explained to students that potential employers may sometimes ask that an application be completed on site, and it is important to present a complete application.

For the second objective, students in the group observe the role play between staff members of a job interview in which many things "go wrong." Students are asked to critique the interviewee's performance. Then students work one-on-one with a staff member practicing an interview. An additional staff member is present to observe and provide feedback. Role plays involve deliberately provocative and difficult interview situations. This is the time to provide feeback and support to the student who has anger control issues or who is prone to rejection sensitivity. In addition, this allows the student an opportunity to prepare for a worst case scenario interview. Staff members also discuss with students how to deal with not hearing from a potential employer and how to deal with not getting a job after an interview.

For the third objective, students discuss workplace expectations. Specific expectations discussed include (1) responsibility (e.g., being on time, coming to work when scheduled, dressing appropriately, definitions and examples of sexual harassment, behavior at work and on breaks), (2) communication skills (e.g., the importance of making eye contact, use of language, accepting feedback, and understanding different contexts and how communication styles need to change based on context), and (3) problem-solving skills (e.g., knowing how to obtain answers to questions and knowing and using proper chain of command). In addition to discussing these issues, students practice role plays with staff. In these role plays, students practice skills in difficult job situations, such as a problem with a customer or coworker. Toward the end of the curriculum, the staff discusses budgeting and financial planning issues with students.

Throughout the course of the curriculum, students learn that reliability, responsibility, and accountability are important in finding and keeping a job. Once students obtain a job, staff members check in with them to monitor their progress and to see how they are balancing work and school.

EXAMPLE OF ALUMNI DYNAMICS

Basically, the dynamics of the alumni group are similar to the CPR group except that initially the boys have to reconnect with each other outside the context of the behavior academy. In the academy, the context of toughness is so pervasive that when they meet at a neutral site (University of Pennsylvania), they are wary of the rules of the new environment. Eventually, they can put the distance politics away and begin to reconnect with each other. Various alumni group activities have included exposure to college events such as fashion shows, step shows, college student educational events, and field trips to the Blacks in Wax Museum in Baltimore. An amazing aspect of these field trips is the boys' wonderment at seeing other worlds outside of their own. The visceral experience of these boys as "boys" can be seen no clearer than when they are excited about how Black college students live out their creativity and still are trying to get an education. This kind of exposure can promote the potential for the future and stimulate the boys to consider many possible future identities or outcomes for themselves, but it's ability to do so is undervalued. The boys ask so many questions as they watch these events, and their questions reveal how "sheltered" within dangerous contexts they have been.

Of all of the alumni group experiences, perhaps the most exciting were the trips to the Blacks in Wax Museum in Baltimore. In one case, a half-asleep student couldn't understand toll booths and angrily asked why we kept having to stop so frequently as we drove back and forth on the turnpike. Another was so excited about the menu at a restaurant, and yet with so many choices for eating, a rapidly growing sense of hunger, and the all-encompassing stimulation of the Hard Rock Café, deciding what to eat seemed impossible.

The Blacks in Wax Museum has one exhibit of a slave ship and another showing lynching. The exposure to these two concepts created more questions from the boys than any lesson on enslavement in a classroom could ever stimulate. Many couldn't understand why these events occurred. Others were astonished at the cramped spaces for captive Africans in the cages of the slave ships. The stories were read aloud by tour guides and by PLAAY staff members. Anger and hostile comments were expressed without hesitation by some of the boys. Those who knew some of the historical facts were still emotionally stunned by the visual aspects of the exhibits. The exhibits touted the accomplishments of Black men and women as they either outwitted their captors (coping with antagonism and discrimination alertness); developed innovative and useful inventions, products, and knowledge (cultural pride reinforcement and cultural legacy appreciation); or blazed trails in predominantly White contexts (mainstream socialization). The museum, with its up front, in your face, life learning you can touch with your hands atmosphere, was the best place to teach the boys and see their natural boyhood expressions come to the surface.

WHAT HAVE WE LEARNED?

To do this work, there have to be staff members who have a personal vision for supporting the emotional development of Black youth. To help young Black boys the interventionists must not be simply technically skilled, they must have hearts that are committed to appreciating the boys' extreme expressions of anger and hostility and interpreting these expressions as emotional cries for help. Staff members must be willing to self-critique their fears about race, racism, difference, Black male images, and the emotional pain attached to these phenomena. To fulfill the village concept mandate, staff should include persons with different personalities, ages, and life experiences. People who are unable to access their own unique gifts, are personally going through enormous personal life crises, or who cannot work independently and make "in-the-moment" caring decisions will not make great staff members for this type of project. Age is not as much a factor as many would believe. We have seen young undergraduates provide excellent intervention responses to the boys and older staff fail to respond to these emotional outcries. Staff members are the emotional life-lines or ropes to these boys by how they interact with the boys and their families in the "small moments."

There have to be funds that support the comprehensive and multifaceted nature of interventions that focus on individual, family, and neighborhood politics in culturally relevant and gender-specific ways. To focus only on the athletic movements of TEAM and MAAR and not focus on cultural socialization in the CPR groups would have less meaningful impact on the boys' coping emotions. Future work has to uncover how PLAAY and its components fare when compared with other intervention strategies without cultural socialization as a focus. The videotaping of the various sessions is invaluable in not only illuminating the various cultural aspects of intervention but in showing images of boys that run counter to the animalistic images that society is more familiar with when Black boys are the focus. Also, the images allow us to remind the world that talking and writing about the emotional survival of Black boys does not compare with actually witnessing it.

We have learned that even with the funds and the staff, hope is still needed. The ROPE and alumni group experiences allow us to ponder more deeply the fact that we are not reaching certain boys and that their lives are much more complex than we can see during the times that we are with them. But these experiences also affirm our belief in the need to see these young boys as boys, not men and that they really do want to be hugged, challenged, supervised, and appreciated in direct and humane ways. We are ever strengthened in our belief in their potential but we are fearful about their futures and their ability to dodge the bullets meant especially for them. At times, watching the boys negotiate these hurdles, we realize that as a staff, we need ropes too—ropes that will keep our hopes alive and our feet sure to continue this work. This hope is built into the last thing that we say as a group to the boys in the rites of passage ceremony. It is meant as a tribute but also as a realization that we can't be with them always.

PASSAGE

Having fully participated in the PLAAY program, and publicly confessed to care for your people, your community, and yourself, we pray God's blessings on your future and your life and we present you to the larger community of the world with our highest hopes, that maybe you might remember our moments together and remember us—because we will not forget you.

—The PLAAY Team

Again, inspiration has benefits if it is grounded in relationship and in the alumni group, many of us are inspired to continue working and learning with these boys and we eventually hope to include girls. The next chapter, "Raising Boys to be Men: Absence Does Not Make the Heart Grow Fonder" is meant to be challenging to anyone working with boys. It reflects a reliance on inspiration if or when social science and educational politics fail African American boys.

REFERENCES

Constantine, M. & Blackmon, S. (2002). Black adolescents' racial socialization experiences: Their relations to home, school, and peer self-esteem. *Journal of Black Studies, 32(3),* 322–335.

Deffenbacher, J., Lynch, R., Oetting, E., & Kemper, C. (1996). Anger reduction in early adolescents. *Journal of Counseling Psychology, 43(2),* 149–157.

Family Resource Trend Report. (2000). Philadelphia Unified School District. Philadelphia, PA.

Johnson, E., & Greene, A. (1991).The relationship between suppressed anger and psychosocial distress in African American male adolescents. *Journal of Black Psychology, 18(1),* 47–65.

Johnson, E., Spielberger, C., Worden, T., & Jacobs, G. (1987). Emotional and familial determinants of elevated blood pressure in Black and White adolescent males. *Journal of Psychosomatic Research, 31,* 287–300.

Johnson, E., Schork, N., & Spielberger, C. (1987). Emotional and familial determinants of elevated blood pressure in Black and White adolescent females. *Journal of Psychosomatic Research, 31,* 731–741.

Renouf, A. & Harter, S. (1990). Low self-worth and anger as components of depressive experience in young adolescents. *Development and Psychopathology, 2,* 293–310.

Roberts, R., & Sobhan, M. (1992). Symptoms of depression in adolescence: A comparison of Anglo, African, and Hispanic Americans. *Journal of Youth and Adolescence, 21(6),* 639–651.

Siegel, J. (1984). Anger and cardiovascular risk in adolescents. *Health Psychology, 3,* 293–313.

Stevenson, H. C. (1997). Managing Anger: Protective, Proactive, or Adaptive Racial Socialization Identity Profiles and Manhood Development. Special Issue on Manhood Development. *Journal of Prevention and Intervention in the Community, 16,* 35–61.

Stevenson, H.C., Cameron, R., Herrero-Taylor, T., & Davis, G. Y. (2002). Development of the Teenage Experience of Racial Socialization Scale: Correlates of race-related socialization from the perspective of Black Youth. *Journal of Black Psychology, 28*, 84–106.

Stevenson, H.C., Herrero-Taylor, T., Cameron, R., & Davis, G. (2002). Mitigating Instigation: Cultural Phenomenological Influences of Anger and Fighting among "Big-Boned and Baby-Faced" in African American Youth. *Journal of Youth and Adolescence, 31*, 473–485.

Stevenson, H.C., Hassan, N., Lassiter, C., Davis, G., Abdul-Kabir, S., Cassidy, E., Fry, D., Mendoza-Denton, R., Yancy, R., Purdie, V., & Best, G. (2001). The PLAAY project: Preventing long-term anger and aggression in youth. In the *Conference Proceedings of the National Men's Health and Fitness Conference, June, 1999, Philadelphia Department of Public Health.*

Stevenson, H.C., Reed, J., Bodison, P,. & Bishop, A. (1997). Racism stress management: Racial socialization beliefs and the experience of depression and anger for African American adolescents. *Youth and Society, 29*, 197–222.

Stevenson, H.C., Davis, G. Y., Cassidy, E., Zamel, P. C., & Williams, V. (2003). *Reduction of rejection sensitivity in Black male youth through a randomized cultural socialization intervention.* Unpublished manuscript: University of Pennsylvania.

CHAPTER 8

Raising Boys to Be Men: Distance Does Not Make the Heart Grow Fonder

Howard C. Stevenson Jr.

What does a parent say to a son about being male in an American society that demands rugged manhood and cool headedness while at the same time rejecting boys who can't behave like "The Man"? For many young growing boys, this Catch-22 is the ultimate straightjacket. It's not just that young boys or men find it impossible to be cool, calm, and collected all of the time. It's that they are supposed to do it while they are wearing the straitjacket. The real dilemma is that while everyone knows it's impossible to *be* The Man, we still expect our boys to play the role of Houdini.

TO BE THE MAN OR NOT TO BE THE MAN

We can see our struggle with manhood in the sitcoms we have watched over decades of television. Take Ralph Kramden of the *Honeymooners*, Dennis the Menace, or Weezy's Mr. Jefferson. Or what about JJ from *Good Times* or Fred Flintstone from Bedrock or Fred Sanford and his son? Then there's Fresh Prince, Keenan and Kel, or Archie Bunker. We laugh at the image of the boy or man who pretends to have it all together or know everything and who eventually makes bad decisions and screws life up (temporarily, I might add)—always for our amusement. As a society, we are able to play with the image of the flawed man, but it must remain a joke. It cannot be true. Ironically, the great man fear of being flawed is that recurring nightmare that, maybe, this joke is really no joke at all. No wonder then that little boys grow up to avoid the great fear of being flawed and pretend to control the uncontrollable.

Instead of Archie Bunker, the true symbol of American male humanity is the Marlboro Man. This icon rules the hearts and minds of males from the suburbs to the ghetto, from the school playgrounds to the Wall Street corporate boardroom, from the blue-collar neighborhood to the mansions of the rich and famous.

Can you see this image in your mind's eye? Here we have a rugged man with a cowboy hat and a horse and in the background are a range of beautiful mountains and some rolling plains. This picture says a real man can conquer the untamed environment without any help. All he needs is a horse. Oh, yeah I forgot, he needs a cigarette too. That's it. That's the ticket. That's all a real man needs is a horse and a cigarette—those secret weapons of survival that will help him conquer the untamed wilderness. A real man takes risks with his life and at the same time maintains control. That we know this image is absolutely ridiculous does not scare us away any more than knowing cigarettes cause cancer will stop folks from smoking!

Yet, boys, men, and women cuddle up to the image of someone who is cool, unemotional, unmoved by catastrophic events, and undaunted by the tumultuous environment. One who is "shaken, not stirred"!

Isn't it interesting to watch boys (or men who have not left boyhood) struggle with the straitjacket of the "ultimate cool"? "You the Man." "No, You the Man." Ironically, a very real and present danger in the Marlboro Man icon is that the ultimate is unattainable. Yet, men and boys trying to be men are duped daily into believing that one way to attain the ultimate is to be cool, not stirred. To me, to be unmoved is to reject one's humanity. It is robotic. To be emotional is essential. It is human. We see too many examples of boys and men who try desperately to be something they are not—"human doings" rather than "human beings," as a friend of mine once called them. We measure manhood by what a man does, not who he is, and we do it again, and again...

We stand by helplessly as we watch boys and men who are in so much desperate need of emotional nurturance that they fill their emptiness with aggression, anger, and physical outbursts. We are witnesses to boys and men who will justify behaviors in the name of divine right and manifest destiny, just for the purpose of proving (temporarily I might add) to the world that they are in fact, the man. The only real way (or so we think) to be the man is to keep pretending until one day, one very sad and pitiful day, the image crumbles and it scares away our loved ones, our livelihoods, and maybe our lives.

It has been said that "All men are great in their imagination." Unfortunately, it's the nightmare of inadequacy that haunts the American male. Let's go back to our picture of the American wilderness. What if as you are imagining this great Wyoming landscape it suddenly transforms into a fairy tale in which all the colors are pastel and the Marlboro Man is shape-shifted into a big, round, overconfident roly-poly fellow sitting on a wall, until without warning, he loses his balance and falls helpless to the ground, only to shatter into shards of eggshell. And imagine further that all the King's horses and all the King's men were left helpless to put him back together again. Oh, what an image that is! This is the great man fear—that behind every Marlboro Man lurks a Humpty Dumpty waiting to fall!

Safe spaces, sanctuaries, and room to breathe. That's what boys need. That's what men need. Why? Because we are fragile, and we break, and we need so desperately to be put back together again—even if we won't admit we are broken.

Boys and men who can honestly feel their own pain and reject the "man" straitjacket can and will inevitably feel fulfilled and secure in themselves. We must applaud the boys who ask questions, who cry, who use their voice to challenge us with logic and emotion, and who tell us they are afraid. We must embrace the little lions that we see on school playgrounds, Wall Street boardrooms, and blue-collar neighborhoods, tussling with each other and expand their current images of best, brightest, swiftest, or strongest.

If we can embrace a newer tougher image, our boys will have a chance to feel safe and be less fragile. They need sanctuary. Not a shelter so they can hide and avoid facing hardship and pain but a place to struggle with their frailty, embracing it with a balanced confidence. If our boys can embrace this newer tougher image, they will be able to rewrite the script of insecure manhood. If not now, when? If so, then they will be able to safely reject The Mantle of pretense and James Bond-dom. Boys need everything. They need and deserve love and encouragement and correction without humiliation. They need to realize that girls will need and deserve the same love and encouragement and correction without humiliation. Safe space, sanctuary, and room to be. The road from boyhood to manhood is paved with the words, "To Be 'The Man' or Not to Be 'The Man.' That is the question." What do we say to our sons about becoming men? Anything and everything. We can say, "Let me tell you my story." We can say, "Be yourself." We can say, "I will be there with you as long as I can." We need to say anything and everything.

DISTANCE DOES NOT MAKE THE HEART GROW FONDER

What does a father say to his son about being an African American male in a society that does not appreciate that fact? Should he ignore racism and discrimination or should he tell it like it is? There is a wise and relevant African proverb that says "A lion's story will never be known as long as the hunter is the one to tell it." To truly contemplate this dilemma we must first realize that raising boys to be men is a matter of the heart.

Today, Black males are portrayed as endangered, aggressive, angry, superhuman, subhuman, lazy, hyperactive, jailed, paroled, on probation, lost, loveless, incorrigible, or just simply self-destructive. Despite the reality that anyone can be described by any of these adjectives during their lives, too often our society understands them to be endemic to Black manhood. This is more than a Catch-22, it's a Catch-33: "Damned if you do, damned if you don't, and just damned!"

Despite the images of the outside world, however, a father's relationship with his son can rewrite the script that society projects for many Black boys. In other words, it is the image of Black manhood that is developed, nurtured, and shaped within the context of a father-son relationship (real or imagined) that dictates the relative influence of those negative societal images.

As Black men, we have always struggled with our identity development on two fronts. These fronts pit self-definition (e.g., "What I think of myself") against others-perception (e.g., "What others think of me"). Our sons need to learn how to fight both battles—but not simultaneously. Unfortunately, I do not think that our sons can grow healthy, wealthy, and spiritually wise if we fail to spend adequate time on self-definition.

It means that Black fathers must actively seek for their sons the kinds of images they want them to refer to and from which their life choices will grow. It also means that we must engage in more "us" discussions than "they" discussions.

There is a time for "they" or "them" discussions. Racism and discrimination are real and their relative impact on Black males is excessive compared with other ethnic and gender groups. But, to forgo "us" discussions is to leave our young boys searching for completion in all the wrong places. Nothing can take the place of a father's message to his son about how to appreciate himself, how to treat women respectfully, and how to assert himself from a position of security rather than doubt. "Us" means that a father's distance is as much a loss for fathers than a loss for sons. It's a loss for us as fathers and a loss for our sons as fathers to be.

As artful griots, Black men must challenge their sons to be brave enough to wrestle with and manage the complexity of the anger bubbling in their veins as well as the hostility foisted on them daily. This balance comes from the reality that people cannot contribute to their community if they are not alive or emotionally available. Furthermore, Black men must teach their children (and yes, even Bay-Bay's kids) that a child cannot *be* alive if he is not giving back to his community, to his children.

Fathers have a responsibility to reject and challenge any definition of Black manhood that contributes to the self-destruction of their children or their community. Power and respect or "juice" does not come from the barrel of a gun or from the ability to develop a harem of women and other children. Nor does juice come from an 80-hour work week. A father may work overtime to give his boy a good life, but forget that life without Dad is rarely good or worth living no matter how many DVDs or video playstations a person can buy.

We must "get with" our little boys and our big boys to usher them through what is, for some, a short roller coaster ride. As fathers and mothers, we must be bodacious enough to love them with our presence, challenge them with our ideals, and touch them with our hugs and kisses. These are the matters of the heart that last! Before we send our little lions into the world where the hunters hide behind bushes of institutional authority and deceitful pomp and circumstance, let us not send them without our stories, our dreams, our definitions, our stripes, and *our* images.

We must teach them how to live instead of die. Death cannot be avoided, but we can teach them as the great poet laureate, Claude McKay, suggests, that "If we must die, let it not be like hogs hunted and penned in an inglorious spot." No, "let us nobly die" for a cause that perpetuates our existence instead of one that pushes us closer to extinction.

Fail, we will. As parents, as fathers, it is our privilege to fail. It is our honor to admit it. But, with God's help, no task is impossible. No child is worth losing to drugs, to gun shots, to racism, to someone stepping on their shoes, to lack of direction, to anything. What must we say to our sons? We must say that we are willing to die for them and take their place if we have to—no greater mission awaits us. But whatever we say and do, let us not believe for one moment that anybody can take *our* place or even worse—that our distance makes their hearts grow fonder.

Index

About the Contributors

SABURAH ABDUL-KABIR serves as the community research coordinator of the COPE (Community Outreach through Parent Empowerment) project at the University of Pennsylvania. She has twelve years of experience as a community coordinator and consultant on funded projects serving urban low-income families. She has served as a panelist on research forums in early childhood and is known for her wisdom and competence on raising Black children in a racially hostile world. She has copresented on parenting issues at several childhood intervention conferences. She has received several awards from national organizations for her outstanding professional and volunteer services. Abdul-Kabir brings an expertise regarding the role of spirituality and religion in child rearing and discipline. She is also a coauthor with Howard C. Stevenson and Gwendolyn Y. Davis on the book, *Stickin' To, Watchin' Over, & Gettin' With: An African American Parent's Guide To Discipline*, 2001.

GARLAND BEST is a third year graduate student in the developmental psychology program at Wayne State University in Detroit, Michigan. He holds a B.S. degree in psychology from Morgan State University. His research interests include developing interventions aimed at improving parenting skills and the relationship between families and schools.

ROBERT CARTER has over twenty-five years of experience working with educators, parents, and children, many challenged with socioemotional and behavioral issues. Considered by many as a leader among practitioners and educators who serve children and parents, Robert Carter (known by many as Brother Robb) has been a keynote speaker and workshop leader at numerous national and international conferences. Robert is the founder of the Peace World Performance Art and Leadership Charter School, scheduled to open in September 2004.

ELAINE F. CASSIDY, Ph.D., is a postdoctoral researcher at the Center for Health, Achievement, Neighborhood, Growth, and Ethnic Studies of the Graduate School of Education at the University of Pennsylvania. She teaches courses in human development and adolescent development at the University of Pennsylvania and is involved in research on adolescent development. Her research and clinical interests focus on gaining an understanding of the internalized, often hidden, psychological factors affecting adolescents living in low-income, urban areas; the meaning underlying the personas adolescents choose; the gender differences in adolescent aggression; and health-related behaviors, including athletic participation and emotional expression. She has presented on coping styles among children and adolescents in urban contexts at numerous national conferences.

GWENDOLYN Y. DAVIS, MSW, Ph.D., received her master's degree from the University of Pennsylvania School of Social Work in 1988 and her Ph.D. in school, community, and clinical child psychology from the University of Pennsylvania Graduate School of Education in 1999 where she was awarded federal research funding for completing her dissertation project on parent involvement. She has several years of experience as a research coordinator and manager of community action research projects conducted in school and community-based settings. In particular, she has managed projects in the areas of reciprocal peer tutoring, culturally sensitive AIDS education and intervention, parent involvement, racial socialization, and anger and aggression among urban youth. She also helped to coordinate a program whose goal was to reduce isolation and stress among parents and families of preschool-age children. In these projects, she helped to shape research design and intervention and has been responsible for collecting, analyzing, and reviewing data; communicating the results of the data to community leaders and colleagues; and disseminating in written form the findings of the research. Along with team members and coworkers, she has also constructed assessment tools to measure the impact of programs and research projects. In addition to her research skills, she has served as a therapist, case manager, behavioral specialist, program evaluator, school psychologist, and educational consultant working primarily with families, schools, social service agencies, and penal institutions. Through these roles she has provided individual, group, and family counseling, sought out and made referral for additional service, designed treatment plans, performed psychological and psychoeducational evaluations, prepared final program evaluation reports, and consulted with school teachers to help them develop and implement student and classroom-wide behavioral plans. She is committed to working with urban, marginalized populations whose life chances are compromised by a host of complex individual, family, community, and societal issues. She is also a coauthor with Howard C. Stevenson and Saburah Abdul-Kabir on the book, *Stickin' To, Watchin' Over, & Gettin' With: An African American Parent's Guide To Discipline*, 2001.

SONIA ELLIOTT, M.S. Ed., is currently a full-time doctoral student in educational studies in the College of Education at Temple University. She has served at the University of Pennsylvania as dean of the W.E.B. DuBois College House and as an admissions officer for fourteen years.

ERICK ESPIN is a graduate from the University of Pennsylvania with a B.A. in African American studies and a M.S. Ed. in teacher education. His professional interests include novel, culturally relevant teaching methods to children and adolescents in urban schools. He currently teaches in the New York City Public School System. He was a teacher and counselor in the African-centered, undergraduate student-directed Saturday School for middle schoolers, *ASE,* of the W. E. B. DuBois College House at the University of Pennsylvania during his undergraduate experience.

JUANA GATSON is a graduate of the University of Pennsylvania with a B.A. in psychology. Her professional and research interests include the investigation of racial identity and mental health among African American youth in African-centered school environments. She has been a teacher and counselor in the African-centered, undergraduate student-directed Saturday School for middle schoolers, *ASE,* of the W. E. B. DuBois College House at the University of Pennsylvania for four years.

DIANE M. HALL, Ph.D., is a child clinical psychologist, lecturer, and program coordinator of the Master's Program in Psychological Services at the University of Pennsylvania where she received her Ph.D. from the School, Community, and Child Clinical Psychology Program She teaches courses in the psychology of women, psychological intervention, and psychological practice. Her clinical and research work explores the roles of race, gender, development, and violence on adolescents in their romantic and interpersonal relationships and the roles of race and gender on marginalized individuals within institutions, such as schools.

NIMR HASSAN is a graduate of Jamestown College where he majored in sociology and psychology. He began his studies in martial arts in 1957. Hanshi Hassan is certified by the Institution of Certified Martial Artists and the National Black Belt League. He has received the rank of tenth degree Black Belt and is a Grand Master. Hanshi Hassan has studied many different forms of martial arts, such as judo, karate, aidido, jujitsu, boxing, and kempo. He is currently the martial arts instructor in three Philadelphia public schools and recently completed an educational and behavioral research project within the Thomas Jefferson University Hospital, Department of Psychiatry and the School District of Philadelphia. Hanshi Hassan is also involved in a five-year joint research project, called PLAAY (Preventing Long-term Anger and Aggression in Youth) with the University of Pennsylvania. Hanshi Hassan has received numerous honors and awards from organizations, institutions, and fraternal orders. He is committed to teaching youth the use of martial arts as a means of gaining control over their behavior and emotions.

TERESA HERRERO-TAYLOR, Ph.D., is a school psychologist currently practicing in central New Jersey. As a postdoctoral fellow and research consultant at the University of Pennsylvania, she has been involved in the PLAAY intervention/research project funded by the National Institute of Mental Health for the past several years. Her research has primarily concentrated on the areas of anger and the cultural-ecological factors affecting the psychological adjustment of minority youth and families. She has also taught graduate courses in developmental psychology, multicultural counseling, and assessment. Her group work includes having both developed and conducted an adolescent anger management program (Strategic Training for Anger Reduction in Teenagers, START) and a psychoeducational support group program for families impacted by mental illness. Herrero-Taylor received her masters in multicultural counseling and counseling psychology from Teachers College at Columbia University. She obtained her doctoral training in school, community, and clinical child psychology from the University of Pennsylvania.

CHAD LASSITER, MSW, is a former student of the University of Pennsylvania Graduate School of Social Work. Currently, he serves as a social worker, health educator, and research fellow at the Center for Health Achievement Neighborhood Growth and Ethnic Studies (CHANGES) at the University of Pennsylvania Graduate School of Education. He is the founder of B.O.Y.S. (Bright Outstanding Young Scholars), a nonprofit mentoring program of professional African American men working with at-risk African American males in elementary schools around racial socialization, identity, and academic achievement. He has seven years of experience counseling families and children.

DELORES McCABE Ph.D., is pastor of Millcreek Baptist Church of Philadelphia where she serves a growing congregation in an impoverished African American community. Prior to her pastorate she spent twenty-six years at Eastern University where she was first associate dean of students and director of the Cushing Center for Counseling and Academic Support and later associate professor of counseling and social justice. McCabe has been the national president of Black American Baptist, ABC USA, a national board member for American Baptist Churches, USA, and currently serves the Baptist World Alliance as a member of the Freedom and Justice Commission. McCabe participated in meetings in Cuba, Spain, and Brazil and some of the other countries on her travel itinerary have included Rwanda, South Africa, the Czech Republic, Holland, Germany, and France. Recently, McCabe was selected as a participant in the Lott Carey Pastoral Excellence Program, which is an international missions immersion program.

RUSSELL MORRIS has over eighteen years of experience with providing psychological services to children, youth, and families in school and clinic settings. He is a school psychologist for the Philadelphia Unified School District and a member of the Delaware Valley Association of Black Psychologists. His work has involved the development of emotional resources for Black youth struggling to achieve academically and socially within traditional school settings. He also provides training, supervision, and the development of community-based psychology programs within urban neighborhood and nontraditional settings.

GALE SEILER is an Assistant Professor at the University of Maryland Baltimore County where she teaches and supervises student teachers. She was a high school science teacher for 16 years, teaching culturally diverse students in a variety of settings from South America to Baltimore. Her research looks at how curricula and classrooms can be restructured to build on the cultural resources and strategies of urban, African American male students and at culturally-specific ways in which African American students participate in school science.

HOWARD C. STEVENSON JR., Ph.D., is an associate professor with tenure in the Graduate School of Education at the University of Pennsylvania. He is the director of the School, Community, and Clinical Child Psychology Doctoral Training Program in the Psychology in Education Division. In 1993, Stevenson received the W. T. Grant Foundation's Faculty Scholar Award, which is a national research award given to only five researchers per year and funds five years of research. He was Faculty Master of the W. E. B. DuBois College House at the University of Pennsylvania from 1994 to 2002. In 1995, Stevenson served as a member of a twelve-member academic panel to consult on the development of a National Strategic Action Plan for African American Males sponsored by the National Drug Control Policy Office in the Office of the President. He teaches courses in African American psychology, adolescence, and family therapy and has written several articles on how families cope under extreme social and economic duress, how adolescents make sense of their world, and how race and culture influence psychological and societal functioning in America. His research and consultation work is designed to identify cultural strengths that exist within families and mobilize those strengths to improve the psychological and educational adjustment of children and adolescents using communities and neighborhoods as the major vehicles of support and social change. Stevenson directed the PLAAY Project (Preventing Long-term Anger and Aggression in Youth), which is a five year National Institute of Mental Health (NIMH) funded study to investigate the impact of cultural socialization intervention and is the substance for this book. PLAAY involved reducing anger in teenage males through cultural socialization and athletic movement. A second NIMH funded project involved investigating the academic and emotional experiences of African American students in independent schools. Stevenson has seventeen years of experience as a clinical supervisor and therapist in family and child psychotherapy.

He has been invited to provide keynote speeches and expertise to audiences as diverse as Presidential task force social scientists as well as local gatherings of urban and rural Head Start parents. He holds a faculty appointment in the Interdisciplinary Studies in Human Development Program, also in the Psychology in Education Division at the University of Pennsylvania. Stevenson obtained a Ph.D. in clinical psychology at Fuller Graduate School of Psychology and a master's of arts in theology from Fuller Theological Seminary, both in 1985. Finally, he is a coauthor with Gwendolyn Y. Davis and Saburah Abdul-Kabir on the book, *Stickin' To, Watchin' Over, & Gettin' With: An African American Parent's Guide To Discipline*, 2001.

VERNITA R. WILLIAMS, ED.M., is a graduate student in the doctoral training program in school, community, and clinical child psychology at the University of Pennsylvania. She received her bachelor's degree from Yale University and her master's degree in human development and psychology from the Harvard Graduate School of Education. Her work experiences as a classroom teacher in public and private institutions and as a juvenile probation officer reflect a continum of care, assessment, education, prevention, and intervention. Her research and clinical interests include risk and resiliency, identity, and the role of cognitive factors in the development of aggression and delinquency.

PAMELA C. ZAMEL, ED.M., is a doctoral candidate in the School, Community and Clinical Child Psychology Program at the University of Pennsylvania. She received her master's degree in psychological counseling from Columbia University in 1995. Her clinical work has included working with emotionally challenged boys in residential settings and incarcerated fathers around parenting issues including communication, child development, and discipline. Prior to her doctoral work, she worked several years as an intensive case manager helping to maintain troubled youth at home with their families through crisis prevention, linkage to community resources, and school advocacy.